D1263443

# Bridge Secrets

# THE TIMES

# Bridge Secrets

## Andrew Robson

**TIMES
BOOKS**

Published in 2007 by Times Books

HarperCollins Publishers
77-85 Fulham Palace Road
London
W6 8JB

www.harpercollins.co.uk
Visit the book lover's website

© Andrew Robson 2007

Reprint 10 9 8 7 6 5 4 3 2 1

*The Times* is a registered trademark of Times Newspapers Ltd

ISBN 13  978-0-00-724939-8
ISBN 10  0-00-724939-X

British Library Cataloguing in Publication Data
A catalogue record for this book is available from the British Library.

Collins uses papers that are natural, renewable and recyclable products made from wood grown
in sustainable forests. The manufacturing processes conform to the environmental regulations
of the country of origin.

Designed by Susie Bell.

Printed and bound in Great Britain by Clays Ltd, St Ives plc.

# Contents

To my wife Lorna,
and my two daughters Hannah and Mimi

# Introduction

I am sure that you will learn many new tactics and techniques within the game from this book. However I hope that *Bridge Secrets* will go further than that and deepen your appreciation of Bridge as a force for good in the modern world.

Aimed at a higher level than my earlier book *Common Mistakes – and How to Avoid Them*, *Bridge Secrets* makes an ideal follow-on for those who enjoyed that book and want more (and, judging by the number of such requests, I hope that number may be large).

I make no apology for basing this book on my daily Bridge columns in *The Times*. A one-deal column format is the perfect way to read Bridge: perhaps in bed before falling asleep (I have been told by many spouses that *Common Mistakes* has frequently been found in bed the morning after, as sleep arrived prematurely) or at the breakfast table.

The final chapter of *Bridge Secrets* consists of entirely new material. It is a very personal reflection of my life in the world of International Bridge, interwoven with triumphs and disasters at the table. The remainder of the book is an assortment of my favourite *Times* columns, selected from Mondays and Tuesdays (the 'Pot Pourri' days), then grouped into themes.

Before we embark, I would like to take this opportunity to thank all my partners, for enabling me to have such a fantastic, worthwhile journey in Bridge. To James Robson, Graham Hartley, Mike Huggins, Glyn Liggins, Oliver Segal, John Pottage, Tony Forrester, Rita Shugart, Zia Mahmood, David Bakhshi, Alexander Allfrey and all others whom I have sat opposite.

# CHAPTER 1
# Partnership

What marks out Bridge as ultimately the most enduringly fascinating and alluring of all games? Picking up each new hand creates endless variety, excitement and challenge. But the most compelling aspect of Bridge is surely the total cooperation that must exist between you and the person sitting opposite.

That person is your partner. Never forget – they have precisely the same goals as you. You must at all times nurture them, encourage them, help them. Ask yourself how you can make your partner's life easier. Ask yourself why (not why on earth!) they have bid/played what they did. There must be a reason.

This challenge of cooperative communication is at the heart of the game of Bridge. If you are a good partner, then you will do well (and have a full diary), even if you are but an ordinary (say) declarer. If this challenge excites you, then read on. If not, well, there are plenty of good poker books on the market.

# Believe it or Not

Bridge is a very suitable choice of name for the game we love. As a game of communication and cooperation, it is the creation of a bridge between the minds of the two partners. It is not fully known why it is called Bridge, but there are a few theories.

The name may have been derived from the nineteenth-century Russian game called Biritch; or from the Turkish game Britch, of the same period. More likely, it might be a combination of the two.

Here is another possible explanation, one that I had not encountered until I saw a letter from reader Gordon Ferguson. The letter informs us that in Ripley's *New Believe It Or Not* (Stanley Paul, 1945) there is the following most appealing excerpt:

'Bridge came to England in 1884 when two families at Great Dalby, Leicestershire, used to visit each other on alternative evenings to play. They had to cross over a rickety old bridge, which was unsafe at night, and the visiting party used to exclaim with a sigh of relief: 'Thank goodness it is your bridge, tomorrow night.' Gradually it became 'Bridge Whist' and then simply 'Bridge'.

Our first deal sees East make the key bid that opened the bridge between the defenders. As a passed hand, he could hardly have a natural Five Club bid. Instead the bid was showing a hand with diamond support and a desire for a club lead, in case North-South bid on to Five Hearts.

If West had led a diamond against Five Hearts, declarer would have ruffed, finessed the jack of spades, cashed the ace of trumps (felling East's king), ruffed a second diamond, finessed the queen of spades, then cashed the ace (noting the even split). He would have cashed the two long spades and merely conceded a club at the end. Twelve tricks.

But, aided by East's Five Club bid, West kicked off with the nine of clubs. East won the king, cashed the ace, then, reading West for a doubleton club for his nine-then-eight plays, led a third round of the suit. West ruffed with the precious five of trumps, forcing out dummy's ace, and East's king of trumps was promoted into the setting trick. Down one.

**Dealer: East    Vulnerability: Neither**

Pairs

|  | North | |
|---|---|---|
| | ♠ A Q J 9 4 | |
| | ♥ A 4 3 2 | |
| | ♦ 6 5 | |
| | ♣ 10 5 | |

West:
♠ K 5 2
♥ 5
♦ A K Q J 9 8 3
♣ 9 8

East:
♠ 10 8 6
♥ K
♦ 10 7 4 2
♣ A K 7 6 3

South:
♠ 7 3
♥ Q J 10 9 8 7 6
♦ –
♣ Q J 4 2

| S | W | N | E |
|---|---|---|---|
| | | | PASS |
| 3♥ | 4♦ | 4♥ | 5♣ (1) |
| PASS | 5♦ | 5♥ | END |

(1) Logically showing diamond support, and asking for a club lead.

**Contract: 5♥    Opening lead: ♣9**

# Crafty Texan

When partner leads and your card will not affect the winning of the trick, you should signal to partner to give him as much information about the suit as possible.

(a)          Dummy
            A 5 3
                 You
                 (i) K 9 2
4 led             (ii) 9 5 2

Partner leads the four and dummy plays the ace. With (i) play the nine ('throw high means aye'); with (ii) play the two ('throw low means no'). These are called 'Attitude Signals'.

Sometimes, however, your attitude is clear. On those occasions you should give partner the count – i.e. whether you hold an even or an odd number of cards.

(a)          Dummy
            J 10 3
                 You
                 (i) 8 2
4 led             (ii) 9 5 2

Dummy's ten is played on partner's four. The fact that you cannot beat that card tells partner that your attitude is negative. Instead give the count– playing high from an even number – the eight in (i); and low from an odd number – the two in (ii). Acronym: HELO (High-Even; Low-Odd).

On this deal declarer, Texan Chris Compton stole a Three Notrump contract that would have been defeated easily using this count signal.

West led the five of spades and dummy's jack won the trick, East playing low (?). The nine of diamonds was led to West's jack and West's club return was won by dummy's ace.

## Dealer: South     Vulnerability: East-West

```
Teams          ♠ J 9
               ♥ Q 7 5
               ♦ 9 2
               ♣ A 10 6 5 4 2

♠ A Q 7 5 3          N          ♠ 10 8 4 2
♥ 10 8 4        W        E       ♥ K 9 2
♦ Q J 6 4            S           ♦ 7 3
♣ 7                              ♣ Q J 8 3

               ♠ K 6
               ♥ A J 6 3
               ♦ A K 10 8 5
               ♣ K 9
```

| S | W | N | E |
|---|---|---|---|
| 1♦ | 1♠ | 2♣ (1) | 2♠ |
| 3NT | END | | |

(1) Marginal – Pass is the textbook alternative.

**Contract: 3NT**        **Opening lead: ♠9**

A second diamond was led to the ten and West's queen.

Still unwilling to play a second spade (and see declarer's presumed guarded king of the suit be promoted), West switched to the ten of hearts. Declarer craftily ducked in both hands, and the unwitting second heart that followed enabled declarer to score three tricks in the suit (thanks to the 3–3 split), to go with a spade, three diamonds and two clubs. Nine tricks and game made.

However if East had signalled with the eight of spades at Trick One (announcing an even number of cards – presumably four for his support), West would have known to have plonked the ace of spades on the table as soon as he won the lead. Declarer's king is felled and the game easily beaten.

# Mind Sports

For our third deal we see defence at its most cooperative, care of English Internationals (both formerly of Scotland) Victor Silverstone (West) and Gerald Haase (East), on a deal from the Mind Sports Olympiad.

West led the ace of spades against Three Notrumps – the least committal opening salvo as it allowed for a look at dummy and a signal from partner without losing the lead. He could continue with spades or switch to any other suit depending on what he saw.

In the event East signalled discouragement by playing the two of spades ('throw low means no'). He did not hold the equal honour to partner's presumed ace-king (i.e. the queen) so, in spite of holding relatively decent spades, this was the correct play.

At Trick Two West switched to the three of hearts. This was not certain to be best – a club switch would be necessary if East held the king-queen – but it was definitely the percentage play and one which would trivially beat the game should East hold the king of the suit. No – declarer won dummy's ten and led the ten of clubs.

East knew that declarer held seven diamond tricks – even if his partner held the missing king it was finessable. One club trick – together with the ten of hearts – would bring declarer's trick total to nine. East therefore flew in with his ace of clubs. But which major-suit should he lead at this point?

The key lay in West's choice of heart lead. As he led his lowest card ('lead low for like') East knew to return a heart. West took South's jack with the queen, cashed the ace (felling South's king) and tabled the established eight. The king of spades soon followed and the game was down two. Poetry in motion.

**Pairs**

|  | Pairs |
|---|---|
| ♠ | 7 |
| ♥ | 10 9 5 |
| ♦ | A Q J 7 6 4 3 |
| ♣ | 10 7 |

West:
♠ A K 4 3
♥ A Q 8 3
♦ 9 5 2
♣ J 3

East:
♠ J 9 8 2
♥ 7 6 4
♦ 10
♣ A 9 6 4 2

South:
♠ Q 10 6 5
♥ K J 2
♦ K 8
♣ K Q 8 5

| S | W | N | E |
|---|---|---|---|
| 1NT | PASS | 3NT (1) | END |

(1) A gamble, of course, but one with two ways to win. 3NT might make (with seven diamond tricks available unless East holds the king of the suit – rendering the finesse a losing proposition); alternatively East-West might have a contract – even a game – of their own (with the 3NT bid inhibiting them from bidding it).

In fact neither way to win proves the case – East-West can make but 2♠ and the deal belongs to North-South in 3♦. However it took the finest defence to beat 3NT...

**Contract: 3NT**      **Opening lead: ♠A**

# Champagne Cashing

**Teams**

|  |  |
|---|---|
| ♠ J 10 | |
| ♥ A K 4 | |
| ♦ Q 6 5 3 | |
| ♣ A K Q 6 | |

|  |  |  |
|---|---|---|
| ♠ Q 9 8 | **N** | ♠ A K 7 5 |
| ♥ 7 | **W    E** | ♥ 10 9 8 6 5 3 2 |
| ♦ 10 9 4 2 | **S** | ♦ 8 |
| ♣ 9 8 5 3 2 | | ♣ 7 |

|  |  |
|---|---|
| ♠ 6 4 3 2 | |
| ♥ Q J | |
| ♦ A K J 7 | |
| ♣ J 10 4 | |

One of the reasons for entering the bidding is to indicate a lead for partner should you end up defending. The converse of this is that you should be loath to enter on a marginal hand when you do not wish your suit to be led.

Look at East's hand from the Lederer Memorial Trophy. Although it would take precious little from partner (in the right places) to make Four Hearts (e.g. ♠xx and ♥Axx), East kept quiet in the hope that his partner would find an opening spade lead, rather than a heart, against the opposing contract.

And so it came to pass. The Canadian North-South pair came uneasily to rest in Four Notrumps and West led his stronger of the two unbid majors, spades. His spot cards in the suit were unfortunate, however, because the lead of a high spot card normally indicates a lack of interest in the suit ('Lead Low for Like; Lead High for Hate').

East went 'into the tank' after winning the eight of spades lead with the king. But he had no real hope of four tricks without partner having specifically ♠Q98, so he correctly returned the five of spades at Trick Two. West won the hoped-for queen and East could overtake the nine with the ace and cash the seven. Down one.

East-West won the Best Defended Hand award for this effort, but several plaudits commented, 'They won for cashing four top tricks'. True – and the judges were rightly looking for something a little more intricate to win the prize. But in a sense the defence began during the auction when East kept his mouth shut and did not mention hearts for fear of a heart lead from partner. Anyway whether or not it was worth the award, David Bakhshi and I enjoyed the prize of a bottle of champagne!

| S | W | N | E |
|---|---|---|---|
| | | | PASS (1) |
| 1♦ (2) | PASS | 2♣ | PASS (1) |
| 2NT | PASS | 3♦ | PASS |
| 3NT | PASS | 4NT (3) | PASS |
| PASS (3) | PASS | | |

(1) Not wishing to attract an unfavourable opening heart lead should he end up defending, East keeps silent.

(2) Playing Five-card Majors and Strong Notrump. But is this really an opening bid, with those dubious heart values, and dreadful spades?

(3) Quantitative slam invite, hurriedly rejected by South.

**Contract: 4NT**          **Opening lead: ♠8**

# Italian Girths

Lest you think this book will be a procession of past glories of the author, this deal redresses the balance of the last. It sees me humiliated by the Bridge equivalent of Tiger Woods or Roger Federer: the all-conquering Italians.

The scene was the Champions Cup (the Bridge equivalent of football's Champions League, in which national trophy winners in the top ten European countries battle it out for a hugely prestigious – and indeed huge – trophy).

Won for a third year by Rome's Tennis Club Parioli (although the girths of the team members suggest that they would have struggled rather more at their club's supposed sport), their star pair were world champions Alfredo Versace and Lorenzo Lauria. Watch them collect an 800 penalty after (or so I thought at the time) a perfectly reasonable bid.

West led the ace of clubs and East signalled with the eight. Because a club continuation was out of the question (dummy having the king and declarer a likely singleton), this was meant as, and taken as, a suit-preference signal for hearts (high card requesting the higher-ranking outside suit).

West did not waste the jack (top of his internal sequence), instead switching to the two of hearts. East won the ace and returned a heart, West beating my queen with the king and following with the jack.

Had East discarded – the normal thing to do on partner's winner – West would have had to play a fourth heart (his only safe exit). Declarer would ruff and bang down ace and a second spade. West would win but now be forced to lead a diamond, promoting my king (or lead a club to dummy).

However East ruffed his partner's jack of hearts (key play) and led his other trump.

**Dealer: West    Vulnerability: East-West**

**Teams**

|  | North |
|---|---|
| ♠ | 5 2 |
| ♥ | 8 6 5 4 |
| ♦ | 9 7 6 3 |
| ♣ | K 6 3 |

| West | | East |
|---|---|---|
| ♠ K 6 | | ♠ 8 3 |
| ♥ K J 10 2 | N | ♥ A 3 |
| ♦ J 10 4 | W   E | ♦ A Q 5 2 |
| ♣ A J 9 2 | S | ♣ Q 8 7 5 4 |

|  | South |
|---|---|
| ♠ | A Q J 10 9 7 4 |
| ♥ | Q 9 7 |
| ♦ | K 8 |
| ♣ | 10 |

| S (ROBSON) | W (VERSACE) | N (BAKHSHI) | E (LAURIA) |
|---|---|---|---|
|  | 1♣ (1) | PASS | 2♣ (2) |
| 4♠ (3) | PASS | PASS | DOUBLE |
| END | | | |

(1) Playing Strong Notrump and Five-card Majors.

(2) Inverted raise – 10+ pts and a club fit.

(3) Didn't seem too rash given the favourable vulnerability. This assessment was soon proved wrong – I lost 800 pts with E-W unable to make game.

**Contract: 4♠ doubled    Opening lead: ♣A**

What could declarer do? I rose with the ace and led a second trump (finessing my queen would have seen West win and return the six of trumps, infuriatingly beating dummy's five). West won the king, exited with the ten of hearts, and I was forced to ruff and lead away from my king of diamonds. Down four and 800 points to those brilliant Italians. We lost the match 25-0.

# Cui Culpa

'Cui Culpa?' East-West can defeat South's Six Heart slam if East wins the first trick with the ace of spades and switches to a club, West ruffing. It did not happen that way. Assess the blame.

At the table West led the king of spades and East let him hold the trick. The slam was no longer beatable. West actually continued with a second spade and declarer ruffed, drew trumps and claimed twelve tricks, scoring five trump tricks, ace-king-queen in both minors and the spade ruff in the short trump hand.

Let us eavesdrop East-West's post-mortem:

West: 'Why didn't you overtake the spade? Surely our only chance of a second trick (looking at dummy) was for you to lead a club in the hope that I was void.'

East: 'I did consider that, but I was concerned that you might have preempted with a six-bagger (six-card suit) and that a second spade trick was cashing.'

West: 'Unlikely. Anyway – didn't you think that South was likely to have a singleton spade for his Five Heart bid? You knew he was aceless, so he surely needed something to excite him.'

East: 'Maybe. But do you know how you could have made me do the right thing? How about leading the queen of spades?'

It is true – the queen of spades opening lead (implying the jack but not the king) would have forced East to win and, placing the king with declarer, he would surely have played for the club ruff. Down one.

Though the blame initially seemed to lie with East, closer analysis does make West more of the culprit. Say 80-20.

At another table – this was a duplicate at my Club – North chose to overcall Four Hearts and it was he who declared the Six Heart slam. East cashed the ace of spades at

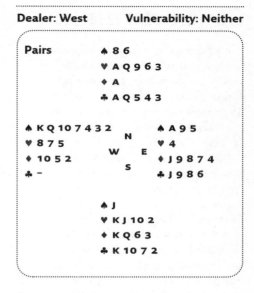

| Pairs | ♠ 8 6 |
| | ♥ A Q 9 6 3 |
| | ♦ A |
| | ♣ A Q 5 4 3 |

♠ K Q 10 7 4 3 2    ♠ A 9 5
♥ 8 7 5    ♥ 4
♦ 10 5 2    ♦ J 9 8 7 4
♣ –    ♣ J 9 8 6

♠ J
♥ K J 10 2
♦ K Q 6 3
♣ K 10 7 2

| S | W | N | E |
|---|---|---|---|
| | 3♠ | DOUBLE (1) | 4♣ |
| 5♥ (2) | PASS | 6♥ (3) | END |

(1) Take-out.
(2) Aggressive, holding just a four-card suit.
(3) Praying his partner has a spade control.

**Contract: 6♥**          **Opening lead:** ♠K

Trick One. Dummy (South) tabled his singleton spade, and West signalled with a suit-preference two (calling for the lower-ranking suit). East had no difficulty switching to a club for West to ruff – down one.

# Good not Best

**Dealer: East**     **Vulnerability: Both**

The old chess player's adage 'When you have found a good move, try to find a better one' should have been ringing in East's ears during the defence of this deal – from the Brighton Pairs. Cover up West's and South's hands and try to find the best defence to Four Spades.

West led the two of diamonds and you as East win your queen, declarer following. Because partner would lead top from a doubleton, you can deduce that his two of diamonds is a singleton. Proceed.

At the table declarer cashed the ace of diamonds at Trick Two and followed with a low diamond. Declarer ruffed with the nine of trumps, West discarding, and led a trump to dummy's jack. East won the ace and led another low diamond. Declarer ruffed with the eight of trumps and West could only discard again.

Declarer led to dummy's king-queen of trumps, drawing the opposing trumps, then cashed the ace of hearts, overtook the jack with his queen, cashed the king of hearts discarding dummy's last diamond, and successfully led a club to dummy's queen. The last two tricks were made with dummy's ace of clubs and the final trump. 10 tricks and game made.

East's defence of leading diamonds at each turn would have worked if West had held a doubleton trump including the eight rather than the seven. In that case he would be able to overruff declarer on the fourth diamond. It was a good plan...

But it was not the best one. In fact you as East can defeat the contract if West has any doubleton spade – even the three-two. After winning the queen of diamonds, switch at Trick Two to your singleton heart. Declarer wins in dummy and leads the jack of trumps. Win the ace and lead a low diamond, forcing

**Pairs**

|  | ♠ K Q J 4 |  |
|---|---|---|
|  | ♥ A J |  |
|  | ♦ J 10 9 8 7 |  |
|  | ♣ A Q |  |

| ♠ 7 3 | | ♠ A 10 6 |
| ♥ 10 9 8 6 4 2 | N | ♥ 7 |
| ♦ 2 | W   E | ♦ A K Q 6 4 |
| ♣ K 6 3 2 | S | ♣ J 8 5 4 |

|  | ♠ 9 8 5 2 |  |
|---|---|---|
|  | ♥ K Q 5 3 |  |
|  | ♦ 5 3 |  |
|  | ♣ 10 9 7 |  |

| S | W | N | E |
|---|---|---|---|
|  |  |  | 1♦ |
| PASS | 1♥ (1) | DOUBLE | 2♣ |
| 2♠ | 3♣ | 4♠ | END |

(1) The modern style. If partner has a suitable maximum one-level opener with a heart fit, Four Hearts could be on; if he has a minimum, then responding could steal the bidding from the opponents who may have a game of their own.

**Contract: 4♠**          **Opening lead: ♦2**

West to ruff. West leads a second heart, reading your heart switch as a singleton, and you ruff. Down one.

It was an exercise in timing. How did you fare?

# Flying to Vegas

The Las Vegas Cavendish Tournament attracts all the Bridge world's high-rollers. The entry fee is huge but the rewards are commensurate.

The defence had three hurdles to overcome in order to defeat Four Hearts on this deal from the event. Read on and, if you think that you and your favourite partner would have passed all the three tests, then maybe you should book your flights for next year...

Hurdle No 1: West must lead the ace of diamonds. Leading ace from Ax is not that popular a strategy amongst experts. The possibility of a third-round ruff is often more than offset by seeing the ace catch only low cards. But on this occasion it is the unbid suit, there is no attractive alternative, and the relative feebleness of West's hand should tilt him in favour of the attacking approach.

After leading the ace of diamonds and seeing East play the six (a scrutiny of the spot cards visible to West reveals that this is likely to be an encouraging signal), West leads his second diamond to East's queen. East cashes the king and now we come to...

Hurdle No 2: West must discard a discouraging low card in spades. He does not want to attract a spade lead, his partner playing him for the ace. Instead he hopes that his partner will have the right trump holding and that his partner will jump over...

Hurdle No 3: East must play a fourth round of diamonds. This will give declarer the dreaded 'ruff-and-discard' – usually only a sensible strategy when the defence have no more tricks to take outside trumps. But West's discouraging spade signal and dummy's strong clubs make this virtually certain from East's perspective. And East is looking at his promotable trump holding...

At Trick Four East leads a fourth diamond,

**Dealer: South**      **Vulnerability: Neither**

Teams

| | | | |
| --- | --- | --- | --- |
| | ♠ K 7 4 3 | | |
| | ♥ K J 2 | | |
| | ♦ 9 7 4 | | |
| | ♣ A J 2 | | |

♠ Q 6 5 2　　　　N　　　♠ J 10 9 8
♥ Q 3　　　W　　E　　♥ 10 9 7
♦ A 8　　　　　S　　　♦ K Q 6 5 2
♣ 9 7 5 4 3　　　　　　♣ 8

♠ A
♥ A 8 6 5 4
♦ J 10 3
♣ K Q 10 6

| S | W | N | E |
| --- | --- | --- | --- |
| 1 ♥ | PASS | 1 ♠ | PASS |
| 2 ♣ (1) | PASS | 4 ♥ (2) | END |

(1) Implying (at least) five hearts and four clubs.
(2) Upgrading his hand in the light of his fitting honours in partner's suits.

**Contract: 4♥**          **Opening lead: ♦A**

and West ruffs with the queen of trumps (the key trick). Though dummy overruffs with the king, East cannot be denied a third round trump winner with his ten. Down one.

Left to his own devices declarer would pick up the trumps without loss (finessing West for the queen), and so chalk up his game. But not against you... see you in Vegas next year.

# CHAPTER 2

# Double Trouble

You are pretty sure that the opponents will fail in their contract. You double, right?

Probably. Those red double cards inside bidding boxes usually look brand new, unsoiled by human contact. They should be used more. To players who boast that they have not doubled the opponents into game all year, the correct retort is not one of congratulation, rather pointing out that they are almost certainly not doubling enough. The odd unpleasant doubled into game score is more than compensated for by all those 500s that would otherwise have been mere 200s.

But not necessarily. First you must check your double really is for penalties – as opposed to for take-out. Even if it is, you must be wary: perhaps the opponents will run to safer havens; perhaps, tipped off by your double, they will make a contract in which they were otherwise likely to fail. And do not double prematurely – like East on our first Double Trouble deal.

# Pleasure or Pain

Have you ever found the opposing auction so hard to believe that you have had to look at the backs of the cards to check you were using the same pack? This East was amazed that his opponents ended up with hearts as trumps (look at his hand). But would his amazement turn to pleasure or to pain?

West led the jack of clubs and declarer saw that, though his combined trump holding was barely adequate, he did have eight top tricks (should they all cash). All he needed was one extra trump trick to make his redoubled contract.

Declarer rose with dummy's ace of clubs, crossed to the king of spades, then cashed the king-queen of clubs, discarding a spade from dummy. Pleased to see East (who clearly had very long trumps for his double) follow suit, declarer next crossed to the king of diamonds, returned to his ace of spades, then crossed to the ace of diamonds (East again following).

Declarer had picked off all East's plain cards (non-trumps) to perfection, leaving him with just his six trumps. He now led a third diamond from dummy. East ruffed with the nine of trumps (though, interestingly, ruffing low and giving declarer a cheap overruff would work better) and declarer discarded his last spade (best).

East now led the king of trumps and declarer won the ace (West discarding) and ruffed his last club with dummy's ten of trumps. East overruffed with the jack and (holding queen-six-two) led the six of trumps (to beat dummy's remaining trump, the five). Declarer (holding eight-seven-three) won the seven, led back the eight to East's queen and had the pleasure of seeing his three of trumps take East's two on the last trick. Ten tricks and redoubled contract made with an overtrick.

**Dealer: South      Vulnerability: East-West**

Rubber

|  | ♠ 9 7 6 4 |  |
|---|---|---|
|  | ♥ 10 5 4 |  |
|  | ♦ A K 4 2 |  |
|  | ♣ A 7 |  |
| ♠ Q 10 8 5 | N | ♠ J 2 |
| ♥ – | W   E | ♥ K Q J 9 6 2 |
| ♦ Q J 8 7 3 | S | ♦ 9 5 |
| ♣ J 10 9 3 |  | ♣ 8 4 2 |
|  | ♠ A K 3 |  |
|  | ♥ A 8 7 3 |  |
|  | ♦ 10 6 |  |
|  | ♣ K Q 6 5 |  |

| S | W | N | E |
|---|---|---|---|
| 1 ♥ | PASS | 1 ♠ | PASS |
| 1 NT | PASS | 3 ♥ (1) | DOUBLE (2) |
| PASS | PASS | REDOUBLE | END |

(1) Showing a game-going hand with delayed heart support (i.e. three cards). South is expected to raise to 4♥ with five hearts, bid 3♠ with three spades, otherwise bid 3NT.
(2) Pointless (though tempting). If N–S stop off to redouble 3♥, you have no guarantee of defeating the contract. If they bid on to 3NT or 4♠, you have given them free information.

**Contract: 3♥ Redoubled   Opening lead: ♣J**

To rub salt into the wound, Three Notrumps, the contract N–S would have reached without the double, looks likely to fail. Declarer can garner no more than his eight top tricks.

# Dutch Lesson

*Question*: the opponents bid to slam and you are sure it will fail. Do you double?
*Answer*: unless you are confident of defeating all other slams that the opponents might escape to, definitely not.

East on this deal – from a match between Holland and Denmark – learned this lesson the hard way. North-South had a long, hesitant auction to Six Diamonds. East's double was most unwise.

Look at it from a mathematical perspective. Assuming Six Diamonds will fail by one trick (East's expectation looking at his hand), he will get 50 points should he pass and defend. If he doubles and the opponents stay in Six Diamonds, he will earn an extra 50 points (assuming that South, tipped off that East holds good trumps for his double, will not now be able to make the contract).

But if the opponents run to safer havens and make their new slam, they will score 990 points (the chicago/duplicate score for making Six Notrumps). His double will have cost 1040 points (net) in an effort to gain 50. Thus his opponents would only need to rescue to a making slam about one time in 20 for his double to be a loser.

Six Diamonds would have lost (at least) two trump tricks. But Six Notrumps was easy. If West had led a diamond, declarer could have beaten East's queen with the ace and driven out the king of the suit to set up the suit. On West's spade lead, declarer won in hand, cashed the ace of clubs, then finessed the jack. East won the queen and switched to the king of diamonds but declarer could claim his slam. Two spades, four hearts, a diamond and five clubs made the required 12 tricks. Slam made.

**Dealer: North      Vulnerability: Neither**

Teams

|  | North |
|---|---|
| ♠ | J 8 5 |
| ♥ | A Q J 3 |
| ♦ | – |
| ♣ | K J 10 5 4 2 |

West: ♠ 7 6  ♥ 10 9 8 6 4 2  ♦ 7 5 3  ♣ 8 7

East: ♠ Q 10 9 4 2  ♥ 7  ♦ K Q 6 2  ♣ Q 9 3

South: ♠ A K 3  ♥ K 5  ♦ A J 10 9 8 4  ♣ A 6

| S | W | N | E |
|---|---|---|---|
|  |  | 1♣ | 1♠ |
| 2♦ | PASS | 2♥ | PASS |
| 2♠ (1) | PASS | 3♣ | PASS |
| 3♦ | PASS | 4♣ | PASS |
| 4♦ (2) | PASS | 5♦ (3) | PASS |
| 6♦ | PASS | PASS | DOUBLE (4) |
| 6NT (5) | PASS | PASS | DOUBLE (6) |
| END |  |  |  |

(1) Setting up a game-force and asking for more information.
(2) Overstressing the suit facing no support.
(3) Trying to wrap things up, although raising with a void looks highly dubious to me.
(4) Wrong in theory. Wrong in practice.
(5) Delighted to have a second chance.
(6) In a fit of pique.

**Contract: 6NT doubled   Opening lead: ♠7**

# More than a Lifetime

Last deal we saw the dangers of a double of a small slam when holding little defence to other small slams. But surely you can double Six Notrumps when you are on lead with an ace-king. After all, the opponents can hardly run to a grand slam – can they...?

So thought East on this deal – a cautionary tale from the Crockfords Final. But when (after some agonising) West led a heart against South's removal to Seven Clubs, he was less sure. Declarer won in dummy, drew trumps finishing in hand, finessed the jack of diamonds, cashed the other top hearts throwing one spade from hand, crossed back to hand in trumps, finessed the queen of diamonds, then cashed the ace of diamonds discarding his other spade. Doubled grand slam made.

Perhaps West should have found the spade lead – East could not have the ace-king of diamonds and was arguably more likely to have the ace-king of spades than hearts because he rated to hold more of them (West being shorter). But East was more guilty – with so little to gain by doubling Six Notrumps and so much to lose.

East-West were soon writing –2330 (teams/duplicate scoring) on their scorecards. East's double had cost 2430 points (+100 from Six Notrumps down one into -2330) in order to gain 100 (+100 from Six Notrumps down one undoubled into +200 from Six Notrumps down one doubled). He would need the doubling to pass off peacefully 24 times before he even broke even – more than a lifetime away.

**Dealer: North**  **Vulnerability: Both**

**Teams**

```
              ♠ Q 10 6
              ♥ A K Q
              ♦ A Q J 4
              ♣ K 9 8

♠ 9 8 5           N        ♠ A K 4 3 2
♥ J 9 6 5 3 2   W   E      ♥ 10 8
♦ K 8 5           S        ♦ 10 7 6 2
♣ 5                        ♣ J 7

              ♠ J 7
              ♥ 7 4
              ♦ 9 3
              ♣ A Q 10 6 4 3 2
```

| S | W | N | E |
|---|---|---|---|
|   |   | 2NT | PASS |
| 6NT (1) | PASS | PASS | DOUBLE (2) |
| 7♣ (3) | PASS | PASS | DOUBLE (4) |
| END |   |   |   |

(1) A gamble, of course, but quite a clever one. South wishes to have his partner declare the slam. Further, he would like a passive opening lead (traditionally favoured against 6NT) rather than an aggressive one, such as cashing an ace or leading away from a king (traditionally favoured against a suit slam). This way 6NT may succeed even if missing the ace-king of a suit unless both are on lead... and even then you might survive if they greedily double...

(2) Wanting to convert +100 into +200.

(3) Realising that East has an ace-king, South cleverly converts the declarership to put West on lead.

(4) Less happily – belatedly seeing the error of his former double.

**Contract: 7♣ doubled   Opening lead: ♥5**

# Brilliant and Daring

The theme of not doubling Six Notrumps with an ace-king on lead – in case they run to Seven-of-a-Suit with partner on lead – swings SO many points that it is worth revisiting.

Our second such deal comes from the Brighton Summer Festival and sees East in a position to beat North's Six Notrumps by five tricks (all six hearts are cashing – with the queen falling). Instead he snatched defeat from the jaws of victory by doubling – allowing North to reassess.

It did not require great insight for North to work out why East had doubled – he had to hold the ace-king of hearts. North had nothing to lose – and everything to gain – by running out of Six Notrumps into Seven-of-a-Suit. But – and this was the clever bit – he had to make sure his partner was declarer. This was to put West – not East with his ace-king – on lead.

Clubs had already been bid by North (the Two Club opener), but diamonds had been bid (as the negative) by South. North removed Six Notrumps to his three-card diamond suit – a brilliant and daring shot. And a successful one too.

West had a pure guess on opening lead and eventually led the ten of spades (East wincing inwardly). Declarer won, cashed the ace-king of trumps (pleased West's singleton was the nine), ran the ten, crossed to the jack of clubs, cashed the queen of trumps felling East's jack, and ran his top tricks in the black suits. Five trumps and four top tricks in each black suit made 13 – grand slam made. East is still waiting to score his top hearts – a salutary lesson.

**Dealer: North**    **Vulnerability: Both**

Teams

|  | ♠ A K J 2 |  |
|---|---|---|
|  | ♥ Q 6 |  |
|  | ♦ A K 10 |  |
|  | ♣ A K 9 8 |  |

| ♠ 10 9 5 4 |  | ♠ 8 7 |
|---|---|---|
| ♥ 10 7 5 2 | N | ♥ A K J 9 8 4 |
| ♦ 9 | W    E | ♦ J 7 5 2 |
| ♣ 10 7 6 2 | S | ♣ 5 |

|  | ♠ Q 6 3 |  |
|---|---|---|
|  | ♥ 3 |  |
|  | ♦ Q 8 6 4 3 |  |
|  | ♣ Q J 4 3 |  |

| S | W | N | E |
|---|---|---|---|
|  |  | 2♣ (1) | PASS (2) |
| 2♦ (3) | PASS | 2NT (4) | PASS |
| 4NT (5) | PASS | 6NT (6) | DOUBLE (7) |
| PASS | PASS | 7♦ (8) | DOUBLE (9) |
| END |  |  |  |

(1) 23+ points or any game-force.
(2) Wisely keeping schtoom, although it is tempting to enter the bidding for disruptive reasons.
(3) 0-7 points, the negative response.
(4) 23-24 balanced.
(5) Questionable: short of the 33 points for a notrump slam, and surely worried about hearts.
(6) Accepting – holding a maximum.
(7) Greedily. And soon to regret it...
(8) The master bid (see text).
(9) Less confidently than his last double, in spite of his ♦Jxxx.

**Contract: 7♦ doubled    Opening lead: ♠10**

# No More Frivolity

Do you remember the days – not so long ago – when four down doubled non-vulnerable scored -700, five down doubled non-vulnerable scored -900, six down doubled non-vulnerable scored -1100 etc?

US star Jeff Meckstroth certainly does! It was as a direct result of his contribution (as South) to this historic deal – from the final of the 1981 World Championships against Pakistan – that the penalty for non-vulnerable doubled undertricks (from four down) was increased from 200 to 300. Four down doubled non-vulnerable now scores -800; five down scores -1100; six down scores -1400 etc.

The opponents sailed into Seven Hearts and the bidding returned to Meckstroth. There was little in his hand to suggest that Seven Hearts would fail, so he assumed that he would score -2210 if he passed. To show a profit by sacrificing in Seven Spades (doubled), he only needed to make two tricks (-2100)!

Against Seven Spades doubled West led the ace-king of clubs, and switched to the ace-queen of hearts. East overtook the queen of hearts with the king, cashed the jack (West discarding a diamond), then switched to the ace of diamonds and a second diamond. West ruffed (with the king) cashed the ace of trumps, then led a club (perforce). Declarer ruffed with dummy's ten of trumps and, whether or not East overruffed, he had to score a total of four trump tricks. Down nine meant that he lost 'only' 1700 points. With teammates duly recording +2210 (Seven Hearts makes easily by establishing clubs), his decision won 11 imps for his side.

A scoring system that rewards such – almost frivolous – bids could not be right. Or so, reasonably, the Bridge authorities decided. Six years later, in 1987, the fairer (if slightly more complex) system was introduced. Today Meckstroth would have lost 2300 points. He would not have even contemplated bidding Seven Spades.

**Dealer: West    Vulnerability: East-West**

**Teams**

```
              ♠ 10 3
              ♥ 9 7 3
              ♦ Q 8 7 6 3 2
              ♣ Q 8

♠ A K              N        ♠ Q 7 6 4
♥ A Q         W       E     ♥ K J 10 6 2
♦ J 9              S        ♦ A 10 5
♣ A K 10 9 6 4 2           ♣ 7

              ♠ J 9 8 5 2
              ♥ 8 5 4
              ♦ K 4
              ♣ J 5 3
```

| S | W | N | E |
|---|---|---|---|
| | 2♣ | PASS | 2♥ |
| PASS | 3♣ | PASS | 3♥ |
| PASS | 4NT (1) | PASS | 5♥ (2) |
| PASS | 7♥ | PASS | PASS |
| 7♠ (!) | DOUBLE | END | |

(1) Roman Keycard Blackwood – agreeing hearts.
(2) Two of 'five aces' (including ♥K), no ♥Q.

**Contract: 7♠ doubled    Opening lead: ♣A**

# Shall We Dance?

Remember the Gershwin song from the musical *Shall We Dance?*, 'You say tomahto, I say tomayto... Let's call the whole thing off'? East-West called their partnership off after this deal. They were both good players, but two good players do not a partnership make, and that their styles were clearly mismatched was evidenced by what happened.

Perhaps East should not have overcalled Two Clubs. Perhaps West should not have doubled Four Spades. Doubtless West, a sound overcaller, would not have contemplated overcalling Two Clubs with East's cards; and East, a light overcaller, would not have doubled Four Spades with West's cards. The combination was fatal.

Declarer won West's club lead – to dummy's seven and East's jack – with his ace. He cashed the ace of trumps, both following low, and then paused for thought. If he played a second trump and West held both honours (as expected from the double), West would win and switch to a diamond. He would then have to lose a diamond, a heart, and two trumps.

Instead declarer sought to set up a fourth round heart winner in dummy to discard a diamond. Abandoning trumps, declarer cashed the ace-king of hearts and led a third heart. West won the queen and switched to a diamond. Declarer rose with dummy's ace and led the established jack of hearts discarding his second diamond. West ruffed with his queen but the only remaining trick he could score was the king of trumps. Doubled game made.

It was clever – and correct – for declarer to go after hearts after cashing the ace of trumps, rather than leading a second trump in the hope that the two missing honours would crash. But would he have found this line if West hadn't doubled? East made

Teams

| | ♠ 8 5 |
| ♥ J 5 4 3 |
| ♦ A 10 8 6 |
| ♣ Q 9 7 |

♠ K Q 9      N      ♠ 3
♥ Q 7 2   W     E   ♥ 10 8 6
♦ Q J 7 5      S      ♦ K 9 4
♣ 10 6 3             ♣ K J 8 5 4 2

♠ A J 10 7 6 4 2
♥ A K 9
♦ 3 2
♣ A

| S | W | N | E |
|---|---|---|---|
| 1♠ | PASS | 1NT | 2♣ (1) |
| 4♠ | DOUBLE (2) END | | |

(1) Skimpy. Some players love a light overcalling style. Some hate it.
(2) Facing a sound overcaller, this is a reasonable double. But not facing this particular East!

**Contract: 4♠**          **Opening lead: ♣3**

unhappy noises about his partner's double. And then it was West's turn.

'If you had kept your mouth shut instead of overcalling Two Clubs on those tram tickets, I would have led the queen of diamonds at Trick One. Now make Four Spades!'

*Postscript*: For the curious, my style is very much to overcall on East's hand, and therefore not to double with West's. Most important, though, is harmony of partnership style – the theme of our opening chapter.

# CHAPTER 3

# Opening Lead

Over half of all contracts that start life in the balance are decided one way or the other by the opening lead. The choice of first defensive card – uniquely played without a sight of dummy – can swing three, four, five tricks from one side to the other. Indeed the 2006 Hawaiian Nationals saw a highly dubious Six Notrump contract declared by USA's Larry Cohen. Had Italian World Champion Fulvio Fantoni found the best lead (a spade), the defence would have made all thirteen tricks. When he chose a heart, it was declarer who made all thirteen tricks.

The opening leader is blind, in the sense that they cannot see dummy. So they fall back on tried-and-tested strategies such as leading fourth from the top of the longest suit in notrumps; and a singleton, or top of a sequence against a trump contract. However there are clues from the bidding – did partner utter? What did the opponents bid? What did they not bid? Which of their bids were made confidently? Which hesitatingly?

No player makes the best lead all the time, but this chapter will unveil the inner workings of the expert mind in this area. On our first deal we see one such expert fall flat on his face. One Andrew Robson...

# Eleven-hour Retrospect

Travelling to Las Vegas for a weekend is a long way to go. Especially when you don't gamble. And more especially when your chances in the Bridge tournament (the reason for my trip) were wrecked on an early deal by an unfortunate choice of opening lead (as West on this featured deal).

Cover up the other three hands, study the auction, and see if you can make your journey more worthwhile than your author.

There is no case for a trump lead against the Six Club slam but the other three suits all have merit:

(a) A spade. If partner holds the king, then a spade might be necessary – to force out the ace and so establish the second round winner.

(b) A heart (the king). A 'safe' choice. Plus it might be important to cash one round before it runs away.

(c) A diamond. Partner might hold the ace, and be able to give us a quick ruff.

After weighing up the pros and cons of each alternative, I eventually settled for the rather wet king of hearts. Wrong!

Declarer won the ace, cashed the ace of trumps, and then led a low diamond to my ten, dummy's jack, and partner's ace. Partner tried a second diamond but my trump had been extracted. Declarer won his queen, drew the remaining trumps, and ran dummy's diamonds. Slam made.

Either an opening spade lead (setting up our second round winner) or a diamond (enabling me to score a second round ruff) would have defeated the slam.

What do I think in retrospect (and there was plenty of retrospect on the 11-hour return flight)? Was I unlucky or did I make a poor choice?

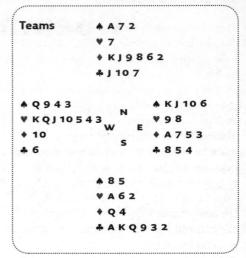

| Teams | ♠ A 7 2 |
| | ♥ 7 |
| | ♦ K J 9 8 6 2 |
| | ♣ J 10 7 |

♠ Q 9 4 3          ♠ K J 10 6
♥ K Q J 10 5 4 3   ♥ 9 8
♦ 10               ♦ A 7 5 3
♣ 6                ♣ 8 5 4

♠ 8 5
♥ A 6 2
♦ Q 4
♣ A K Q 9 3 2

| S | W (ROBSON) | N | E |
|---|---|---|---|
| 1♣ | 4♥ | 5♣ | 5♥ |
| 6♣ | END | | |

**Contract: 6♣**

**Opening lead: ♠3/♥K/♦10**

I do not think a diamond lead is sound – only working when partner holds the ace. Leading a singleton against a slam is a sound choice, but only when you have more than one trump – because you succeed if partner has either the ace of the singleton suit or the ace of trumps.

I now believe that I should have led a spade – essential if partner has the king, or ace-jack sitting over dummy's king, and probably doing little harm on other layouts.

# Rita's Ace

There is a saying in Bridge, applying to the opening lead to a trump contract, 'When you have an ace-king, you do not have a lead problem.'

The ace from ace-king lead is even better than a singleton because it keeps all your options open (assuming the ace isn't ruffed). You see dummy and partner's signal, and can make an informed decision as to whether to continue with the king or to switch (probably to your singleton). The singleton lead, on the other hand, risks losing the initiative, with the distinct possibility that declarer will win the trick and promptly draw your trumps.

Sometimes, because it keeps options open, even an unsupported ace is preferable to a singleton lead if there is a possibility that partner is singleton. Take this deal, from the NEC Invitational Teams in Yokohama.

At one table West led his singleton club. Declarer made no mistake, rising with dummy's ace and crashing his king. This was necessary so that he could be in dummy to take the trump finesse. The jack of trumps won Trick Two, a second trump was led to the king and ace, and declarer merely conceded two spades and a diamond. Ten tricks and game made.

USA's Rita Shugart preferred the ace of diamonds opening lead, continuing (when a look at dummy revealed the pointlessness of the club switch) with a second diamond (leading the jack – a high card – as a suit preference signal for spades – the higher ranking suit). East ruffed, cashed the ace of spades, then led a second spade. West won the king and led a third diamond, East overruffing dummy's jack of trumps with his bare king. Down two.

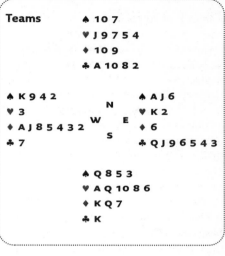

**Dealer: South   Vulnerability: North-South**

Teams

```
            ♠ 10 7
            ♥ J 9 7 5 4
            ♦ 10 9
            ♣ A 10 8 2
♠ K 9 4 2              ♠ A J 6
♥ 3          N        ♥ K 2
♦ A J 8 5 4 3 2  W  E  ♦ 6
♣ 7          S        ♣ Q J 9 6 5 4 3
            ♠ Q 8 5 3
            ♥ A Q 10 8 6
            ♦ K Q 7
            ♣ K
```

| S | W | N | E |
|---|---|---|---|
| 1♥ | 3♦ (1) | 4♥ | END |

(1) Weak Jump Overcall.

**Contract: 4♥**          **Opening lead: ♦A**

# Top of Partner's Suit?

Leading top of partner's bid suit used to be standard defensive policy. However the passing of time has revealed that this is too costly on many deals. Take these suit layouts for example:

(i)
```
            x x
    K x x        Q 10 9 x x
            A J x
```

or

(ii)
```
            x x
    Q x x        A 10 9 x x
            K J x
```

The lead of the honour (the king in (i) and the queen in (ii)) both present declarer with a second trick in the suit (the jack in both cases).

However there can be times when leading top of partner's suit is necessary. One reason – certainly the appropriate one on this deal – is to retain the lead to allow for an informed switch after a look at dummy. The deal comes from the Swiss Pairs at the wonderful Peebles Congress in December.

West was international Andrew McIntosh, originally from Inverness but now living in North London. He unerringly selected the king of diamonds – rather than a low one – as his opening lead.

A look at dummy suggested that spades was the suit for the defence to attack. But in case McIntosh had any doubt, his partner (Edinburgh's Les Steel) contributed a suit-preference queen of diamonds (high card asking for higher ranked suit) under the king.

At Trick Two West switched dutifully to the jack of spades. Declarer suspected he was doomed, but covered with dummy's king. East won the ace, cashed the queen, and led a third spade to West's ten. The defence had taken the first four tricks so, although declarer took the remainder by finessing in

**Dealer: East**          **Vulnerability: Neither**

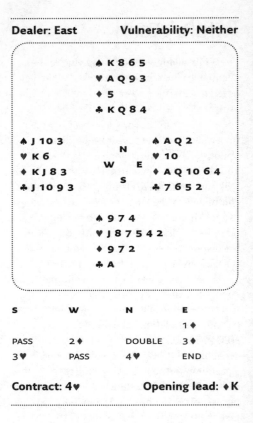

|       |        |        |       |
|-------|--------|--------|-------|
| **S** | **W**  | **N**  | **E** |
|       |        |        | 1♦    |
| PASS  | 2♦     | DOUBLE | 3♦    |
| 3♥    | PASS   | 4♥     | END   |

**Contract: 4♥**          **Opening lead: ♦K**

trumps (leading and passing the jack), the game was down one.

Note that Four Hearts would have been undefeatable had West led a low diamond. East (not his partner) would win the trick and be unable to attack spades profitably from his side. At his leisure declarer could discard two losing spades on dummy's clubs.

# Irish Sneak

Cover up all hands bar West's on this deal from the World Transnational Teams. Your partner opens 1♦ and your vulnerable right-hand opponent leaps to 5♣. What do you lead?

Surely a diamond – partner's suit – right? WRONG!

Have a look at all four hands. You lead a diamond and declarer is home – his ten of diamonds is promoted as partner's jack is finessed, and seven trump tricks (when the jack cooperates) ensure that his only losers are his two major-suit singletons.

Is it being wise after the event to suggest that West should not have led his partner's suit?

I don't think so. South's vulnerable leap to 5♣ is a rare action. Is it not likely that his hand is improved by the diamond bid; that he is banking on a diamond lead?

Ireland's Hugh McGann managed to sneak home after a more prudent opening lead from West, the ace of hearts, followed by a less prudent heart continuation (a spade or jack of trumps switch at Trick Two would beat the game).

Declarer ruffed the second heart and led out all his trumps and two top diamonds to reach:

```
                ♠ J 9
                ♥ Q
                ♦ 9
                ♣ –
    ♠ Q 7 5    N      ♠ A 10
    ♥ 8     W     E   ♥ –
    ♦ –              ♦ J 8
    ♣ –       S      ♣ –
                ♠ 8
                ♥ –
                ♦ Q 10
                ♣ 4 (led)
```

West threw a heart, dummy having the boss card in the suit (set up by West's heart

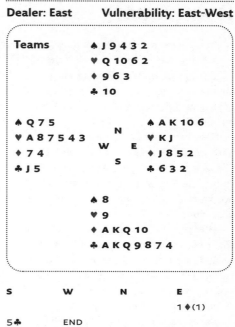

```
Teams        ♠ J 9 4 3 2
             ♥ Q 10 6 2
             ♦ 9 6 3
             ♣ 10

♠ Q 7 5              ♠ A K 10 6
♥ A 8 7 5 4 3   N    ♥ K J
♦ 7 4        W    E  ♦ J 8 5 2
♣ J 5           S   ♣ 6 3 2

             ♠ 8
             ♥ 9
             ♦ A K Q 10
             ♣ A K Q 9 8 7 4
```

| S | W | N | E |
|---|---|---|---|
|   |   |   | 1♦(1) |
| 5♣ | END | | |

(1) Playing Five-card Majors and Strong Notrump.

**Contract: 5♣**          **Opening lead: ?**

continuation). Dummy threw a diamond, and it was over to East.

Having to retain both diamonds, a spade had to go. East had already thrown the king to retain the ten (afraid of being endplayed), but now had to commit.

If East threw his ace of spades, declarer would lead to dummy's jack and restrict West to his queen. And if he (as he did) threw the ten of spades, declarer could exit with a spade to East's ace and wait for the forced diamond return, enabling declarer to score both his ♦Q10. Game made.

# If in Doubt

What is your view of the motto for a defender on opening lead, 'If in doubt, lead a trump?' In general I am quite a believer in this passive approach – guessing which side-suit to break open before viewing dummy is a precarious business.

However on this deal the defence could have taken four tricks – and so defeat the Four Spade contract – on any lead but a trump: the king of trumps, ace of hearts and ace-king of clubs are unavoidable losers. But on a trump lead...

After playing dummy's jack of trumps at trick one, it is tempting for declarer to lead a second round of the suit to discover the split. He would find out that East held a singleton and rise with the ace. What next?

Faced with the four obvious losers, declarer would need to discard a club from dummy on his fourth diamond. But after cashing ace-king-queen of diamonds (observing the even split) and leading the master ten, West would not be so kind as to ruff with his king of trumps. Instead he would discard. Declarer would lead a heart to dummy's queen and East's ace and East would continue the fine defensive recovery by underleading his club honours. West would win the king, cash the king of trumps (crucially drawing dummy's last trump), then lead a second club to his partner. Down one.

However at the table declarer – Herefordshire's Tony Forrester – did not play a second round of trumps. Anticipating the likely trump split, he immediately led four rounds of diamonds (key plays), discarding a club from dummy on the fourth round. West ruffed low (as good as anything), but declarer could either discard a club from dummy or overruff. He chose to discard (more elegant) and won West's king of trumps exit with the ace. He then conceded a club, knowing that

he could safely ruff his second club with dummy's last trump. Game made.

**Teams**

```
                 ♠ J 7 5
                 ♥ K Q 10 7 3
                 ♦ K 8 3
                 ♣ 10 6

♠ K 6 4                        ♠ 2
♥ J 6 2          N             ♥ A 9 8 4
♦ 9 4 2       W     E          ♦ J 7 5
♣ K 4 3 2         S            ♣ A Q J 8 7

                 ♠ A Q 10 9 8 3
                 ♥ 5
                 ♦ A Q 10 6
                 ♣ 9 5
```

| S | W | N | E |
|---|---|---|---|
| 1♠ | PASS | 2♠ (1) | DOUBLE |
| 4♠ (2) | END | | |

(1) Playing Five-card Majors.
(2) Clearly South does not have the points for game, but he expects the opponents to have a heart game (er... not this time!).

**Contract: 4♠**          **Opening lead: 4♠**

# Cultural Divide

The opening lead against a notrump contract of 'Fourth highest of your longest and strongest suit' is one of the longer lasting and more universally played mottoes.

Its plus is that it establishes winners by virtue of length. Its minus is that it can give a cheap trick to declarer en route. Normally a strong five-card suit is worth leading, but it pays to think twice before leading a strong four-card suit. It might be better to sit tight with the holding and wait for someone else (partner?) to lead it.

Interestingly there is something of a cultural divide here. Most Americans, led by 'Meckwell' (World Champions Meckstroth and Rodwell), prefer to lead the strong four-card suit; at least it makes the subsequent defence clearer (partner returns the lead when in doubt). However many European countries, led by the Poles, are unwilling to give a cheap trick to declarer at trick one. They prefer a more passive approach, typically choosing to lead from three small cards.

My instinct tells me that the Polish method is slightly better in theory. But, because in practice it requires partner to be absolutely spot on with his subsequent defence, the old favourite 'fourth highest of your longest and strongest' is probably more practical.

On this deal it was the Polish approach that won the day. West led the six of diamonds (leading high from rubbish) to South's One Notrump and East won the ace and found the killing switch at trick two – he led the queen of clubs (key play). Had he led low, declarer would have played low from hand and prevented the defence from running four tricks in the suit, East being unable to regain the lead to play a second round.

Declarer covered the queen with the king

**Dealer: South** **Vulnerability: Both**

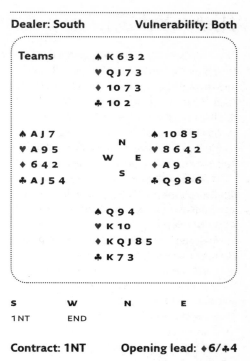

Teams

|  |  |  |  |
|---|---|---|---|
| | ♠ K 6 3 2 | | |
| | ♥ Q J 7 3 | | |
| | ♦ 10 7 3 | | |
| | ♣ 10 2 | | |

♠ A J 7           ♠ 10 8 5
♥ A 9 5    N    ♥ 8 6 4 2
♦ 6 4 2   W   E   ♦ A 9
♣ A J 5 4    S    ♣ Q 9 8 6

| | |
|---|---|
| ♠ Q 9 4 | |
| ♥ K 10 | |
| ♦ K Q J 8 5 | |
| ♣ K 7 3 | |

| S | W | N | E |
|---|---|---|---|
| 1NT | END | | |

**Contract: 1NT** **Opening lead: ♦6/♣4**

but West won his ace, cashed his jack, felling dummy's ten, then led to East's nine-eight. East switched to a heart and West defeated the contract with his two major suit aces. Four club tricks and three aces meant down one.

The 'fourth highest' approach would be less successful. If West leads the four of clubs, declarer wins his king, flushes out the ace of diamonds, and loses just three clubs and three aces.

# Rise and Shine?

Cover up the East-West cards and declare Six Hearts on the two of diamonds lead, the only opposing bid being a weak jump overcall in spades from East. Bear in mind that it is Rubber Bridge, so the overtrick is irrelevant.

The key decision is whether or not to rise with dummy's ace of diamonds at Trick One. Make your decision before reading on.

The two of diamonds looks suspiciously like a singleton, making rising with dummy's ace seem mandatory. But rising with the ace might be the wrong thing to do if West holds the king and has craftily underled it. Most of the time rising with the ace will only cost you the unimportant overtrick, but there are two layouts where it will cost you the slam:
(a) when East has a void diamond and
(b) when East has a void trump (giving West a trump trick).

The key question is as follows: which is more likely – East holding a red suit void or West holding a singleton diamond?

If West holds a singleton diamond, he has to have ten hearts and clubs (he is known to have just two spades from East's weak jump). Because you cannot make the slam if West holds all four trumps (and a singleton diamond), you must assume that he has fewer. This leaves him with seven (+) clubs – surely he would have preempted in the suit as dealer, non-vulnerable.

Though East holding a red-suit void is unlikely, it is more likely than West holding a singleton diamond. Declarer should play low from dummy at Trick One. He subsequently loses a trump trick to West but avoids losing to the king of diamonds. Slam made.

However declarer should not forget to congratulate West on his fine Machiavellian low diamond lead, tempting him to panic into rising with dummy's ace before he knows there is a trump loser.

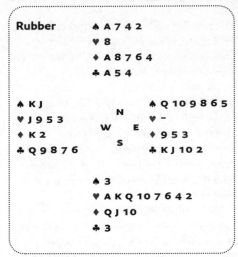

**Dealer: West    Vulnerability: North-South**

Rubber

|  | ♠ A 7 4 2 |
|  | ♥ 8 |
|  | ♦ A 8 7 6 4 |
|  | ♣ A 5 4 |

| ♠ K J | ♠ Q 10 9 8 6 5 |
| ♥ J 9 5 3 | ♥ – |
| ♦ K 2 | ♦ 9 5 3 |
| ♣ Q 9 8 7 6 | ♣ K J 10 2 |

|  | ♠ 3 |
|  | ♥ A K Q 10 7 6 4 2 |
|  | ♦ Q J 10 |
|  | ♣ 3 |

| S | W | N | E |
|---|---|---|---|
|  | PASS | 1♦ | 2♠ (1) |
| 4NT (2) | PASS | 5♣ (3) | PASS |
| 6♥ (4) | END |  |  |

(1) Weak Jump Overcall.
(2) Roman Key Card Blackwood with diamonds agreed. Though he always intends to play in hearts, this enables him to find out about ♦K.
(3) Zero or three of the 'five aces' (including ♦K).
(4) Assumes three so, missing one of ♠A, ♦AK and ♣A, settles for a small slam in hearts.

**Contract: 6♥**        **Opening lead: ♦2**

# He Who Hesitates

You pick up ♠Q985, ♥Q1093, ♥7, ♣A852. You have a slender lead in the semifinals of the English Trials but have a nightmarish decision on which many points are certain to rest.

Right-hand opponent opens a preemptive Three Diamonds, which is promptly raised to Five Diamonds by left-hand opponent (presumably as an advance sacrifice). Partner comes in with a vulnerable Five Heart bid and you have to decide whether or not to bid Six Hearts. Do you or don't you?

After a small but agonising (I can assure you) pause, I summoned up the courage and bid the slam. In the other room the bidding had started identically, including my decision to bid on to Six Hearts. But at that point East-West took the 'phantom sacrifice' (bidding on to stop the opponents from playing a contract that would not have made). They lost 800 points in Seven Diamonds (four down doubled). Perhaps my fractional hesitancy had dissuaded East-West from doing likewise at my table.

Six Hearts is hopeless on a diamond lead, but perhaps our bidding implied a readiness to cope with the expected lead. A friend who rang to find out the result of match said, when given West's lead problem 'I choose between the black suits... stick me down for the jack of spades'.

Had West led the jack of spades, declarer would win his ace, crossed to a trump, ruffed a spade, crossed to a second trump, then led the queen of spades (key play). East would cover with the king but West's ten would be pinned. Declarer would cross to the ace of clubs, cash the established nine of spades discarding his king of diamonds, then lead a club towards the queen. Slam made.

But West, David Burn, unerringly fished out the queen of diamonds. Partner Tony

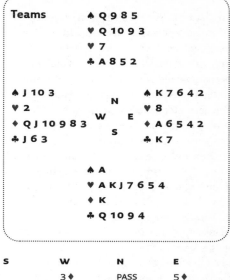

|   | ♠ Q 9 8 5 |
|---|---|
|   | ♥ Q 10 9 3 |
|   | ♥ 7 |
|   | ♣ A 8 5 2 |

Teams

♠ J 10 3     ♠ K 7 6 4 2
♥ 2          ♥ 8
♦ Q J 10 9 8 3   ♦ A 6 5 4 2
♣ J 6 3      ♣ K 7

♠ A
♥ A K J 7 6 5 4
♦ K
♣ Q 10 9 4

| S | W | N | E |
|---|---|---|---|
|   | 3♦ | PASS | 5♦ |
| 5♥ | PASS | 6♥ (?) | END |

**Contract: 6♥**          **Opening lead: ♦Q**

Forrester naturally thanked me for my dummy, but we had been playing together for close to ten years and I could sense his disappointment. East won the ace, switched safely to a trump, and declarer was left hoping that West held a singleton king of clubs. He led low to dummy's ace of clubs, but there was no joy. He led a second club, East won the king, and everybody put their cards back in the wallet. Down one.

I cursed. We all knew the match was now on a knife-edge.

# Underrated Primates

**Dealer: East**    **Vulnerability: Neither**

**Teams**

```
              ♠ 8 5
              ♥ Q J 6 4
              ♦ Q 9 8 7 4
              ♣ A 5
♠ 10 9 7 3 2        N        ♠ A K Q J 6
♥ A 9 7 2      W       E     ♥ K 10 8 5 3
♦ -                S         ♦ -
♣ 9 8 7 3                    ♣ J 10 2
              ♠ 4
              ♥ -
              ♦ A K J 10 6 5 3 2
              ♣ K Q 6 4
```

I remember a deal from a recent European Championships where Norwegian star Boye Brogeland held two aces on opening lead against a grand slam. Lead either ace and declarer would have made all 13 tricks (both would have been ruffed). Instead Boye led a neutral trump, and his partner scored the setting trick, would you believe it, with his ace (yes – a third missing one).

This deal – from London's Young Chelsea Bridge Club Teams – demonstrates the danger of falling for the temptation to plonk your ace on the table against a grand slam.

West's (understandable) choice of the ace of hearts against Seven Diamonds (doubled) was a disaster. Declarer ruffed it, and did not need to get rid of the opposing trumps, for the unusual reason that there were none. Instead he crossed to the ace of clubs and led the queen of hearts for a ruffing finesse.

If East had covered the queen of hearts with the king, declarer would have ruffed, cashed the king of clubs, ruffed a club, then discarded his singleton spade on dummy's promoted jack of hearts. At the table, East chose to play low on the queen of hearts (hoping declarer would ruff). No good – declarer discarded his spade and was soon chalking up his doubled grand.

On any other lead – even an improbable low heart – declarer would have been unable to dispose of his spade loser, and would have gone down one. A monkey (selecting a card at random from West's hand) would have had a 12/13 chance of defeating the grand – these primates are not to be underrated.

Next time, of course, the ace will cash, and be the only lead to defeat the grand slam. Your studious neutral alternative strategy will fall flat on its face, as declarer gratefully wins, draws trumps, and runs a long side-suit, discarding all his cards in the suit in which

| S | W | N | E |
|---|---|---|---|
|  |  |  | 1♠ |
| 5♦ (1) | 5♠ | 6♦ | 6♠ (2) |
| 7♦ (2) | DOUBLE (3) | END | |

(1) Very strong for a preempt, but South desperately wants to silence his opponents and declare the deal.

(2) Bidding one more – the safe approach on such wild deals in which both sides have a big fit.

(3) With a hopeful eye on his ace.

**Contract: 7♦ doubled    Opening lead: ♥A**

you hold the ace. Partner will look incredulously at you, as you write down minus 2210 or similar, having 'gone to bed' with your ace. That's Bridge!

# CHAPTER 4

# Count Winners not Losers

Bridge is a game about winning tricks. It therefore seems to me entirely logical to count winners, rather than losers, when planning the play as declarer. Count your top tricks, those you can make before losing the lead, and you know how many extra ones are required for your contract. This is (rightly) the accepted wisdom in a notrump contract; but many declarers prefer to count losers in a trump contract.

Whilst ideally a quick tally of both winners and losers is recommended to declarer in a trump contract, I would rather just count winners than just count losers. This chapter exposes the flaws of the loser approach. It has to be said however, that the relationship between winning and losing (tricks) is often curiously blurred. Take the words of Pyrrhus on defeating the Romans at Asculum in 279 BC:

'One more such victory and we are lost.'

# Two Plus Two

You are West (cover up South and East) and have confidence that you will defeat Five Hearts. You lead the king of clubs and await your two natural trump tricks – plus whatever partner is destined to make in diamonds.

Declarer wins the ace of clubs and leads a trump. You naturally play low, to ensure you make both your trumps and...

Oops. You will not enjoy the rest of the defence. Look at all four hands and see what is about to happen. Declarer wins dummy's jack of trumps (partner discarding) and ruffs a club; he crosses to the ten of spades and ruffs a third club; he crosses to the queen of spades and ruffs a fourth club; finally, over to the ace of spades and declarer scores his last low trump by ruffing dummy's final club.

Declarer's last four cards are ace-queen of trumps and two losing diamonds. You as West hold king-ten-nine of trumps and a club. Declarer exits with a diamond and you postpone the agony by discarding your last club. But when partner wins and tries to cash a second diamond winner, you are forced to ruff and lead away from your king of trumps around to declarer's ace-queen. Eleven tricks and game made.

Rise with the king of trumps at Trick Two and declarer has no chance. Partner has to score two diamond tricks at the end and the game is down one.

Funny old game – you have two 'certain' trump tricks by ducking your king at Trick Two; partner has two certain diamond tricks. But does two + two = four? Not a bit of it: two + two = two. Where did the third and fourth defensive tricks go?

One trick was taken twice – West perforce ruffing his partner's second winning diamond; the second trick (a trump) was lost because West had to lead away from his king at Trick 12.

**Dealer: East**        **Vulnerability: Neither**

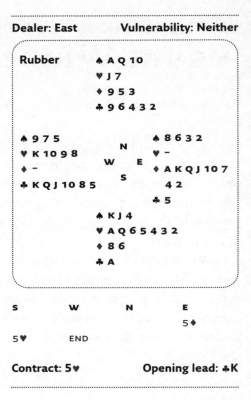

Rubber

|  | ♠ A Q 10 |  |
|---|---|---|
|  | ♥ J 7 |  |
|  | ♦ 9 5 3 |  |
|  | ♣ 9 6 4 3 2 |  |

| ♠ 9 7 5 | | ♠ 8 6 3 2 |
| ♥ K 10 9 8 | N | ♥ – |
| ♦ – | W    E | ♦ A K Q J 10 7 |
| ♣ K Q J 10 8 5 | S | 4 2 |
| | | ♣ 5 |

|  | ♠ K J 4 |  |
|  | ♥ A Q 6 5 4 3 2 |  |
|  | ♦ 8 6 |  |
|  | ♣ A |  |

| S | W | N | E |
|---|---|---|---|
|  |  |  | 5♦ |
| 5♥ | END |  |  |

**Contract: 5♥**        **Opening lead: ♣K**

This apparent paradox illustrates our theme: that it is better for declarer to think in terms of winners rather than losers. After all, Bridge is a game all about winning tricks.

# Bucolic Leap

Those declarers who prefer to count losers (in a trump contract) might miss the winning line on this deal, taken from a Duplicate at my London Club (www.arobson.co.uk).

South's leap to Six Diamonds may have been rather bucolic, but it is far from clear that a slower route would have enabled the partnership to reach the superior Six Club contract (which would make by ruffing a diamond in dummy).

In Six Diamonds, declarer was faced with two seemingly certain losers, West with a trump trick and East with a club trick. Watch one disappear.

He trumped the opening heart lead, cashed his three top trumps (East discarding a spade on the third round), then followed with his two top clubs. He crossed to dummy's king of spades, cashed the two top hearts (discarding clubs), ruffed a heart, crossed to the ace of spades and, at trick twelve, ruffed dummy's fifth heart (West helplessly following suit).

Declarer's last card, a club loser, was beaten both by West's jack of trumps and by East's queen of clubs.

Note that West's opening heart lead gave declarer an extra entry to dummy, enabling him to ruff all three hearts. He could not have succeeded on a black suit lead.

♠ 8
♥ J
♦ J 9
♣ J 8

♦ A K Q 10 8 6
♣ A K 6 5 4

| S | W | N | E |
|---|---|---|---|
|  |  | 1♥ | PASS |
| 2♦ (1) | PASS | 2♠ | PASS |
| 6♦ (2) | END |  |  |

(1) Correctly not jump shifting with a two-suiter.

(2) Three Clubs would be Fourth Suit Forcing, not natural, so South simply bids what he thinks he can make.

**Contract: 6♦**     **Opening lead: ♥4**

...Spades (the deal ...e Olympic semifinals) ...u count winners. The ...r was obviously thinking ...ent lines, for he missed the best ...finished up down one – can you do ...ter?

Bear in mind the following homily: When you are seeking to score trumps separately, count up your top tricks in the side-suits; you will then know how many trump tricks you need for your contract.

Here there are just three side-suit tricks (the aces), so you need to score all seven trumps. This may sound a tall order, but ruffing two hearts will make tricks with both dummy's trumps and, if East (the non-preemptor) holds the king of trumps, all your five trumps in hand can be promoted. But only with careful timing.

The correct line is to win the ace of hearts in hand, and immediately play to the ace of clubs and ruff a club (you need to shorten your trumps in hand before ruffing in dummy). Then (preferably cashing the ace of diamonds at – or before – this early stage) ruff a heart, and ruff a third club (pleased to see East follow, or he could throw a heart and overruff dummy on the third heart: a risk that must be taken). Next ruff a third heart, and ruff a fourth club.

You have scored the first eight tricks and still have ace-queen of trumps in your hand. Simply exit with a red card, and wait to be given the finesse of the queen of trumps. Ten tricks and game made – on a complete crossruff.

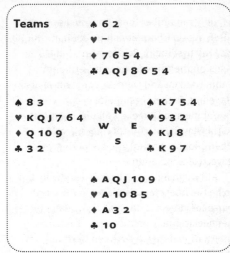

**Dealer: West**      **Vulnerability: Both**

**Teams**

North:
- ♠ 6 2
- ♥ –
- ♦ 7 6 5 4
- ♣ A Q J 8 6 5 4

West:
- ♠ 8 3
- ♥ K Q J 7 6 4
- ♦ Q 10 9
- ♣ 3 2

East:
- ♠ K 7 5 4
- ♥ 9 3 2
- ♦ K J 8
- ♣ K 9 7

South:
- ♠ A Q J 10 9
- ♥ A 10 8 5
- ♦ A 3 2
- ♣ 10

| S | W | N | E |
|---|---|---|---|
|  | 2♥ (1) | PASS | 3♥ |
| 3♠ | PASS | 4♣ | PASS |
| 4♠ (2) | END | | |

(1) Weak Two – 5-10 points and a good six-card suit.
(2) Tricky choice. An improbable raise to 5♣ with the singleton support is the winner (5♣ makes on any lead but an unlikely diamond).

**Contract: 4♠**      **Opening lead: ♥K**

# Sabine and Daniela

I vividly remember the plane journey to the 1986 World Championships in Miami – it was my first major Bridge event. In nearby seats on the same plane, sat Germany's Sabine Auken and Daniela Von Arnim, also travelling to their first major event.

Sabine and Daniela, still playing together to this day, have won countless World Championship titles, and are both great advertisements for the game.

Although Sabine is acknowledged by many to be the finest female player in the world, her partner Daniela is no weak link. Just look at her declarer play on this deal – from an international match between Germany and the USA.

With 25 points between the partnership and an eight-card major fit, you would think it was a normal Four Heart contract for North-South. Think again! South's light opener and the presence of such excellent controls in all four suits caused the partnership to reach the dizzy heights of Six Hearts.

West led a devious six of clubs, though an unlikely trump lead would have worked best. Declarer won dummy's king of clubs, cashed the ace of spades, ruffed a spade, cashed the ace of diamonds, ruffed a diamond, ruffed a third spade and ruffed a third diamond. She cashed the ace of clubs, ruffed a fourth spade (with the ten), then led her fourth diamond.

Down to just her four trumps, West ruffed low. Declarer overruffed with dummy's bare king, then led a third club. Though East had the boss card in the suit, West was forced to ruff, and lead from her queen-nine of trumps into declarer's ace-jack.

Don't consider Dani's losers. She made twelve tricks, and that was all that mattered. Slam made!

**Dealer: South     Vulnerability: East-West**

Teams

|  |  |
|---|---|
| | ♠ A J 9 8 7 |
| | ♥ K 8 7 |
| | ♦ 3 |
| | ♣ A K 5 2 |

| ♠ K 10 5 2 | | ♠ Q 6 4 |
|---|---|---|
| ♥ Q 9 6 2 | N | ♥ 4 |
| ♦ Q 10 5 | W    E | ♦ K 9 8 6 2 |
| ♣ Q 6 | S | ♣ J 9 7 4 |

|  |  |
|---|---|
| | ♠ 3 |
| | ♥ A J 10 5 3 |
| | ♦ A J 7 4 |
| | ♣ 10 8 3 |

| S | W | N | E |
|---|---|---|---|
| 1♥ (1) | PASS | 1♠ | PASS |
| 2♦ | PASS | 3♣ (2) | PASS |
| 3♥ | PASS | 4NT | PASS |
| 5♥ | PASS | 6♥ | END |

(1) Light but all her honours are in long suits and there are no rebid problems.
(2) Fourth Suit Forcing – more information please.

**Contract: 6♥          Opening lead: ♣6**

# Style Points

A Two Diamond opener has more different meanings amongst tournament players than any other opening bid.

In traditional Acol it shows a strong hand ('eight playing tricks') with a good diamond suit; in Standard American it shows a weak hand (6-10 points) and a six-card suit; other meanings include Multi (either a weak hand with a six-card major or certain strong hands); Flannery (four spades, five hearts and a minimumish opening hand); Benjamin Two (an eight playing trick hand in any suit)... and there are more!

Because I prefer a natural approach to the game, but like to bid with weak hands to make life awkward, my favoured use for the bid is as a Weak Two in diamonds (the US method). However I would be the first to admit that the bid was not successful on this deal.

West's four of diamonds opening lead was a clear singleton (East having opened a Weak Two in the suit), so declarer was not tempted to ride the lead around to his queen. He rose with dummy's ace and led a trump to his ace. This revealed the bad news (East discarding).

It appeared that West had two certain trump tricks in addition to East's king of diamonds. Could declarer condense these three losers into two? Focus, as usual, on winners.

At Trick Three declarer cashed the ace of spades and at Trick Four he cashed the ace of hearts (earning style points by playing aces to each of the first four tricks). He then ruffed a heart.

He crossed to the king of spades, ruffed a third heart, ruffed a spade, ruffed his fourth heart, then led dummy's fourth spade. When East discarded declarer could ruff low, knowing that West was following.

He was now home and dry, with the king

Dealer: East  Vulnerability: Neither

**Teams**

|  | ♠ 9 8 6 3 |  |
|---|---|---|
|  | ♥ 7 |  |
|  | ♦ A 8 6 2 |  |
|  | ♣ 9 7 5 2 |  |

| ♠ Q J 7 4 | N | ♠ 10 5 2 |
|---|---|---|
| ♥ Q 10 8 3 | W E | ♥ K 6 5 4 |
| ♦ 4 | S | ♦ K J 10 9 7 3 |
| ♣ Q J 8 3 |  | ♣ - |

|  | ♠ A K |  |
|---|---|---|
|  | ♥ A J 9 2 |  |
|  | ♦ Q 5 |  |
|  | ♣ A K 10 6 4 |  |

| S | W | N | E |
|---|---|---|---|
|  |  |  | 2♦ (1) |
| DOUBLE | PASS | 2♠ | PASS |
| 3♣ | PASS | 4♣ | PASS |
| 5♣ | END |  |  |

(1) Weak Two. Purists would object to holding a four-card major on the side. I believe the disruptive factor probably outweighs the risk of missing a heart fit.

**Contract: 5♣**  **Opening lead: ♦4**

of trumps scoring his eleventh trick. He conceded the last two tricks, West holding the master queen-jack of trumps and East the master king of diamonds, and rather enjoyed the overkill! Eleven tricks and game made.

# Shape not Points

By bidding and making slam with just 24 high-card points, Alexander Allfrey from Dorset and his London partner Andrew McIntosh demonstrated why Bridge is more about shape than high-card points, on this deal from the European Champions Cup.

West kicked off with a somewhat soft defence, leading ace and another heart (even though the bidding surely indicated that South held at most one card in the suit). Ruffing the second heart, declarer counted his winners.

With two top spades and two top diamonds, declarer sought to score all his eight trumps separately to bring his total to twelve. He cashed the ace-king of diamonds discarding spades from dummy, then ruffed a diamond.

Keen to score dummy's remaining low trump as soon as possible – before playing a third heart and giving East the chance to discard a spade/diamond, then overruff that suit – declarer played king of spades-spade to his ace-ruff a third spade (West discarding a diamond). He then ruffed a third heart (East discarding), ruffed a fourth diamond (with the king), a fourth heart (with the ten), a fifth diamond with the ace and a fifth heart with the queen. Twelve tricks and slam made.

Declarer timed the hand very well, but would he have succeeded on an opening trump lead? He would not be able to score all his trumps separately, however twelve tricks are still possible; declarer must finesse East for the queen of spades, plus set up his fifth diamond (by ruffing twice), taking advantage of the four-four diamond split. Dicey stuff.

**Dealer: South  Vulnerability: North-South**

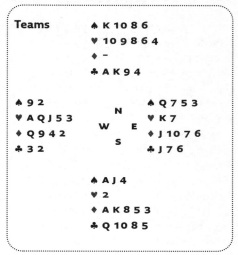

| Teams | ♠ K 10 8 6 |
| | ♥ 10 9 8 6 4 |
| | ♦ – |
| | ♣ A K 9 4 |

|  ♠ 9 2 |  | ♠ Q 7 5 3 |
| ♥ A Q J 5 3 | N | ♥ K 7 |
| ♦ Q 9 4 2 | W   E | ♦ J 10 7 6 |
| ♣ 3 2 | S | ♣ J 7 6 |

| | ♠ A J 4 |
| | ♥ 2 |
| | ♦ A K 8 5 3 |
| | ♣ Q 10 8 5 |

| S | W | N | E |
| --- | --- | --- | --- |
| 1♦ | 1♥ | 1♠ | PASS |
| 2♣ (1) | PASS | 2♥ (2) | PASS |
| 3♠ (3) | PASS | 6♣ (4) | END |

(1) Showing his five-four shape.
(2) I have a good hand – tell me more.
(3) Showing real (if delayed) support (i.e. three cards). Bidding 2♠ would sound like mere preference – on a doubleton.
(4) Partner being marked with at most one heart, North realises that the two hands will fit like gloves.

**Contract: 6♣**          **Opening lead: ♥A**

# Overcomplicating

**Dealer: South**      **Vulnerability: Both**

Sometimes an apparently simple bridge hand actually requires quite complex technique. But in my experience the converse is far more likely to be the case – that declarer over-complicates matters, and misses a relatively easy line of play. Take this declarer, for example.

West led a club – actually the most awkward lead – and it was over to declarer. At the table he won dummy's ace, led the nine of trumps to his ten, trumped his second club with dummy's ace, then cashed the ace and king of diamonds. Disaster! East trumped the second round. He exited with his last trump to declarer and now declarer was forced to try the spade finesse for his twelfth trick. He ran the queen but it lost to East's king. Down one.

Let us go back to basics. What should you do before playing from dummy at trick one? Right – count top tricks (again, focusing on winners rather than losers, even in a trump contract). You have a spade, seven trumps, two diamonds and a club. Total eleven. By far the easiest route to twelve tricks is to establish a second trick in spades.

The correct line of play after winning the opening lead with dummy's ace of clubs is to cash the ace of spades and follow with a second spade. Let East (it doesn't matter which defender) win the king, for dummy's jack is now established. You can win any return from East (ruffing a third spade high), draw trumps, cross to dummy in diamonds, then throw your club loser on the jack of spades. Twelve tricks and slam made.

Perhaps declarer was lured into a false sense of security. On a red suit lead he would have made Seven Hearts – he draws trumps, then starts on diamonds. He has the two black aces as late entries to establish the suit.

**Rubber**

|  | North |
|---|---|
|  | ♠ A J 8 3 |
|  | ♥ A 9 |
|  | ♦ A K J 9 8 3 |
|  | ♣ A |

| West | | East |
|---|---|---|
| ♠ 10 5 4 | | ♠ K 9 7 6 |
| ♥ 8 | N | ♥ 5 4 2 |
| ♦ Q 10 7 2 | W  E | ♦ 4 |
| ♣ J 10 4 2 | S | ♣ K Q 8 7 6 5 |

|  | South |
|---|---|
|  | ♠ Q 2 |
|  | ♥ K Q J 10 7 6 3 |
|  | ♦ 6 5 |
|  | ♣ 9 3 |

| S | W | N | E |
|---|---|---|---|
| 3♥ | PASS | 6♥ (1) | END |

(1) No need for exploration, as he already knows the essence of his partner's hand: weak with a good seven-card heart suit. Six Hearts must have play.

**Contract: 6♥**      **Opening lead: ♣J**

# Losers – pah!

I do not advocate many conventions. Having to bid naturally improves your judgment more than if you have an artificial tool for every occasion. That said, if a convention crops up often enough, plus it's easy to understand and effective, it is worth playing.

One of my favourite conventions is the Splinter Bid. The most basic scenario is a double jump in a new suit in response to an opening bid. The bid shows a singleton or void in the suit bid, primary support for partner's suit, and at least a game-going (are you listening, North?) hand.

No one likes to finish in Five-of-a-Major under their own steam, and here it was North 'splintering' with insufficient values that was the culprit.

Declarer looks certain to lose three tricks (with trumps 3-1) – a heart, a diamond and a trump... Or does he? Focus on winners.

Declarer ducked West's queen of hearts opening lead, won the queen of trumps switch with the ace, crossed to the king of trumps (East discarding a diamond) then cashed the ace of hearts. He followed by cashing the ace of diamonds, crossing to dummy's king of diamonds, returning to the ace of clubs, then trumping a club. He trumped a third heart, trumped a third club, trumped his last heart, and finally trumped his last club. He had scrambled eleven of the first twelve tricks. Game made.

You know you have played a hand well when both opponents can lay claim to the final trick. Here declarer had a losing diamond in each hand and East held the master diamond. But it was West who actually took the trick with his remaining trump.

The moral of the deal, indeed of the chapter? Losers – pah! Focus on winners.

**Dealer: South**      **Vulnerability: Both**

**Rubber**

|  | North |
|---|---|
| ♠ | A 8 7 5 3 |
| ♥ | 8 5 3 2 |
| ♦ | K 8 6 |
| ♣ | 4 |

| West |  | East |
|---|---|---|
| ♠ Q J 10 | | ♠ 9 |
| ♥ Q J 9 7 | | ♥ K 10 6 |
| ♦ Q 10 | | ♦ J 9 7 5 4 |
| ♣ K 10 8 5 | | ♣ Q J 9 7 |

|  | South |
|---|---|
| ♠ | K 6 4 2 |
| ♥ | A 4 |
| ♦ | A 3 2 |
| ♣ | A 6 3 2 |

| S | W | N | E |
|---|---|---|---|
| 1♠ | PASS | 4♣ (1) | PASS |
| 4♦ (2) | PASS | 4♠ (3) | PASS |
| 5♣ (2) | PASS | 5♦ (4) | PASS |
| 5♥ (2) | PASS | 5♠ (3) | END |

(1) Very (too) light Splinter bid.
(2) Ace-showing cue bids, looking for the spade slam.
(3) No more to say.
(4) Cue bidding a king, facing partner's ace (previous cue bid).

**Contract: 5♠**      **Opening lead: ♥Q**

# Twixt Optimist and Pessimist

*'Twixt optimist and pessimist, the difference is droll.*
*One sees the doughnut, the other the hole.'*

In Bridge you must be both. When things look bleak, and you have just one hope for your contract, or just one way to defeat their contract, you must be an optimist. Hope for the layout to exist and play for it. If things look plain sailing on the other hand, you must be a pessimist. What can go wrong? Can you take the requisite precautions?

Before we look at some wonderful deals that I have assembled over the years, it is worth pointing out that specifically Matchpoint Duplicate, scored completely differently to other forms of the game, requires different thought-processes. If you are in a near-hopeless contract, you are probably better off settling for down one, rather than pursuing some unlikely hope for the contract that will usually see you go more than down one. Take your medicine. Equally, when things are looking great, go for broke and do as well as you can. There's rarely a place for the Safety Play at Duplicate, say catering to a five-nil split at the cost of giving up a trick when the suit is more normally divided.

At Rubber, Chicago, and Teams Bridge, however, be prepared to imagine the doughnut when things are grim, but the hole when you appear to be romping to success.

# Worst-Case Scenario

On our first deal of the chapter you must focus on the hole – the worst case scenario.

West leads the ace of clubs against your Four Spade contract, and continues with the king and queen. You are only in danger in your Four Spade contract if the trumps are 3-0 and East has the king of diamonds (if West has the king then a diamond loser can be avoided by leading the queen and finessing). You will still succeed if you can guess which opponent has three trumps – the top honour can be led on his right, exposing him to a marked finesse. But which opponent should you play for the three trumps?

In fact you can absolutely guarantee your contract at this point. Ruff the third club and cash the ace of trumps. If both opponents follow, you draw the remaining trump with dummy's king, and cross to hand in hearts to take the diamond finesse for the overtrick. If East discards on the ace of trumps, then you run the jack of spades, draw West's queen with dummy's king, then later take the diamond finesse as before.

The danger comes if West discards on the ace of spades. In that case, cross to dummy's king and, leaving East's queen outstanding, cash the hearts, starting with the queen. Ruff the fourth heart in dummy and, if East hasn't yet ruffed, simply exit with a trump. East is now fatally forced either to lead a diamond around to dummy, or to lead a club, in which case you discard a diamond from your hand and ruff in the dummy. Either way East does not score his king of diamonds.

West could have made life harder for you by switching to a diamond at Trick Three. In that case you would have to lose to East's king and would have to guess to start trumps by leading dummy's king first.

**Rubber**

|  | ♠ K 10 6 5 3 |  |
|---|---|---|
|  | ♥ Q 4 |  |
|  | ♦ A J 3 |  |
|  | ♣ J 7 4 |  |

| ♠ – | | ♠ Q 8 7 |
|---|---|---|
| ♥ 10 8 5 2 | N | ♥ J 9 3 |
| ♦ 9 8 7 6 5 | W    E | ♦ K 10 2 |
| ♣ A K Q 10 | S | ♣ 9 8 6 5 |

|  | ♠ A J 9 4 2 |  |
|---|---|---|
|  | ♥ A K 7 6 |  |
|  | ♦ Q 4 |  |
|  | ♣ 3 2 |  |

| S | W | N | E |
|---|---|---|---|
| 1♠ | PASS | 4♠ (1) | END |

(1) Three-and-a-half Spades, but the fifth trump swings it. For Losing Trick Count fans, remember to restrict its use to balanced hands.

**Contract: 4♠**          **Opening lead: ♣A**

# No Morale Boost

If you are told 'I have good news and bad news', which do you tend to ask for initially?

Asking first for the good news on our next deal – from the high stake Rubber table at London's TGR Bridge Club – you would receive the following reply: 'The good news is that you bid to a super grand slam which would make more than 99 times out of 100. The bad news is your partner went down.' Such a fate befell North, David Price. Losing in the final of the English Trials by a tiny margin just a few days earlier, David was looking to receive a morale boost. There was no justice on this deal.

West led the queen of clubs and declarer won dummy's king. A three-one trump split or better would render the grand slam easy. With twelve top tricks (five trumps, three hearts, two diamonds and two clubs), he would garner his thirteenth by ruffing a third club (or a fourth heart) with the remaining trump dummy (after the trumps had been drawn in no more than three rounds).

But when, at Trick Two, West discarded on dummy's ace of trumps, declarer had to think again. Seven Spades was still an excellent contract, though, and declarer looked no further than the club ruff. At Trick Three he led dummy's second club, preparing to ruff his third club with a high trump in dummy. He could have survived a six-two club split; but not a seven-one split. In the event East ruffed the second club. Down one.

Of course declarer (and David Price, dummy) were terribly unlucky. But there is a slightly better line available – a Dummy Reversal. After winning the king of clubs and cashing the ace of trumps to receive the bad news, declarer cashes the ace of diamonds, then ruffs a low diamond. He crosses to the queen of hearts, then ruffs the jack of diamonds (with the ten). He cashes the queen

**Rubber**

|  | ♠ A K J 2 |
|  | ♥ Q 10 3 |
|  | ♦ A K J 4 |
|  | ♣ K 10 |

| ♠ – | | ♠ 9 7 6 4 |
| ♥ 9 8 6 2 | N | ♥ J 5 |
| ♦ 8 5 | W    E | ♦ Q 10 9 7 6 3 |
| ♣ Q J 9 8 4 3 2 | S | ♣ 5 |

|  | ♠ Q 10 8 5 3 |
|  | ♥ A K 7 4 |
|  | ♦ 2 |
|  | ♣ A 7 6 |

| S | W | N | E |
|---|---|---|---|
| 1♠ | PASS | 4NT (1) | PASS |
| 5♥ (2) | PASS | 5NT | PASS |
| 6♦ (2) | PASS | 7♠ | END |

(1) Regular Blackwood.
(2) Two aces and one king.

**Contract: 7♠          Opening lead: ♣Q**

of trumps, leads over to the king-jack drawing all East's trumps, then cashes the king of diamonds, and leads over to the ace-king of hearts and the ace of clubs. Grand Slam made.

By ruffing twice in hand in addition to the four trumps in dummy, declarer scores a sixth trump trick without needing to ruff in dummy and risk the seven-one club split.

*Postscript*: I always ask for the bad news first!

# If Only

'If only' is a dangerous place to be at the bridge table. This declarer – from the Malta Festival – saw dummy and immediately thought, 'If only I was in 7♠.' He promptly played the hand as though he needed all thirteen tricks – and so failed to make the twelve he needed. Can you find a way to virtually guarantee the Small Slam, at the cost of the overtrick?

At the table declarer won the trump lead (a clever choice by West, who suspected that declarer had a void somewhere, perhaps in diamonds, because of his failure to use Blackwood) in his hand and led a second trump to dummy, East discarding. He then crossed to the king of hearts and led out the ace, preparing to ruff the suit good on a three-two split and so chalk up all thirteen tricks. But West ruffed the second heart honour, and declarer now found himself unable to make even twelve tricks. West switched to a club to East's king and declarer's ace; declarer ruffed a third heart, ruffed a club, but had to give up the fourth heart to East. Down one.

There are various ways in which declarer could have done better – including running dummy's ten of hearts on the first round of the suit. But one way shines above all others, as it succeeds on every layout apart from hearts five-nil.

Win the trump lead (it doesn't matter where), cash the ace of hearts, and then follow with a low heart (key play). If both follow on the second heart, you have lost an unnecessary trick. But it is only the overtrick. However if the hearts are splitting four-one, it is imperative that the second heart led is a low one. Leading the other top honour runs the risk that an opponent will ruff and lead a second round of trumps. There will now be just one trump in dummy to ruff two losing

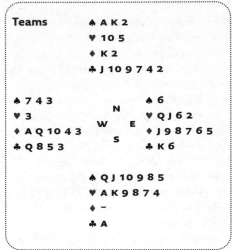

**Dealer: North**     **Vulnerability: Neither**

Teams
♠ A K 2
♥ 10 5
♦ K 2
♣ J 10 9 7 4 2

♠ 7 4 3
♥ 3
♦ A Q 10 4 3
♣ Q 8 5 3

♠ 6
♥ Q J 6 2
♦ J 9 8 7 6 5
♣ K 6

♠ Q J 10 9 8 5
♥ A K 9 8 7 4
♦ –
♣ A

| S | W | N | E |
|---|---|---|---|
|  |  | 1♣ | PASS |
| 1♠ (1) | PASS | 2♠ (2) | PASS |
| 6♠ (3) | END |  |  |

(1) Always a mistake to make a strong-jump-shift when holding a two-suiter, however massive.
(2) More helpful than a 2♣ rebid.
(3) It will be hard to find out whether partner has the right heart holding for a grand slam (in addition to ♠AK), so South settles for a small slam.

**Contract: 6♠**          **Opening lead: ♠3**

hearts. Leading a low heart means that you can stand an opponent winning and leading another trump – now just one more heart needs to be ruffed (with dummy's one remaining trump). Slam made.

Were you able to see the hole, when the doughnut was staring you in the face?

# Five Over Five

'Don't bid Five over Five.' 'Believe a vulnerable opponent.' These are two of several sayings designed to assist the player in the heat of a bidding battle. The trouble was that in this deal the mottoes gave conflicting advice.

The question was whether or not South should bid on to Five Spades over East's leap to Five Diamonds. Eventually he decided to believe his vulnerable opponent; that East would probably have a great hand to bid Five Diamonds and may very well be able to make his contract (scoring 600 points – including 500 for the vulnerable game).

South was absolutely correct – East would have romped home in Five Diamonds, losing just a heart and a club (and not even a club if South led a spade). South could therefore afford to go as many as three down in Five Spades doubled and show a profit. He was to do rather better...

West led a diamond to East's ten and East switched correctly to a heart (choosing the ten). Declarer looked certain to lose a heart and the ace of trumps, and you would not bet against him losing a club either. He looked like going down two for a loss of 300 points (still a good sacrifice if East was making). But in Bridge, you never know...

Declarer rose with the ace of hearts at Trick Two and, rather than lead a trump, decided to play for a miracle layout, knowing that East was bound to have extreme shape for his vulnerable bid (remember the saying). He cashed the ace of clubs at Trick Three and noted the fall of the queen from East. He stared at this card and eventually decided to play this card to be a singleton, and prayed that East did not hold a small trump (if he did then declarer would go an extra one down – but even losing 500 was better than the 600 he would have lost defending Five

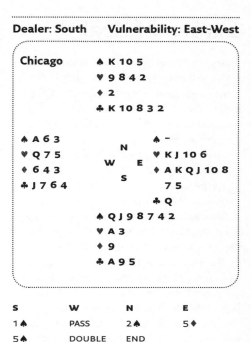

**Dealer: South    Vulnerability: East-West**

**Chicago**

|   | S | W | N | E |
|---|---|---|---|---|
|   | 1♠ | PASS | 2♠ | 5♦ |
|   | 5♠ | DOUBLE | END |   |

**Contract: 5♠ doubled    Opening lead: ♦4**

Diamonds). Can you see what his plan was?

Declarer next led the nine of clubs and ran it. When East discarded (a diamond), he smiled. The miracle layout did indeed exist. He followed by leading his third club to dummy's ten, then cashed the king of clubs discarding his heart loser. The defence were helpless. All they could take was the ace of trumps – declarer's last seven cards were all trumps. The sacrifice bid had turned into a most improbable make.

# Excess of Zeal

An excess of zeal from North – on this deal from the Easter Festival – resulted in South having to make no fewer than eleven tricks in clubs. With three likely spade losers – not to mention the third round of hearts – this was a gargantuan task.

*Question*: Is there any chance of making Five Clubs. If so, what is it?

At the table declarer won West's king of diamonds lead with the ace. He drew trumps in three rounds, then used his only entry to hand, the king of hearts, to lead a spade to the ten. East won the king and led the queen of diamonds, ruffed in dummy. Declarer then cashed the ace of hearts and exited with a third heart. West won and switched to the jack of spades. Declarer covered with dummy's queen, East winning the ace and exiting with the jack of diamonds. Declarer ruffed, but still had a spade to lose (the fourth could be ruffed with his last trump). Down two.

Let us replay the deal. Declarer needs to score two spade tricks with just one entry to hand to lead towards dummy's broken honours.

*Answer* (to the above question): Yes, there is one chance. East needs to hold specifically ace-king doubleton of spades.

The correct line to take advantage of this favourable spade layout is: win the ace of diamonds, draw trumps in three rounds, then lead a low spade from dummy. East wins the king and switches to the jack of hearts (best). Win the ace and lead a second low spade. East wins the ace and leads his second heart. Win your king, finesse dummy's ten of spades, cash the queen discarding your last heart, ruff dummy's losing heart, and claim the remainder. Eleven tricks and game made.

**Dealer: East    Vulnerability: North-South**

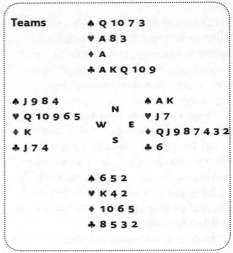

Teams

| | | |
|---|---|---|
| | ♠ Q 10 7 3 | |
| | ♥ A 8 3 | |
| | ♦ A | |
| | ♣ A K Q 10 9 | |
| ♠ J 9 8 4 | N | ♠ A K |
| ♥ Q 10 9 6 5 | W    E | ♥ J 7 |
| ♦ K | S | ♦ Q J 9 8 7 4 3 2 |
| ♣ J 7 4 | | ♣ 6 |
| | ♠ 6 5 2 | |
| | ♥ K 4 2 | |
| | ♦ 10 6 5 | |
| | ♣ 8 5 3 2 | |

| S | W | N | E |
|---|---|---|---|
| | | | 1♦ (1) |
| PASS | 1♥ | DOUBLE (2) | 2♦ |
| PASS | PASS | DOUBLE (3) | 3♦ |
| PASS | PASS | DOUBLE (4) | PASS |
| 4♣ | PASS | 5♣ (5) | END |

(1) Too strong to preempt.
(2) Take-out – for the black suits.
(3) More of the same.
(4) Yet more.
(5) Grossly optimistic. North has wrung a bid out of a most unwilling partner, who has shown nothing. Pass is indicated.

**Contract: 5♣**        **Opening lead: ♦K**

The key was leading low spades from dummy on the first two rounds, preserving the queen-ten for a finesse against West's jack.

# Achilles Heel

Six Clubs, reached after a massive 'punt' by North, would have been easy to make if West had led his partner's suit, diamonds. Declarer would trump the lead in dummy, force out the ace of trumps, then cash dummy's spades (all winners thanks to the three-three split) discarding his hearts. Slam made for just the loss of the ace of trumps.

Wisely, however, especially bearing in mind his length in the suit, West concluded that dummy's majestic leap to Six Clubs was based in part on a diamond void. A surprise attack was called for and on that basis the ten of hearts hit the table.

As dummy was laid down, declarer thanked his partner with a hard-to-hide air of pessimism. The heart lead – to East's queen and declarer's ace – had really found his Achilles Heel. He was staring at a second round heart loser in addition to the ace of trumps.

In fact there was a glimmer of hope, just a glimmer. Can you spot it?

Declarer crossed to dummy's queen of spades at Trick Two, then followed with the ace-king of the suit. Both opponents followed (first hurdle overcome) and declarer threw two of his hearts away. Still left with the losing jack of hearts, however, the end looked nigh. But because West held a void trump (the second – and biggest – hurdle) declarer could actually scramble home. Watch!

He led a fourth (winning) spade from the dummy. With West holding no trumps, the onus was entirely on East. He had to trump the spade with a low trump (if he discarded or trumped with the ace then declarer's jack of hearts would be thrown). Declarer overtrumped, crossed to dummy by trumping a diamond, then led a fifth spade. East trumped with his second low trump and

**Rubber**

|  | North |
|---|---|
| ♠ | A K Q 6 3 2 |
| ♥ | 8 7 |
| ♦ | – |
| ♣ | J 9 8 7 3 |

| West | | East |
|---|---|---|
| ♠ J 9 4 | N | ♠ 10 8 7 |
| ♥ 10 9 6 5 3 | W   E | ♥ K Q |
| ♦ 10 9 7 5 4 | S | ♦ A K J 8 6 |
| ♣ – | | ♣ A 5 4 |

|  | South |
|---|---|
| ♠ | 5 |
| ♥ | A J 4 2 |
| ♦ | Q 3 2 |
| ♣ | K Q 10 6 2 |

| S | W | N | E |
|---|---|---|---|
|  |  |  | 1♦ |
| 2♣ | PASS (1) | 6♣ (2) | END |

(1) Rather feeble with such a shapely, fitting hand.

(2) You could not use the word 'feeble' to describe North's contribution.

**Contract: 6♣**        **Opening lead: ♥10**

declarer overtrumped again. He ruffed a second diamond and led dummy's sixth spade.

This time East could only trump with the ace. Away went declarer's losing jack of hearts and now East's king of hearts could be trumped and the rest of the tricks claimed.

Slam made. Phew!

# Long Silk Robe

Dealer: South     Vulnerability: Neither

Rubber

```
                ♠ J 10 8 7 6 4
                ♥ 3
                ♦ K 7 5 4 3
                ♣ 7
♠ -                          ♠ K 5
♥ K Q J 9 2       N          ♥ 8 6 4
♦ A 9 6       W       E      ♦ Q 10
♣ 8 6 4 3 2       S          ♣ K Q J 10 9 5
                ♠ A Q 9 3 2
                ♥ A 10 7 5
                ♦ J 8 2
                ♣ A
```

| S | W | N | E |
|---|---|---|---|
| 1♠ | 2♥ | 4♠ | 5♣ |
| DOUBLE | PASS | 5♠ | PASS |
| PASS | 6♣ | 6♠ | END |

**Contract: 6♠**          **Opening lead: ♥K**

If you walk up Fulham's Munster Road, you will find a wonderful ethnic shop called Thailandia. When not searching the streets of Bangkok or Chiang Mai for a bargain to bring back, its owner, Jeremy Reiss, can usually be found at the Bridge table, typically dressed in a long silk robe.

This deal features Jeremy at the helm in Six Spades – not that he had wanted to be there, having doubled the opponents in Five Clubs. His partner removed the double of Five Clubs (actually a good idea, as Five Clubs would only fail by one trick, and Five Spades is relatively easy), but then had bid on to Six Spades over Six Clubs (not such a good idea – or was it...?).

West led the king of hearts. Declarer won the ace, and had to decide the layout of the missing trumps. Though the odds slightly favour laying down the ace, Jeremy reasoned that West's decision to bid on to Six Clubs was indicative of a void spade. He ruffed a heart at Trick Two and played a spade to the queen.

West duly discarded, and now declarer had to face his second (and most major) obstacle – how to avoid more than one diamond loser. Short of West holding precisely ace-queen doubleton, declarer would need to resort to endplay technique. He cashed the ace of spades felling East's king, then ruffed a third heart. This was sure to have removed East's last heart (in the light of West's overcall), so the time was right for the Throw In. He crossed to the ace of clubs, and led a low diamond. West could not afford to play the ace, or his partner's queen would fall under dummy's king. So he played low and dummy's king won the trick.

East had a sinking feeling at this point. Knowing that he would be left on lead with the queen on the next round, he tried the effect of throwing his queen under dummy's king. This was a good shot that would have succeeded if his second card had not been the ten. When declarer led back a low diamond, playing low from hand under East's ten, (West having to play low to prevent declarer's jack from winning), East could only lead a club. Declarer's jack of diamonds was promptly discarded as dummy ruffed.

The slam had been made, and with it a small portion of the air-fare that would take Jeremy back to his beloved Thailand.

# Tram Tickets

This deal – from a fifth round Gold Cup match – saw both Souths understandably unable to contain themselves. But partner tabled his usual flat collection of tram tickets, and the Six Club slam was near-hopeless.

However there was a chance – on West's ace of spades opening lead (his partner having preempted in the suit). Cover up the East-West cards and see if you can work out a layout of the opposing cards – however unlikely – that allows you to make your slam.

*Question*: how (on earth) can you restrict your diamond losers to one?

*Answer*: you must use Elimination and Throw-in technique.

You have to hope that an opponent holds a singleton ace of diamonds (presumably East given that he has advertised seven spades). If you have robbed him of all his safe exits, a low diamond lead will see him win his bare ace and be forced to yield a ruff-and-discard. Trumps will be required in both hands for the endplay to work (after drawing all the missing trumps), thus a two-two split is required.

The correct line – found at the table – is as follows. Ruff the opening spade lead and cash the ace-king of trumps (noting the even split). Cross to dummy's jack of hearts and ruff a second spade (seeking to eliminate the suit from the dummy). Then cash the ace-king-queen of hearts, discarding dummy's last spade. The scene is set.

Now exit with a low diamond from hand (key play). Can you see what will happen? East wins his bare ace, and has only spades to lead. You discard your remaining low diamond from hand and ruff with dummy's last trump. Twelve tricks and slam made.

Note that the slam would have stood no chance had West not led a spade – enabling you to get rid of all dummy's spades before the diamond throw-in.

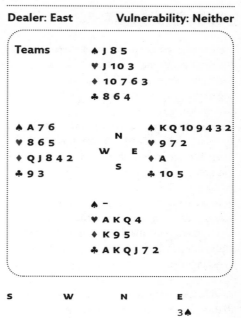

**Dealer: East          Vulnerability: Neither**

Teams

North: ♠ J 8 5  ♥ J 10 3  ♦ 10 7 6 3  ♣ 8 6 4

West: ♠ A 7 6  ♥ 8 6 5  ♦ Q J 8 4 2  ♣ 9 3

East: ♠ K Q 10 9 4 3 2  ♥ 9 7 2  ♦ A  ♣ 10 5

South: ♠ –  ♥ A K Q 4  ♦ K 9 5  ♣ A K Q J 7 2

| S | W | N | E |
|---|---|---|---|
|   |   |   | 3♠ |
| 6♣ (1) | END |   |   |

(1) No claim for the 'Subtle Bid of the Year Award', but how is North supposed to know that ♦QJ is probably enough for the slam?

**Contract: 6♣          Opening lead: ♠A**

# Lucky Mashee

Dealer: North       Vulnerability: Both

Here is yet another appalling slam contract that made. The hand took place on the Internet Bridge Site 'OKBridge' and South, the hero of the show, went under the pseudonym Mashee.

West appears to have two certain trump tricks in the Six Spade contract, holding the king-jack-ten over declarer's queen. But he did not get off to the best start, his lead of the unbid suit, clubs, presenting dummy's queen with an extra trick. And, as it turned out, that was his last chance to defeat the slam.

After successfully rising with the queen of clubs at Trick One, declarer cashed dummy's ace-king of diamonds (discarding a heart from hand), crossed to the ace of clubs, cashed the ace of hearts (discarding a diamond from dummy), ruffed a heart, ruffed a third diamond (both opponents following a third time), ruffed a third heart (noting the fall of the king from East), ruffed a third club (both opponents following again), then led a fourth heart. West followed suit and declarer ruffed with dummy's nine of trumps, in the vain hope that West held all three higher trumps.

When declarer opened his eyes he saw that East had discarded (a club). It looked like a miracle layout existed for declarer. With just three tricks to go, all six opposing trumps were still missing. And from East's inability to overruff dummy's nine, it appeared that West held king-jack-ten and East held three small cards in the suit. Declarer held ace-queen of trumps and the queen of hearts and the lead was in dummy, who held three minor suit cards. Can you see how he managed to wangle two further tricks and so made this most unlikely slam?

At Trick Eleven declarer led a minor suit card from dummy. Though East ruffed with the seven of trumps, declarer simply

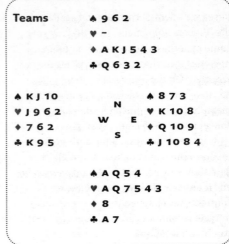

**Teams**

|  | |
|---|---|
| ♠ 9 6 2 | |
| ♥ – | |
| ♦ A K J 5 4 3 | |
| ♣ Q 6 3 2 | |

West: ♠ K J 10 ♥ J 9 6 2 ♦ 7 6 2 ♣ K 9 5

East: ♠ 8 7 3 ♥ K 10 8 ♦ Q 10 9 ♣ J 10 8 4

South: ♠ A Q 5 4 ♥ A Q 7 5 4 3 ♦ 8 ♣ A 7

| S | W | N | E |
|---|---|---|---|
|  |  | 1♦ | PASS |
| 1♥ | PASS | 2♦ | PASS |
| 3♠ (1) | PASS | 4♠ (2) | PASS |
| 4NT | PASS | 5♦ | PASS |
| 6♠ | END | | |

(1) No reason to jump, when 2♠ would be forcing.
(2) North reasonably concludes that South's jump to 3♠ shows a 5-6 shape in the majors.

**Contract: 6♠**       **Opening lead: ♣5**

discarded his heart. West was forced to overruff with his ten of trumps and lead away from his king-jack around to declarer's ace-queen.

Slam made! Declarer scored all seven trumps, the ace of hearts, the ace-king of diamonds, and the ace and queen of clubs. An almost unbelievable twelve tricks.

# Pigeon-hole

Research scientists are all too familiar with the 'Pigeon-hole Effect'. In trying to prove some hypothesis, all positive experiments (the ones that vindicate the hypothesis) get reported. On the other hand, almost all the negative ones get stacked away in some metaphorical pigeon-hole, where they are conveniently neglected.

It is the same with slams and the Bridge media. Who wants to hear about another wild slam venture that meets its predictable end (demise)? No one. But lousy slam contracts that happen to make – either on a miracle layout or brilliant declarer play or a combination of both – make great reading.

So please don't get the impression that bidding frisky slam contracts is the way to win – just because they always seem to succeed in Bridge books. Remember that for each one that makes, there are twenty that lie forgotten in some dusty pigeon-hole of oblivion.

Our last slam was horrendous, yet scrambled home. It looks doomed, with declarer seemingly destined to lose a club and at least one diamond trick. It did not turn out that way...

West led the six of clubs and declarer, knowing from East's Three Club opener that the king was offside, rose with dummy's ace. He drew the trumps in one round, cashed the ace of spades, ruffed the jack of spades in dummy, and then led a low diamond. East followed with the jack and declarer tried the queen with fingers firmly crossed. His luck was in for East held the king and the finesse succeeded. He then cashed the ace of diamonds, and exited with a third diamond to West's ten. But his spirits were still low.

Placing East with seven clubs for his preemptive opening, declarer fully expected West to lead his second club to East's king at

**Rubber**

|  |  |
|---|---|
| ♠ 8 | |
| ♥ A Q J 8 6 3 | |
| ♦ 9 7 3 2 | |
| ♣ A 8 | |

|  |  |  |  |
|---|---|---|---|
| ♠ Q 10 9 7 6 5 3 2 | N | ♠ K 4 | |
| ♥ 9 | W      E | ♥ 2 | |
| ♦ 10 8 6 | S | ♦ K J | |
| ♣ 6 | | ♣ K J 10 9 7 5 4 2 | |

|  |  |
|---|---|
| ♠ A J | |
| ♥ K 10 7 5 4 | |
| ♦ A Q 5 4 | |
| ♣ Q 3 | |

| S | W | N | E |
|---|---|---|---|
| | | | 3♣ (1) |
| 3♥ | PASS | 6♥ (2) | END |

(1) A case for One Club – too good to preempt; or Four Clubs – with the eight cards. Three Clubs would be my third choice.
(2) North looks to have a colossal hand – with his magnificent trumps, ace of the opponents' suit and side singleton. But he is somewhat trump-bound – too much in trumps and too little outside.

**Contract: 6♥**          **Opening lead: ♣6**

this point – and so defeat the contract. But in fact East had an eighth club and West had only spades remaining. Declarer ruffed the spade return in dummy and discarded his queen of clubs (he could equally well have discarded dummy's club loser and ruffed in hand). Slam made and I hope South enjoyed the doughnut!

CHAPTER 6

# Trick One

If the opening lead is the single most important card played in a deal of Bridge, the first trick is the most important trick. By far. Like the serve at tennis, and the drive at golf, it is the early stages of the play that usually matter most.

The techniques of the second, third and fourth cards to that first trick all vary. However there is one common thread. There must be thought before each card. For the knee-jerk card may not be the right one. Top level declarers will always think before playing from dummy at Trick One, even if dummy's card is automatic (e.g. a singleton). They are planning the whole play. Similarly an expert defender playing third to the trick will always think before playing a card, generally acquainting himself with the challenge ahead, as well as deciding which card to play at the all-important first trick.

The variety and number of counter-intuitive cards that need to be played to Trick One is a constant fascination to me. After playing top-level Bridge for over twenty years, I still meet positions that make me say 'Wow!'

On our first deal, declarer learned a salutary lesson that your author has learned on more than one occasion.

# Cautionary Tale

**Dealer: South**  **Vulnerability: Neither**

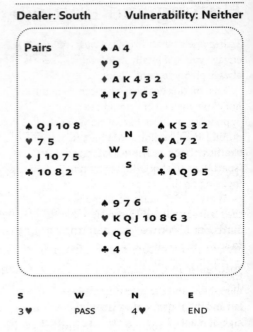

| Pairs | ♠ A 4 |
| --- | --- |
| | ♥ 9 |
| | ♦ A K 4 3 2 |
| | ♣ K J 7 6 3 |

♠ Q J 10 8   ♠ K 5 3 2
♥ 7 5   ♥ A 7 2
♦ J 10 7 5   ♦ 9 8
♣ 10 8 2   ♣ A Q 9 5

♠ 9 7 6
♥ K Q J 10 8 6 3
♦ Q 6
♣ 4

| S | W | N | E |
| --- | --- | --- | --- |
| 3♥ | PASS | 4♥ | END |

**Contract: 4♥**    **Opening lead: ♠Q**

I remember declaring a slam at a crucial stage of an important match. I won the opening lead in my hand and started to think. With clues from the bidding and lead, I was able to reconstruct the opposing hands very accurately. I worked out the one line to make my slam but realised – horror of horrors – that I had needed to win the first trick in dummy rather than in my hand. I had blown it and there was no recovery!

With this cautionary tale in mind, how would you declare this deal from a duplicate at my Club?

At the table declarer won the queen of spades lead with dummy's ace, and started to think. If he led a second spade, the defence would win, cash the ace of trumps, then follow with their third spade winner and the ace of clubs. Down one. So he had to hope the opposing diamonds were three-three.

At Trick Two he led to his queen of diamonds, then led back to dummy's ace-king. But East ruffed the third diamond with a low trump. Declarer overruffed and led a club to dummy's king. East won the ace, cashed the ace of trumps and the king of spades, then followed by leading a spade to West's jack. Down one.

Have you worked out where declarer went wrong? Had he thought *before* winning the first trick with dummy's ace, rather than after, he might well have come up with the correct solution. He needed to duck the queen of spades at trick one (key play). What can the defence do?

(a) If they lead a second spade, declarer wins in dummy (perforce), crosses to the queen of diamonds, then ruffs his spade loser with dummy's singleton trump.

(b) If they switch to a trump to East's ace and then revert to a spade, declarer wins dummy's ace, crosses to the queen of

diamonds, draws the remaining trumps, then cashes the ace-king of diamonds.

(c) If they switch to a trump, East ducking his ace, then declarer wins in hand, forces out the ace of trumps, wins the spade return (best) in dummy, crosses to the queen of diamonds, draws the last trump, then leads to dummy's ace-king of diamonds.

Whichever route the defence choose, declarer can negotiate the play to make his contract... provided he ducks that first spade.

# Huffing and Puffing

To become a better Bridge player, you must engage yourself totally in the game. There is always plenty to think about.

East on this deal was an example of how not to be. Instead of listening to his opponents' auction, he was huffing and puffing, complaining about his cards, chatting about cricket to a kibitzer (spectator). In short, doing anything but focusing on the matter at hand.

West led the queen of diamonds against the slam and dummy played low. East automatically played low, presumably hoping to score his ace on the next round.

The queen winning, West continued with the jack of diamonds. Dummy and East played low and declarer ruffed in hand and led and ran the jack of trumps, breathing a sigh of relief when the finesse succeeded. He led a second club to dummy's queen, East discarding a heart, then cashed the ace of trumps, felling West's king. He ruffed a third diamond, cashed the ace of hearts discarding dummy's king of diamonds, cashed the ace-knave of spades and led the two to dummy's king-queen-ten. Contract made.

You can guess East's reaction – irritation at the luck of his opponents, bidding and making a slam with the aid of a successful finesse.

It was the kibitzer who made the telling comment.

'Hold on a second. Couldn't you (East) have overtaken your partner's queen of diamonds with the ace at Trick One and switched to a spade for partner to ruff?'

'Well, how was I supposed to know my partner was out of spades?,' East replied, now somewhat on the defensive.

The trouble was that East had not been listening to the bidding. South had supported spades and East could see ten spades

**Rubber**

|   | North |
|---|---|
| ♠ | K Q 10 7 5 |
| ♥ | – |
| ♦ | K 9 7 3 |
| ♣ | A Q 9 3 |

| West |   | East |
|---|---|---|
| ♠ – | | ♠ 9 8 6 4 3 |
| ♥ 9 7 6 5 3 2 | | ♥ K 10 4 |
| ♦ Q J 10 8 | | ♦ A 6 5 4 |
| ♣ K 4 2 | | ♣ 6 |

|   | South |
|---|---|
| ♠ | A J 2 |
| ♥ | A Q J 8 |
| ♦ | 2 |
| ♣ | J 10 8 7 5 |

| S | W | N | E |
|---|---|---|---|
| 1♣ | PASS | 1♠ | PASS |
| 2♠ (1) | PASS | 4♣ | PASS |
| 4NT (2) | PASS | 5♦ (3) | PASS |
| 6♣ | END | | |

(1) Limiting his hand to a minimum opener, and thus better than Two Hearts.
(2) Launches into (ordinary) Blackwood, as his hand has improved vastly in the light of the club support opposite.
(3) One ace.

**Contract: 6♣**      **Opening lead: ♦Q**

between his hand and dummy's. West was marked with a void spade.

It was that all-important Trick One – did you get it right?

# Fast or Slow?

So many key decisions at top-level Bridge occur at Trick One. This next deal – a Five Club contract from the Las Vegas Cavendish – was just such a case in point.

West had to decide whether it was going to be a 'fast hand' – one in which the defence would have to score their tricks quickly – or a 'slow hand'. If fast, then the ace of diamonds lead – partner's suit – was a standout. But if the defence could afford to wait for their tricks then it might be imperative to remove dummy's trumps.

Eventually electing to go the latter route, West led the five of trumps. He must have mentally patted himself on the back when he saw dummy – with its singleton diamond.

Wrong! Had West led the ace of diamonds, East would have signalled violently with the king (with dummy holding a singleton, this would be a suit-preference signal for the highest ranking suit). West would duly switch to spades, and East would take his ace-king to beat the game.

The five of trumps opening lead gave declarer a chance, but he had a key decision of his own at Trick One. In order to succeed, he would have to set up dummy's fifth heart. This would require a four-four split and three dummy entries, which would all have to be in trumps. If West held five-three of trumps and East a singleton eight, it would be best to rise with dummy's jack. This would fell the eight and ensure a second entry with dummy's seven (the two would be a ruffing entry).

Declarer (US World Champion Eric Rodwell) played for West to have led from eight-five, a more likely permutation (equivalent to finessing for the king when missing three cards). He inserted dummy's seven (key play) and was pleased to see East follow low. He cashed the ace-king of hearts,

discarding two spades, ruffed a heart, then exited with a diamond.

West won and returned his second trump (as good as anything) but declarer won dummy's jack, ruffed a fourth heart (observing the even split), ruffed a diamond, discarded a loser on the established fifth heart, and gave up just one trick at the end. Eleven tricks and game made.

**Dealer: North    Vulnerability: East-West**

Teams

|  | ♠ J 9 8 5 |  |
|---|---|---|
|  | ♥ A K 9 6 4 |  |
|  | ♦ 6 |  |
|  | ♣ J 7 2 |  |

| ♠ 10 7 2 | | ♠ A K 4 |
| ♥ Q J 8 2 | N | ♥ 10 7 5 3 |
| ♦ A J 10 4 | W    E | ♦ K Q 7 5 2 |
| ♣ 8 5 | S | ♣ 3 |

|  | ♠ Q 6 3 |  |
|  | ♥ – |  |
|  | ♦ 9 8 3 |  |
|  | ♣ A K Q 10 9 6 4 |  |

| S | W | N | E |
|---|---|---|---|
|  |  | PASS | 1♦ |
| 2♣ | 2♦ | 2♥ | 3♦ |
| 4♣ | PASS | 5♣ | END |

**Contract: 5♣**      **Opening lead: ♣5**

# Software

There is little to choose between the best computer software for Bridge. Blue Chip, Q-Plus, Bridge Baron and the many more that are on the market all have similar features. Their bidding and card-play is mostly reasonable but a trifle erratic – nowhere near as good as the top players (unlike in Chess). However, as methods of generating random hands enabling you to practice declarer-play, they are most useful.

This deal was generated by Q-Plus Bridge and contains a point of interest in the early play. See if you can spot it. West led the queen of diamonds. Declarer played low from dummy and East ruffed. Following low from hand, he saw East switch to the eight of clubs at Trick Two (the ace of spades would not run away).

Reading West for the king of clubs, declarer wisely rose with his ace and sought to discard his three remaining clubs on dummy's spades (playing East for the honours – he rated to have the length and strength based on the bidding). Declarer drew three rounds of trumps finishing in dummy and advanced the king of spades.

East covered with the ace of spades, and declarer ruffed. He crossed to the king of diamonds, cashed the promoted queen of spades, discarding a club, then led the ten for a second ruffing finesse. East covered with the jack and declarer ruffed. There were now two established spades sitting in dummy. But, with no way back there, all he could do was lead a club. West pounced on this trick with the king – down one.

Declarer's basic plan was impeccable, but he was one entry short to dummy. Can you see the solution? He must unblock his ace of diamonds at Trick One (key play). He now has a second dummy entry in diamonds (via the marked finesse of dummy's ten), enabling

| | | |
|---|---|---|
| **Computer** | ♠ K Q 10 9 8 | |
| | ♥ A 3 2 | |
| | ♦ K 10 6 | |
| | ♣ J 3 | |

| ♠ 5 | | ♠ A J 7 6 4 3 2 |
|---|---|---|
| ♥ – | N | ♥ 7 6 5 4 |
| ♦ Q J 9 8 7 3 2 | W  E | ♦ – |
| ♣ K 9 7 6 2 | S | ♣ 8 5 |

| | |
|---|---|
| ♠ – | |
| ♥ K Q J 10 9 8 | |
| ♦ A 5 4 | |
| ♣ A Q 10 4 | |

| S | W | N | E |
|---|---|---|---|
| 1♥ | 3♦ (1) | 4♥ (2) | PASS |
| 6♥ | END | | |

(1) Weak Jump Overcall.
(2) North-South were playing Five-card Majors – you can program the software to play your preferred system and conventions.

**Contract: 6♥**      **Opening lead: ♦Q**

him to discard all his losing clubs on the promoted spades after the two successful ruffing finesses. Twelve tricks and slam made.

Only an opening low diamond lead defeats the slam – preventing dummy's ten from being an entry.

# Specific Aces

Your partner opens Four Notrumps. After falling off your chair, you regain your composure and must ask its meaning.

Traditionally the bid showed a huge balanced hand – say 28-30 pts. But because such hands can easily (and preferably) be opened Two Clubs, the following method has become standard: a Four Notrump opener asks for aces, but not merely the number (as in Blackwood). Rather it asks for specific aces – invaluable on those rare occasions where you hold a huge single-suited hand with a void, and merely need to know which ace(s) partner holds.

The responses are as follows:

5♣: *No ace.*
5♦: *Ace of diamonds.*
5♥: *Ace of hearts.*
5♠: *Ace of spades.*
5NT: *Two aces (unspecified).*
6♣: *Ace of clubs.*

This South hand – on a deal from the Shrewsbury Congress – was reasonably suitable for a Four Notrump opener (I say reasonably, not more, because of the problem of the back-suit deuces). To open Two Clubs then bid Four Notrumps (Blackwood or Roman Key Card Blackwood) would not solve his problem. A one-ace response would leaving him guessing which red ace his partner held.

When, in actuality, North reveals the wrong red ace to the specific ace ask, any thought of a grand slam is rejected. But even Six Hearts is precarious on a singleton club lead. Many declarers won in hand with the ace/king and led the king of trumps. But East simply won the ace and led a second club for West to ruff. Down one. Can you spot the winning line?

Declarer must win the opening club lead in dummy with the queen, and cash the ace-

## Dealer: South  Vulnerability: Neither

**Pairs**

|  | ♠ 5 4 |  |
|---|---|---|
|  | ♥ 3 |  |
|  | ♦ A K 8 7 4 2 |  |
|  | ♣ Q 10 6 3 |  |

| ♠ Q J 8 6 5 3 | N | ♠ 9 7 |
|---|---|---|
| ♥ 6 5 4 2 | W E | ♥ A |
| ♦ 9 6 | S | ♦ Q J 10 5 3 |
| ♣ 9 |  | ♣ J 8 7 5 4 |

|  | ♠ A K 2 |  |
|---|---|---|
|  | ♥ K Q J 10 9 8 7 |  |
|  | ♦ - |  |
|  | ♣ A K 2 |  |

| S | W | N | E |
|---|---|---|---|
| 4NT (1) | PASS | 5♦ (2) | PASS |
| 6♥ (3) | END | | |

(1) Asking for specific aces.
(2) Ace of diamonds.
(3) Knowing the partnership is missing the ace of hearts, South settles for Six Hearts.

**Contract: 6♥**       **Opening lead: ♣9**

king of diamonds, discarding his ace-king of clubs (key plays). He then needs to trump his third spade in dummy, cashing the ace-king and ruffing the two with dummy's singleton three of trumps. The bad news is that East can overruff. But the (overriding) good news is that his only trump is the ace. Declarer can then claim the last seven tricks with his top trumps. Twelve tricks and slam made.

# Think First

Whether declaring or defending, it is totally illogical to win a trick and then think what to do next. You must do your thinking before you win the trick – in case it was incorrect to win the trick at all.

On this deal you are East. You hear your opponents bid to Six Notrumps via a Stayman auction, and partner leads the jack of diamonds.

At the table East won Trick One with the ace of diamonds, and, after reflecting that there was no need to switch suits, led a second diamond. Declarer won and tabled his hand. He had twelve easy tricks via three spades, three hearts, two diamonds and four clubs.

Have you spotted East's error? He should duck the opening lead round to declarer's queen of diamonds, and thereby restrict declarer to one diamond winner. Can declarer still succeed?

Actually yes – but in practice probably no. After winning the queen of diamonds, declarer cashes four club tricks, East discarding two diamonds. Declarer guesses to cash three rounds of spades (as opposed to hearts – a pure guess), finishing in hand.

On the third spade East is squeezed: either he bares his ace of diamonds, in which case declarer leads a low diamond to set up his king; or he discards a heart, and so gives dummy the fourth heart trick.

If declarer plays as well as that, good luck to him. If you as East ducked the first trick, you would be writing down a plus-score against most declarers.

Did you think before deciding whether to win your ace of diamonds at the all-important Trick One? It's no use thinking after winning the ace – it's too late.

**Pairs**

|  | ♠ A 8 7 3 |  |
|---|---|---|
|  | ♥ K 7 6 4 |  |
|  | ♦ 6 |  |
|  | ♣ A Q 6 4 |  |

| ♠ J 9 6 2 | **N** | ♠ 10 4 |
|---|---|---|
| ♥ 10 8 | **W**    **E** | ♥ J 9 5 3 |
| ♦ J 10 9 8 | **S** | ♦ A 7 5 4 3 |
| ♣ 10 8 7 |  | ♣ 9 2 |

|  | ♠ K Q 5 |  |
|---|---|---|
|  | ♥ A Q 2 |  |
|  | ♦ K Q 2 |  |
|  | ♣ K J 5 3 |  |

| S | W | N | E |
|---|---|---|---|
| 2NT | PASS | 3♣ (1) | PASS |
| 3♦ (2) | PASS | 6NT (3) | END |

(1) Stayman – a request for four-card majors.
(2) No major.
(3) Knowing of the combined 33 points.

**Contract: 6NT**  **Opening lead: ♦J**

# CHAPTER 7
# Finessing Fun

The finesse is a mysterious and alluring word that implies something creative, something rather Machiavellian. In fact this is not really the case. A finesse is a straight technique of card promotion, whereby you lead from the opposite hand to the card you are trying to promote. It is the relative position of that card, and the opposing higher card, that will determine whether you can promote your card; whether your finesse is successful.

The most basic finesse position is K2 facing 43. You lead to the king, in the hope that the ace is sitting underneath, i.e. playing second. With no clue as to the location of the ace, you have a 50-50 chance of promoting the king. Like tossing a coin – heads I win, tails I lose.

Adopting the same principles – leading from the opposite hand to the card(s) you are trying to promote – will stand you in good stead for more complex situations, and some truly fascinating positions can arise.

How to finesse? Whether to finesse? When to finesse? Which finesse to take? This chapter will delve deep...

# Magnetic Lure

An even money gamble – such as the tossing of a coin – holds great fascination and excitement to all. So it is hardly surprising that the finesse has a magnetic lure for Bridge players.

West led the unbid suit, clubs, and declarer beat East's king with his ace. How should he continue?

At the table he cashed the two top spades to dispose of dummy's club loser, crossed to the jack of trumps, then took the diamond finesse, leading low to his queen. This lost to West's king and West cleverly led the queen of clubs, forcing dummy to ruff. Declarer crossed to his ace of diamonds, returned to dummy's queen of trumps, then ruffed a third diamond with the king of trumps (East discarding his last spade) to set up the suit. He ruffed a third spade with dummy's remaining low trump, but East overruffed and led a top club. Declarer ruffed with the ace and led a spade, but West claimed the last two tricks with the queen of spades and a club. Down three.

By crossing to the jack of trumps at Trick Four in order to take the diamond finesse, declarer wasted a precious dummy entry. Let us replay the deal.

Win the ace of clubs and cash the top spades discarding dummy's club (as before), then, spurning the diamond finesse, cash the ace of diamonds and lead the queen (key play).

West wins the king and leads the queen of clubs, so ruff in dummy, ruff a diamond (high if necessary), draw trumps finishing in dummy on the third round, then enjoy the three established diamonds.

Did you fall for the lure of the diamond finesse?

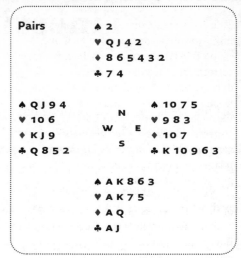

**Pairs**

|          |                |
|----------|----------------|
| ♠ 2      |                |
| ♥ Q J 4 2 |               |
| ♦ 8 6 5 4 3 2 |           |
| ♣ 7 4    |                |

| West | | East |
|------|--|------|
| ♠ Q J 9 4 | | ♠ 10 7 5 |
| ♥ 10 6 | | ♥ 9 8 3 |
| ♦ K J 9 | | ♦ 10 7 |
| ♣ Q 8 5 2 | | ♣ K 10 9 6 3 |

|          |
|----------|
| ♠ A K 8 6 3 |
| ♥ A K 7 5 |
| ♦ A Q   |
| ♣ A J   |

| S | W | N | E |
|---|---|---|---|
| 2♣ (1) | PASS | 2♦ (2) | PASS |
| 2♠ | PASS | 3♦ | PASS |
| 3♥ | PASS | 4♥ | PASS |
| 6♥ (3) | END | | |

(1) 23+ points, unrelated to clubs.
(2) Negative – up to seven points.
(3) Not guaranteed, but partner would avoid raising a second suit without four-card support.

**Contract: 6♥**                    **Opening lead: ♣2**

# Three Finesses

This declarer had three possible finesses to take. How many do you think he took?

West led the ten of hearts and declarer correctly spurned the first finesse, rising with dummy's ace. Though the odds in trumps favour taking a first round finesse (running the queen and hoping East holds the king), he correctly spurned the second finesse, instead leading to his ace of trumps. He knew it was relatively unlikely that the king would drop, but he had good chances when it didn't.

One option was to finesse dummy's queen of clubs. If successful, he would be able to cash the ace and discard his jack of hearts. But declarer spurned the third finesse also, preferring to use his diamonds to discard dummy's two hearts.

So the answer to the question 'How many finesses did declarer take?' was 'None at all'. Indeed with all three kings offside, declarer had given himself the only chance of making the contract.

At Trick Three declarer cashed the ace-king of diamonds, discarding a heart from dummy, then he trumped a third diamond. He cashed the ace of clubs and trumped a second club. He ruffed a fourth diamond, but smelt disaster when West hurriedly discarded the jack of clubs. He had to trump a club to return to hand but West was able to overtrump and lead to his partner's king of hearts. Down one.

Declarer was very much on the right track, but had fractionally mistimed the play. The winning line after rising with the ace of hearts is to lead to the ace-king of diamonds and trump a third diamond at Tricks Two, Three and Four (key plays). Then return to the ace of trumps, and follow by ruffing a fourth diamond (West discarding a club).

Cash the ace of clubs, trump a second club (West following), then lead the established

fifth diamond discarding dummy's queen of hearts as West – too late – trumps with the king. Twelve tricks and slam made.

**Dealer: South**      **Vulnerability: Both**

**Rubber**

|  | ♠ Q J 8 5 3 |  |
|---|---|---|
|  | ♥ A Q 2 |  |
|  | ♦ 4 |  |
|  | ♣ A Q 5 3 |  |
| ♠ K 10 | **N** | ♠ 7 |
| ♥ 10 9 8 5 3 | **W E** | ♥ K 7 6 5 |
| ♦ J 7 2 | **S** | ♦ Q 10 8 5 |
| ♣ J 9 7 |  | ♣ K 10 8 6 2 |
|  | ♠ A 9 6 4 2 |  |
|  | ♥ J 4 |  |
|  | ♦ A K 9 6 3 |  |
|  | ♣ 4 |  |

| S | W | N | E |
|---|---|---|---|
| 1♠ | PASS | 4NT (1) | PASS |
| 5♥ (1) | PASS | 6♠ | END |

(1) Regular Blackwood, eliciting a two-ace reply.

**Contract: 6♠**      **Opening lead: ♥10**

# Eight Ever?

It is important for you, as declarer, to know the correct percentage play taking one suit in isolation. Take eight cards between your hand and dummy, missing just the queen: the best chance of avoiding losing a trick to the lady is to cash one high honour then take a finesse. Thus with Kx facing AJxxxx (the trump suit), the percentage play is to cash the king then finesse the jack.

However – and this is the lesson – you must always take the whole deal in context. Frequently there are other, overriding factors. Don't be a slave to the oft-quoted maxim 'eight ever, nine never' (finesse when holding eight cards missing the queen; 'drop' with nine). The words 'ever' and 'never' imply a certainty where none exists.

This declarer – from the European Pairs – was blinded by the motto. He trumped the club lead, crossed to the king of hearts (West following with the ten), then led to his jack ('eight ever'). West won his queen and led a second club. Declarer trumped, drew the last outstanding trump with his ace, then led and passed the queen of diamonds. East won his king and led a third club, forcing declarer to use his last trump. Declarer cashed dummy's diamonds, but when, at Trick Twelve, he led a spade, West won the ace and cashed a club. Declarer had scored not one spade trick and was down one.

Let us replay the hand. After trumping the club lead, declarer crosses to the king of hearts and returns to his ace (key play). As it happens, he is lucky and the queen falls. He cashes the jack, runs the queen of diamonds to East's king, trumps the club return, and has time to force out the ace of spades. Eleven tricks.

If (as is more likely) the queen of trumps does not drop under the ace (both following low), declarer has time to knock out the king

**Dealer: South     Vulnerability: East-West**

**Pairs**

|  |  |  |
|---|---|---|
| ♠ Q J 10 |  |  |
| ♥ K 8 |  |  |
| ♦ A J 9 8 3 |  |  |
| ♣ 7 6 2 |  |  |

| ♠ A 9 8 2 | N | ♠ 6 4 |
|---|---|---|
| ♥ Q 10 | W    E | ♥ 9 4 2 |
| ♦ 6 2 | S | ♦ K 5 4 |
| ♣ 10 9 5 4 3 |  | ♣ A K Q J 8 |

|  |  |  |
|---|---|---|
| ♠ K 7 5 3 |  |  |
| ♥ A J 7 6 5 3 |  |  |
| ♦ Q 10 7 |  |  |
| ♣ – |  |  |

| S | W | N | E |
|---|---|---|---|
| 1 ♥ | PASS | 2 ♦ | PASS |
| 2 ♥ | PASS | 3 ♥ | PASS |
| 4 ♥ (1) | END | | |

(1) The partial diamond fit and overall shape make the decision to go on to game clearcut depite the low point-count.

**Contract: 4 ♥          Opening lead: ♣10**

of diamonds, and the ace of spades, by dint of leaving the queen of trumps outstanding. Ten tricks and game made.

# Not My Favourite

'Eight ever, nine never', as you will have surmised from the previous deal, is not my favourite motto. Here is a second deal that highlights the danger of slavishly following the ditty. It comes from the European Team Championships, and sees the Bulgarian declarer go down in his slam. Was he unlucky, or did he misplay the contract?

Declarer won West's spade lead with dummy's ace (discarding a club from hand), then crossed to the ace of hearts (in case the queen was singleton). He next returned to dummy's ten of diamonds and ran the jack of hearts. He had optimised the play of the trump suit, taking it in isolation. But West won the queen and declarer found himself unable to make his slam anymore. West switched to the six of clubs and declarer rose with the ace, drew the last trump, then ran the diamonds. But he had to concede a club at the end. Down one.

Declarer had a blind spot. All he had to do (after winning the ace of spades discarding a club) in order to safeguard his contract on any 3-2 trump split, was to bang down the ace-king of trumps. As it happens, the queen of trumps would fall and his problems would be over. But say both opponents follow twice with small trumps. It appears that declarer has a club and a trump to lose. But this is illusory.

Leaving the hypothetical queen of trumps outstanding, declarer simply follows by playing out his five winning diamonds, discarding dummy's two club losers. The defence are welcome to ruff with their queen, for declarer has one trump left in dummy to ruff his club loser from hand. Slam made.

The motto really ought to be changed to 'eight probably, nine probably not'. But I can't see the pedantic revised version catching on, can you?

**Dealer: South    Vulnerability: East-West**

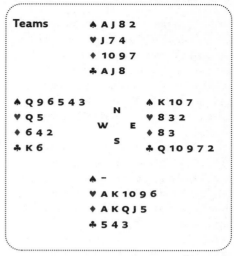

Teams

North:
♠ A J 8 2
♥ J 7 4
♦ 10 9 7
♣ A J 8

West:
♠ Q 9 6 5 4 3
♥ Q 5
♦ 6 4 2
♣ K 6

East:
♠ K 10 7
♥ 8 3 2
♦ 8 3
♣ Q 10 9 7 2

South:
♠ –
♥ A K 10 9 6
♦ A K Q J 5
♣ 5 4 3

| S | W | N | E |
|---|---|---|---|
| 1♥ | PASS | 1♠ | PASS |
| 3♦ (1) | PASS | 3♥ | PASS |
| 4♦ (2) | PASS | 6♥ (3) | END |

(1) Forcing to game.

(2) Showing his 5-5 shape with slam aspirations.

(3) Accepting – aces in both of South's short suits, and fits (and secondary honours) in both his long suits.

**Contract: 6♥**          **Opening lead: ♠5**

# Beating Air

Football may be 'a game of two halves', but Bridge is definitely not. The bidding and play are inextricably involved. Forget the bidding while you are playing at your peril.

West led the four of hearts to East's ace, and won the heart return with his king. At Trick Three West switched to the queen of clubs.

Winning the ace, declarer barely stopped to think, doubtless recalling 'eight ever, nine never'. He banged down the ace and king of trumps (East discarding on the second round), then played a diamond from dummy and inserted his queen. West won the king, cashed the queen of trumps and led a low club to East's nine and declarer's king. Declarer cashed the ace of diamonds and led to dummy's jack, but the 4-2 split meant that he had to lose a club at the end. Down two.

Let us replay the deal. As soon as East shows up with the ace of hearts, declarer knows that West has every other missing high card for his One Notrump opening bid.

Declarer wins the club at Trick Three, cashes the ace of trumps, plays a trump to West's nine and dummy's ten. He cashes the king of trumps felling the queen, then turns his attention to diamonds.

Rather than the normal finesse, he plays to his ace of diamonds and follows with a low diamond (key play). West's king 'beats air', and West returns a second club. Declarer wins, cashes the queen of diamonds, crosses to dummy's seven of trumps, then cashes the jack of diamonds discarding his club loser. Ten tricks and game made.

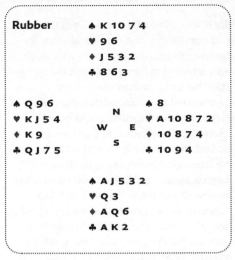

**Rubber**

North: ♠ K 10 7 4 / ♥ 9 6 / ♦ J 5 3 2 / ♣ 8 6 3

West: ♠ Q 9 6 / ♥ K J 5 4 / ♦ K 9 / ♣ Q J 7 5

East: ♠ 8 / ♥ A 10 8 7 2 / ♦ 10 8 7 4 / ♣ 10 9 4

South: ♠ A J 5 3 2 / ♥ Q 3 / ♦ A Q 6 / ♣ A K 2

| S | W | N | E |
|---|---|---|---|
|  | 1 NT | PASS | 2 ♥ (1) |
| DOUBLE | 3 ♥ | PASS | PASS |
| 3 ♠ (2) | PASS | 4 ♠ (3) | END |

(1) Weakness take-out.
(2) Double-then-bid showing a hand too strong to overcall spades immediately.
(3) So North is worth the raise to game.

**Contract: 4♠**          **Opening lead: ♥4**

# Reaching Dummy

On this deal from the World Team Championships, declarer knew he needed to finesse – in trumps. The whole play revolved around whether he could reach dummy to take that precious finesse.

West led the five of hearts to East's jack (a clever play to clarify the layout of the suit to his partner). At Trick Two East switched accurately to the seven of clubs (leading 'high for hate', but cleverly choosing the second-highest so he could follower higher next time to deny the doubleton).

Correctly convinced that the king of clubs was offside (i.e. with West), declarer rose with the ace of clubs and led back the jack of the suit. West won the king, and East followed with the nine (no doubleton).

If West had led the ace of diamonds at this point, declarer would have dumped the king on it and reached dummy via the queen of the suit; if West had led a low diamond declarer would have risen with dummy's queen to the same effect. So West stayed off diamonds, instead cashing the king of hearts and leading a third heart.

Declarer ruffed and led the king of diamonds, but West correctly ducked his ace. Declarer led his second diamond and West won the ace of diamonds and led a third diamond. This was most frustrating for declarer. He could temporarily reach dummy via the queen of diamonds... but his last six cards were all trumps so he had to trump the queen.

Stuck in his hand with just five trumps, declarer finally had no alternative but to cash the ace of trumps in the forlorn hope that the king would drop. Not so. He followed with the queen, and cursed when East won the king and the two-two split revealed itself. He had never managed to reach dummy (nor had it been possible on the fine defence he received). Down one.

**Teams**

|  | ♠ 9 7 |  |
|---|---|---|
|  | ♥ 10 8 3 |  |
|  | ♦ Q 10 3 |  |
|  | ♣ Q 8 6 4 2 |  |

|  | N |  |
|---|---|---|
| ♠ 5 2 | W    E | ♠ K 10 |
| ♥ K 9 5 |  | ♥ A Q J 6 4 |
| ♦ A J 9 7 5 | S | ♦ 8 6 2 |
| ♣ K 10 7 |  | ♣ 9 7 3 |

|  | ♠ A Q J 8 6 4 3 |  |
|---|---|---|
|  | ♥ 7 2 |  |
|  | ♦ K 4 |  |
|  | ♣ A J |  |

| S | W | N | E |
|---|---|---|---|
|  | PASS | PASS | 1 ♥ (1) |
| 1 ♠ | 2 ♦ | PASS | PASS (2) |
| 2 ♠ | 3 ♥ | PASS | PASS |
| 3 ♠ | END |  |  |

(1) Opening light third-in-hand is a profitable business. You indicate a lead to partner, plus the bluff show of strength can be off-putting for the opponents. And don't worry about being weak...

(2) ...for you don't have to make a rebid.

**Contract: 3♠**               **Opening lead: ♥5**

# Cut to the Chase

What would you open on South's hand on our next deal, from an Australian team event? Too strong to open Three Clubs or Four Clubs (both are preemptive and show fewer points), I would opt for One Club. Whilst this does let the opposition into the bidding cheaply, it does have the merit of allowing a meaningful discourse with partner. You have too much defence to expect the opponents to make a game; and too little playing strength to expect to be able to make a game yourself. So I would start simply low and see how things developed.

At the table South, Phil Markey, saw things somewhat differently. Despite being vulnerable, he cut to the chase and opened Five Clubs. West led the king of diamonds, dummy displayed his two huge aces (facing a long suit, aces are worth far more than picture cards), and declarer ruffed in hand. He was faced with finessing options in three suits, each one missing the king. How should he proceed?

There was no reason to delay drawing trumps, and the odds missing three cards including the king favoured the finesse, so at Trick Two declarer made the first key play of leading a low trump to dummy's (precious) eight. East followed low, so the first hurdle was overcome, and, crucially, he had won the trick in dummy.

At Trick Three declarer made the second key play – leading a low spade. It was correct to promote his queen of spades at this point (the heart finesse could wait, not so the spade finesse). If East had played low, declarer would have won his queen, drawn the last remaining trump (West's king) and emerged with eleven tricks. But East flew in with his king of spades, and switched to a heart (best).

Though it looks reasonable to try the finesse, such a play would lead to the demise

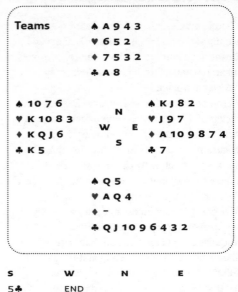

**Teams**

|  | ♠ A 9 4 3 |
|  | ♥ 6 5 2 |
|  | ♦ 7 5 3 2 |
|  | ♣ A 8 |

| ♠ 10 7 6 | | ♠ K J 8 2 |
| ♥ K 10 8 3 | N | ♥ J 9 7 |
| ♦ K Q J 6 | W    E | ♦ A 10 9 8 7 4 |
| ♣ K 5 | S | ♣ 7 |

|  | ♠ Q 5 |
|  | ♥ A Q 4 |
|  | ♦ – |
|  | ♣ Q J 10 9 6 4 3 2 |

| S | W | N | E |
|---|---|---|---|
| 5♣ | END | | |

**Contract: 5♣**          **Opening lead: ♦K**

of the contract. West would take the queen of hearts with the king and return... his king of trumps. Dummy's ace of trumps would be removed before declarer could unblock his queen of spades. Declarer would never reach dummy's ace of spades and the contract would fail.

Declarer spotted the trap, and made his third key play of rising with his ace of hearts on East's heart switch, spurning the finesse (key play). He unblocked the queen of spades, crossed to dummy's ace of trumps, felling West's king, cashed the ace of spades discarding a heart, and eventually conceded the queen of hearts to West's king at Trick Thirteen. Eleven tricks and game made.

# Vulgar Habits

The following snippet of conversation was recently reported to me. It took place in the cardroom of a smart all-male London club, and I must say it amused me greatly.

*Eager new member*: 'But surely if you had run the rest of your clubs, you would have had a perfect count of the hand and known the location of the missing queen'.

*Long-standing member*: 'Dear boy, I don't count. If you ask me, counting is a vulgar middle-class habit'.

I doubt the long-standing member would have emerged victorious on this deal.

West led the nine of hearts against the Four Spade contract – in response to his partner's preemptive opening bid in the suit. Declarer won the ace, crossed to dummy's king of trumps, and returned to his ace (noting the 2-2 split). He then cut loose with a heart.

East won the heart, and switched to a low diamond, dummy's weakness. West beat declarer's ten with the jack, cashed the ace, and followed with a third diamond to East's king, ruffed by declarer.

It was time to broach clubs. The normal play is to bang down the three top honours, hoping for a favourable split. However this declarer did not regard counting as too vulgar; he put on his counting hat. He knew that East began with seven hearts for his preempt, and that he had shown up with two trumps and (at least) three diamonds. That left room for just one club.

At Trick Eight declarer cashed the ace of clubs, to observe the size of East's singleton (it was the seven). He then led the nine of clubs. Had West covered with the ten, he would have won dummy's queen (East discarding), crossed back to a trump, and then finessed dummy's eight. In fact West played low on the nine, so declarer

**Pairs**

|  | ♠ K J 4 2 |
|  | ♥ 7 5 |
|  | ♦ 8 5 4 |
|  | ♣ K Q 8 2 |

| ♠ 10 8 | | ♠ 7 5 |
| ♥ 9 3 | N | ♥ K Q J 10 8 6 4 |
| ♦ A Q J 9 7 | W   E | ♦ K 6 3 |
| ♣ J 10 6 4 | S | ♣ 7 |

|  | ♠ A Q 9 6 3 |
|  | ♥ A 2 |
|  | ♦ 10 2 |
|  | ♣ A 9 5 3 |

| S | W | N | E |
|---|---|---|---|
|  |  |  | 3♥ (1) |
| 3♠ | PASS | 4♠ | END |

(1) Preemptive – showing a weak hand with a good seven-card suit.

**Contract: 4♠**          **Opening lead: ♥9**

simply let it ride. With East discarding, declarer had avoided a club loser. Game made.

# Textbook Call

What would you rebid as South after opening 1♦, and hearing a 1♥ response?

1NT? Show your balanced distribution and 15-16 points in spite of the lack of stopper in the other major.

2♣? A fabrication, intending to show delayed support for hearts and thus worry about spades.

2♦? Implying a sixth card in a one-suited hand, but keeping all options alive.

2♥? A trump shy, but the hand may well play better in hearts than Notrumps.

The textbook rebid is 1NT, and that is what South chose at the table (for me the choice lies between 1NT and 2♥). He soon found himself in 3NT on the dreaded spade lead. He ducked in dummy, but East won the jack and returned a spade to dummy's ace. What next?

Declarer needed to score his nine tricks without losing the lead. Broaching hearts was out for the opponents would win the ace and a flurry of spades would follow. Instead he had to hope for favourable splits in the minors.

The problem was lack of dummy entries in order to take the necessary minor-suit finesses. At the table declarer ran dummy's ten of clubs. He then tried a diamond to the jack, cashed the ace-king of the suit (noting the three-three split) and carried on with his two length winners.

Declarer's only chance was that East began with just a doubleton king of clubs, but no king appeared when he next cashed the ace of the suit. With a resigned air he tried a heart but West won his ace and cashed three spades. Down one.

Declarer needs to repeat the club finesse whilst in dummy, before scoring his five diamond tricks via a finesse. There is only one way to do this. He must lead dummy's

**Dealer: South       Vulnerability: East-West**

**Pairs**

|  | ♠ A 10 |  |
|---|---|---|
|  | ♥ K J 10 6 |  |
|  | ♦ 7 2 |  |
|  | ♣ Q 10 9 4 2 |  |

| ♠ K 9 7 4 2 | | ♠ Q J 8 3 |
|---|---|---|
| ♥ A 7 5 | N | ♥ 8 4 2 |
| ♦ 10 8 6 | W   E | ♦ Q 9 4 |
| ♣ 6 5 | S | ♣ K 8 7 |

|  | ♠ 6 5 |  |
|---|---|---|
|  | ♥ Q 9 3 |  |
|  | ♦ A K J 5 3 |  |
|  | ♣ A J 3 |  |

| S | W | N | E |
|---|---|---|---|
| 1♦ | PASS | 1♥ | PASS |
| 1NT (1) | PASS | 3NT | END |

(1) Though 1NT is the textbook call, showing 15-16 balanced, rebidding 2♦, 2♥ or even 2♣ might well lead to a superior game contract. 4♥, 5♣ and 5♦ all make on the layout.

**Contract: 3NT          Opening lead: ♠4**

queen of clubs at Trick Three and follow with the jack from hand (key play). He next runs the ten and, assuming East plays low a second time (best), is (crucially) in dummy for the diamond finesse. Five diamonds, three clubs and the ace of spades make nine tricks. Game made.

# Duck Soup

Do you think this Three Notrump contract can be made against best defence?

West led the seven of hearts in response to East's (light but acceptable) opening bid. Declarer won with the queen, and clearly needed to make something of dummy's clubs.

At Trick Two declarer led a club to dummy's jack. East won with the ace and, seeing no future in hearts, switched to the king of spades.

Declarer won the ace, played a club to dummy's king, then led a low club. The ten and queen crashed together and, though West led a second spade and East made his queen and ten, the fourth round of spades was won by declarer's nine. Declarer crossed to dummy's ace of diamonds and cashed his two small clubs. Contract made.

East was correct to switch to spades after winning the ace of clubs – if his partner had held the nine of spades and/or four cards then the contract would have gone down. But he had not been correct to win the ace of clubs at Trick Two.

If East had ducked his ace when declarer had led a club to dummy's jack, then declarer would have needed a second dummy entry to set up the clubs. Say he returns to his hand with the king of diamonds at Trick Three to lead a club to dummy's king. East wins his ace this time and switches to the king of spades. Declarer wins, crosses to the ace of diamonds to lead a third round of clubs, but cannot return to dummy to enjoy the clubs.

So the contract cannot be made?

Actually declarer can always succeed by ducking a club completely at Trick Two (key play). Think of dummy's clubs as Axxxx, and you will see the need to duck the first club in order to save an entry.

Even, after winning the first club cheaply,

if East returns his diamond in an attempt to remove dummy's entry, declarer wins his king and leads his second club to dummy's jack.

East wins the ace and switches to the king of spades, but declarer wins the ace, crosses to the ace of diamonds, cashes the king of clubs felling the two remaining clubs, and enjoys his two length winners in the suit. Game made.

---

**Dealer: East**   **Vulnerability: Neither**

Rubber

```
              ♠ J 4
              ♥ 8 4 3
              ♦ A 7 2
              ♣ K J 7 4 2

♠ 6 5 3              N         ♠ K Q 10 8
♥ 7 6                          ♥ J 10 9 5 2
♦ Q 10 8 6 4    W       E      ♦ J
♣ Q 9 6              S         ♣ A 10 8

              ♠ A 9 7 2
              ♥ A K Q
              ♦ K 9 5 3
              ♣ 5 3
```

| S | W | N | E |
|---|---|---|---|
|   |   |   | 1 ♥ |
| 1 NT | PASS | 3NT | END |

**Contract: 3NT**   **Opening lead: ♥7**

# Into the Jaws

On this deal, declarer got so fixated by his finessing options in the heart suit, that he completely overlooked a far superior alternative.

West led the king of spades against the Six Club slam and declarer won dummy's ace. He crossed to the ace of trumps, then led the three of hearts. West played low and declarer began to think.

If West held the ace of hearts, the right play was the queen/king, which would win the trick. He could ruff a heart and lead a diamond to the queen, taking the finesse for an overtrick (ruffing his third diamond in dummy).

But, reflecting that West might have risen with the ace of hearts in the hope of being able to cash the queen of spades, declarer placed the ace of hearts with East. So he tried finessing the ten of hearts. It was a reasonable shot (and playing the queen would have worked no better). But East won the jack and returned a spade. Declarer ruffed and had to go one down when the diamond finesse lost.

Admittedly declarer was unlucky that both the jack of hearts and the king of diamonds were offside, but he had missed an 100% line of play. Can you spot it?

Let us replay the hand. After winning dummy's ace of spades, declarer ruffs a spade. He crosses to dummy in trumps, ruffs a third spade, crosses to another trump, then ruffs dummy's last spade. Only after eliminating spades (key play) does he play a heart to the queen. There is no location of the red suit honours that can beat him.

On the actual layout East has to win the queen of hearts with his ace (or declarer has no heart loser and is finessing the diamond for the overtrick). But he is then endplayed.

If East leads a spade, declarer ruffs in

| Rubber | ♠ A 8 6 5 |
| ♥ K Q 10 |
| ♦ A Q |
| ♣ K J 9 4 |

```
                 N
  ♠ K Q 10              ♠ J 9 7 4 3
  ♥ 8 6 5 4 2    W   E  ♥ A J 9 7
  ♦ J 7 3 2             ♦ K 10 9 5
  ♣ 5              S    ♣ -
```

| | ♠ 2 |
| ♥ 3 |
| ♦ 8 6 4 |
| ♣ A Q 10 8 7 6 3 2 |

| S | W | N | E |
|---|---|---|---|
| 4♣ | PASS | 4NT (1) | PASS |
| 5♦ (1) | PASS | 6♣ | END |

(1) How many aces? Answer: one.

**Contract: 6♣**      **Opening lead: ♠K**

hand and discards dummy's queen of diamonds. And the return of either red suit is into the jaws of dummy's strength, presenting declarer with the two necessary tricks and his slam.

# Exam

For a bit of fun, you are taking an exam. How you would play Six Hearts on the queen of clubs lead?

Let's consider the sensible alternatives:

Plan D: Draw trumps and play a spade to dummy's queen.

Plan C: Draw trumps and lead a low spade from dummy. If the defence win without playing the king, later take a second round spade finesse by leading to dummy's queen.

Plan B: Draw trumps, cash all the minors, cash the ace of spades, cross to hand in trumps, then lead towards the queen of spades.

Plan A: Draw trumps, cash all the minors finishing in hand, then lead a low spade. If West plays the eight, duck in dummy. Otherwise rise with dummy's ace, cross back to hand with a trump, then lead a spade to dummy's queen.

Plan D makes when West has the king of spades – a 50% chance.

Plan C makes all the time Plan D makes, and also when East rises with the king of spades on the first round of the suit – as he may well do with king-doubleton. Plan C is an improvement on Plan D, utilising the power of leading towards the closed hand.

Plan B is better still. It makes all the time Plan C makes and also guarantees the contract (where Plan C relied on a defensive error) when East has a doubleton king of spades. He will be endplayed on the second spade to lead a minor suit. Then you can trump in dummy and discard your last spade from hand.

Plan A is best of all. It makes all the time Plan B makes and also when West plays the eight of spades from a singleton eight, or any doubleton including the eight. In these cases, ducking the first spade in dummy will endplay East.

**Teams**

|  | ♠ A Q 7 3 2 |  |
|---|---|---|
|  | ♥ A Q 10 7 |  |
|  | ♦ K Q |  |
|  | ♣ A 2 |  |

| ♠ J 10 8 | N | ♠ K 9 |
|---|---|---|
| ♥ 8 | W        E | ♥ 6 5 |
| ♦ J 9 7 3 2 | S | ♦ 10 8 6 5 |
| ♣ Q J 9 4 |  | ♣ 10 8 7 6 5 |

|  | ♠ 6 5 4 |  |
|---|---|---|
|  | ♥ K J 9 4 3 2 |  |
|  | ♦ A 4 |  |
|  | ♣ K 3 |  |

| S | W | N | E |
|---|---|---|---|
|  |  | 2♠ (1) | PASS |
| 3♥ | PASS | 4NT | PASS |
| 5♦ | PASS | 6♥ | END |

(1) Old-fashioned Strong. Playing Weak Twos you would have to choose between stetching to Two Clubs, or settling for One Spade and hoping the bidding doesn't proceed pass-pass-pass.

**Contract: 6♥**          **Opening lead: ♣Q**

Plan D = Fail; Plan C = Pass; Plan B = Merit; Plan A = Distinction.

And you?

# Unsophisticated

No one would call South's bidding sophisticated on our last deal of the chapter, but the final contract was certainly reasonable. Six Notrump starts with eleven top tricks, and actually the twelfth trick can (almost) always be made, on the reasonable assumption that West has seven hearts for his barrage bid of Four Hearts. Can you see how?

At the table declarer won the king of hearts lead with the ace and assessed that the deal boiled down to the spade finesse. Not being one to hang around, he crossed to the jack of clubs at Trick Two and played a spade to his ten. This was not a success – West won the king and cashed six heart tricks. Down six!

Clearly declarer's line can be improved upon by cashing more winners before taking the spade finesse. But to claim that twelve tricks are guaranteed as long as East has no more hearts (and neither minor-suit longer than dummy's), regardless of who holds the king of spades, seems rather a rash thing to say...

Try this. Win the ace of hearts, cash the ace-queen of diamonds and the queen of clubs. Cross to the jack of clubs, then lead out dummy's five remaining minor-suit winners. Your last three cards should be ace-queen-jack of spades, East's will be three spades (with or without the king) and West's...?

If West discards a spade, then he is known to have just one spade left. Therefore you can cross to the ace of spades and lead the queen. Either the king will have fallen under the ace from West (as here) or, if East holds the king, you simply lead the queen to flush out East's king and set up your jack for the twelfth trick.

If West does not discard a spade, then his last three cards are known to be two spades and one top heart. Exit with dummy's nine of

hearts to West and wait for West to lead a spade around to your ace-queen.

Neat – eh? – and somewhat appropriate to end a chapter on finessing by refusing to take one!

**Dealer: North   Vulnerability: North-South**

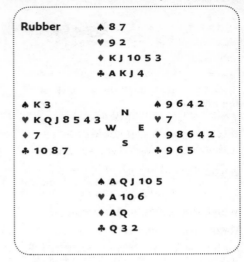

Rubber

|  | North |
|---|---|
| ♠ | 8 7 |
| ♥ | 9 2 |
| ♦ | K J 10 5 3 |
| ♣ | A K J 4 |

West
♠ K 3
♥ K Q J 8 5 4 3
♦ 7
♣ 10 8 7

East
♠ 9 6 4 2
♥ 7
♦ 9 8 6 4 2
♣ 9 6 5

South
♠ A Q J 10 5
♥ A 10 6
♦ A Q
♣ Q 3 2

| S | W | N | E |
|---|---|---|---|
|  |  | 1♦ | PASS |
| 2♠ | 4♥ | PASS | PASS |
| 6NT (1) | END | | |

(1) Hardly gilt-edged, with just one heart stopper, and no ace-king of clubs.

**Contract: 6NT        Opening lead: ♥K**

# CHAPTER 8

# Guess Who?

'One peek is worth two finesses.' Reprehensible behaviour, of course, but how often you wish you could see through the backs of the cards.

So many contracts depend on 'guessing' which opponent holds a particular queen, or other crucial missing card. Take ♥KJ2 facing ♥A103.

Are you going to finesse (i.e. lead to) the jack, or finesse the ten? If you knew which opponent held more hearts, you would play them for the queen... unless their partner opened One Notrump... unless that partner had already shown up with thirteen points in the outside suits... Such sleuthing is one of the skilful, and alluring parts of the game.

Psychological factors play a role too. Say you have ♥KJ9 in hand (note the presence of the nine, which you need for this gambit) facing ♥A103 in dummy. Try leading the jack. Perhaps the next hand will cover ('cover an honour with an honour'). Perhaps he will flinch ('he who hesitates is lost'). If he plays low in bored fashion, go up with the ace and lead low to the nine. Don't ignore your sixth sense either – if you 'feel' more tension from your left, it may well be that it is your left-hand opponent who holds the missing card.

One final thought: how much better it would be to force your opponents to open up the suit, resolving the guess for you.

# King-Jack Guess

Does this position look familiar?

```
            Dummy
             KJ
West                    East
 ??                      ??
           Declarer
             xx
```

You lead low towards dummy and West follows low. Do you play the jack, hoping West holds the queen? Or the king, hoping he holds the ace? An eternal dilemma.

Experts have different approaches, ranging from English star Tony Forrester who agonises over every king-jack guess and tears his hair out when he goes wrong (which is not often, by the way); to Swedish star Magnus Lindqvist who almost always plays the jack, preferring to use his grey cells in situations where there is less guesswork involved, simply shrugging when he is wrong. (Why the jack? Because an opponent playing second and holding the ace might rise with the card, or make a giveaway hesitation.)

This deal featured a king-jack diamond guess for a slam. At the table declarer misguessed, but a small precaution saved the day. Winning the king of hearts with the ace, declarer drew one round of trumps, then played ace-king of spades, and ruffed a spade (setting up the suit when the queen fell).

If declarer had crossed to a second trump, cashed two winning spades discarding diamonds (to leave ♦KJ) and then mis-guessed by leading to the king (playing East, the non-preemptor for the ace), he would have gone down in his slam. For West would beat the king with the ace and, after exiting perforce with a heart (ruffed in dummy as declarer followed with his second heart), East would score his queen of diamonds.

**Dealer: North        Vulnerability: Both**

**Pairs**

```
              ♠ A K 10 9 7
              ♥ 7
              ♦ 10 4
              ♣ A K Q 8 3

♠ 6 5 4              N          ♠ Q 3 2
♥ K Q J 6 4 3 2   W     E       ♥ 10 9 5
♦ A                  S          ♦ Q 8 7 6 5 3
♣ 10 7                          ♣ 2

              ♠ J 8
              ♥ A 8
              ♦ K J 9 2
              ♣ J 9 6 5 4
```

| S | W | N | E |
|---|---|---|---|
|   |   | 1♠ | PASS |
| 2♣ | 4♥ | 4NT (1) | PASS (2) |
| 5♦ (3) | PASS | 6♣ | END |

(1) Blackwood (old-fashioned 'Four Ace'). North gambles on the diamond situation.
(2) Misses the chance to bid 5♥, and interfere with the opposing Blackwood. (The standard approach is to play 'D0P1': in other words, double the interference with no aces, pass with one, make the cheapest bid with two etc.)
(3) One ace.

**Contract: 6♣        Opening lead: ♥K**

However declarer made the key play of ruffing his second heart before cashing a second trump and leading to the king of diamonds. He could now survive the diamond misguess (leading to the king) because, after winning his singleton ace, West's forced heart return gave declarer a ruff-and-discard. He could throw his remaining diamond from one hand as he ruffed in the other. Slam made.

# Heart View

Let us have another look at the dreaded king-jack guess. West switches to a heart during the play and you must decide which of dummy's king-jack to play. Cover up the East-West cards to give yourself the proper challenge.

West leads a trump to your Four Spades and you win in hand, draw a second top trump (they split 2-2), and advance the king of diamonds. West takes the ace and shoots out a low heart. Crux time. Do you play dummy's king, hoping West holds the ace? Or do you play dummy's jack, hoping West holds the queen?

There is a small argument for playing the king of hearts on the grounds that West might have opened with a heart lead from the queen, but surely not from the ace. However there is a far stronger reason for trying dummy's king – what is it?

If you guess incorrectly, you are down (with two hearts, a diamond and at least a club to lose). So assume you guess correctly.

If you guess correctly to play the king (in other words West holds the ace, and the king wins the trick) then your problems are solved. You can run through your diamonds and make your contract easily. But if you guess correctly to play the jack (West holding the queen and East the ace), then you have still not necessarily made your game. For East will undoubtedly switch to a club when he wins the jack of hearts with the ace and you may still go down if you lose two club tricks (either through a losing guess if West holds one of the ace-queen or without the option if West holds them both).

You should take the view in hearts that gains most when correct and, on this occasion, that means playing the king. On the actual layout you are rewarded when it holds the trick. Diamonds are cashed, and

**Teams**

```
              ♠ 10 8 6
              ♥ K J
              ♦ J 9 8 7 4
              ♣ 4 3 2

♠ 5 2                        ♠ 7 3
♥ A 8 6 5        N           ♥ Q 10 9 3 2
♦ A 3 2      W     E         ♦ 6 5
♣ A Q 9 7       S            ♣ 10 8 6 5

              ♠ A K Q J 9 4
              ♥ 7 4
              ♦ K Q 10
              ♣ K J
```

| S | W | N | E |
|---|---|---|---|
| 2♠ (1) | PASS (2) | 2NT (3) | PASS |
| 3♠ | PASS | 4♠ | END |

(1) Slightly shaded for a Strong Two, but if you still play them (as opposed to the increasingly popular Weak variety) then you might as well use them.

(2) Little point in fighting the spade suit, on a hand that has good defensive prospects.

(3) Negative – up to seven points.

**Contract: 4♠**                **Opening lead: ♠2**

eleven tricks made via six trumps, four diamonds and the king of hearts.

# Wishful Thinking

Card Placing by Assumption – or wishful thinking – is a logical process of much importance at the Bridge table. This featured deal is a good illustration. Cover up the East-West cards before proceeding.

Defending the Four Spade contract, West cashed the ace of hearts at Trick One, followed with the king of the suit, and then switched to the three of diamonds (best). Which of dummy's honours should declarer play?

In one sense it is a guess. If West holds the ace of diamonds, playing dummy's king will be the winning view; but if West holds the queen of diamonds and East the ace, the jack has to be played (which will force out the ace and so establish dummy's king).

Declarer reasoned as follows:

'In order to make my optimistic game contract, I will not only need a successful diamond guess, but I will also need to avoid a loser in either black suit. Barring the improbable possibility of a singleton king in West's hand in either suit, I therefore need East to have both black kings. Although I do not know that to be the case, I must assume it to be so for my contract to stand a chance of making.

'Mentally placing both black kings in East's hand, there cannot be any room for him to hold the ace of diamonds as well; for otherwise he would have too much strength (10 points) for his mere raise to Two Hearts (6-9 points). Thus I must play West for the ace of diamonds.'

Flawless reasoning by declarer resulted in him making the correct play of rising with dummy's king of diamonds at Trick Three. When it won the trick (good!), he ran the jack of trumps. When this held the trick, he led a second trump to his queen. He cashed the ace of trumps, felling East's king, then led to

## Dealer: West    Vulnerability: Neither

```
Chicago        ♠ J 10 8 7
               ♥ 4 2
               ♦ K J
               ♣ Q 9 7 3 2

♠ 3                          ♠ K 6 5
♥ A K Q 9 7      N           ♥ J 10 5 3
♦ A 9 8 3 2   W     E        ♦ Q 10 6 5
♣ 8 5            S           ♣ K 6

               ♠ A Q 9 4 2
               ♥ 8 6
               ♦ 7 4
               ♣ A J 10 4
```

| S | W | N | E |
|---|---|---|---|
|  | 1♥ | PASS | 2♥ |
| 2♠ | 4♥ | 4♠ | END |

**Contract: 4♠**          **Opening lead: ♥A**

dummy's ten of trumps in order to take the club finesse. He led the nine of clubs and ran it, smiling inwardly when it won. He led a second (low) club to East's king and his ace, cashed the jack of clubs, overtook the ten with dummy's queen, then tabled dummy's fifth club discarding his second diamond. Eleven tricks made.

Note that if East had held the ace of diamonds, and beaten dummy's king with it at Trick Three, declarer would have known that West held at least one black suit king and that the contract was destined to fail regardless of his choice of diamond honour from dummy. He would go down an extra trick, but that is relatively insignificant at all forms of the game except Matchpoint Duplicate.

# Innocuous Move

Dealer: South       Vulnerability: East-West

Sometimes the most innocuous of moves can turn a whole deal to your advantage. Take this deal – from a home game.

Powering into Six Spades, declarer must have fancied his chances when he saw dummy. Unless West held all three trumps, he would be making twelve or thirteen tricks depending on the location of the king in the minor-suit he chose to finesse.

Indeed so confident was declarer of making Six Spades that he found his thoughts wandering to the issue of how to bid to Seven Hearts. On 2-1 spades and 3-2 hearts, he would have thirteen tricks with hearts as trumps without needing a minor-suit finesse (with a fifth heart trick, making the last two trumps separately after drawing their trumps).

However after winning the heart lead, he cashed the ace of trumps and saw East discard. Even Six Spades was now in jeopardy. He cashed the king of trumps, then led out winning hearts, West refusing to ruff. He then exited with a third trump to West in the hope of a helpful diamond return. West was not so obliging, however, and back came a club.

Should declarer play West for the king of clubs, finessing dummy's queen and, if successful, discarding his queen of diamonds on the ace of clubs? Or should he rise with the ace of clubs and play a diamond to the queen? Eventually he decided that West might be reluctant to lead away from the king of clubs. He rose with the ace and finessed the queen of diamonds. Down one.

Have you spotted the ingeniously simple manoeuvre that avoids this guess? Declarer should cash dummy's ace of clubs (key play), before playing hearts and exiting with a trump. Now he has the free shot of rising with dummy's queen on a club return. He

**Rubber**

```
                ♠ J 10 7 5
                ♥ 10 9 7 4
                ♦ 8 6
                ♣ A Q 2
♠ Q 9 3                         ♠ –
♥ 8 3          N                ♥ 6 5 2
♦ K 10 4 2   W   E              ♦ J 9 7 5 3
♣ K J 9 5      S                ♣ 10 8 7 6 3
                ♠ A K 8 6 4 2
                ♥ A K Q J
                ♦ A Q
                ♣ 4
```

| S | W | N | E |
|---|---|---|---|
| 2♣ (1) | PASS | 2♦ (2) | PASS |
| 2♠ | PASS | 4♠ (3) | PASS |
| 6♠ (4) | END | | |

(1) 23+ points, or any game-forcing hand.
(2) Negative – any hand up to seven points.
(3) Jump support to show a maximum negative.
(4) Intends to play 6♠ whether or not partner holds ♣A, so no need for Blackwood.

**Contract: 6♠**          **Opening lead: ♥8**

will only be defeated when East holds the king of clubs and West the king of diamonds, a 3:1 against shot, where no line of play works.

# Point-counting

As a matter of routine, declarer should work out how many high-card points are missing at the start of play. This is not a hard exercise – simply add your points to dummy's and subtract the total from 40 (the number of points in the pack).

Sometimes the answer will be of little benefit, especially when the opponents hold few points and did not enter the auction. Often it will give you pointers but no categoric answers. But occasionally it will tell you everything, particularly if an opponent made a bid that showed his point-count to within a narrow range. This deal was just such a case in point.

With declarer and dummy holding 26 points, it was easy to work out that the defenders held 14. But East had opened One Notrump and so had shown 12-14 of those points. This meant that West held between zero and two points and therefore could not hold a king.

Bearing in mind that East holds all the missing kings, how would you declare Six Diamonds on a club lead?

You have a certain trump loser – East would not have opened One Notrump with a singleton king of diamonds – so it would be folly to play a low club from dummy at Trick One. East would win his king and wait to score his king of trumps. Instead rise with dummy's ace, and concentrate on discarding your two remaining clubs on dummy's hearts.

At Trick Two lead a low heart from dummy and ruff East's jack. Cross to the ace of trumps (pleased to see West follow but, as expected, no king appears), cash the ace of hearts (discarding a club), and ruff a third heart. Cross to the ace of spades and ruff a fourth heart (more pleasure as East's king falls). Cash the king of spades, ruff a third

**Teams**

|  | |
|---|---|
| ♠ A 3 | |
| ♥ A Q 6 5 2 | |
| ♦ A 9 4 | |
| ♣ A 6 4 | |

| ♠ J 9 5 2 | ♠ Q 8 7 6 |
|---|---|
| ♥ 10 8 7 4 | ♥ K J 9 3 |
| ♦ 10 | ♦ K 7 |
| ♣ J 9 8 3 | ♣ K 10 5 |

|  | |
|---|---|
| ♠ K 10 4 | |
| ♥ – | |
| ♦ Q J 8 6 5 3 2 | |
| ♣ Q 7 2 | |

| S | W | N | E |
|---|---|---|---|
| | | | 1 NT |
| 2♦ | PASS | 3♥ | PASS |
| 4♦ | PASS | 6♦ (1) | END |

(1) Rare to bid a slam after an opponent has opened, but North's hand has the ingredients: controls (i.e. aces), a fit, and a potential source of tricks (his heart suit).

**Contract: 6♦**          **Opening lead: ♣3**

spade, then lead the promoted queen of hearts. East ruffs with his king but it is too late – you discard your queen of clubs on the same trick and take the remaining tricks with your trumps. Slam made.

# Less Likely

This is the one defensive problem of the chapter – from the Brighton Teams. It can be solved by pure logic. You are East – so cover up the West and South hands.

Defending Four Hearts, your partner, having overcalled in the suit, leads the queen of spades. Declarer plays low from dummy and you naturally ruff. So far so good, but you need to reach your partner's hand to receive a second ruff.

Which of the following two options offers a better chance of defeating the game?
(a) Underleading your ace of of clubs, in the hope that partner holds the king. Or...
(b) Leading a diamond in the hope that partner holds the ace.

Make your choice before reading on.

At the table East tried a low club. But declarer rose with the king, drew trumps, and merely conceded a diamond to the ace. Game made – with an overtrick.

Strategy (b) would have succeeded. West would have won the ace of diamonds, given East a second spade ruff, and the ace of clubs would have been the fourth defensive trick. Was East unlucky? Or did he make the wrong play?

Here is the crux. Strategy (b) only requires West to have one specific card – the ace of diamonds. But Strategy (a) requires more than just West to hold the king of clubs. Say the underlead of the ace of clubs succeeds: it sees West win with the king and lead a second spade, ruffed. The game is not yet down – a further trick is required – which can only really come from diamonds. West will need to hold the ace or king of diamonds in addition to the king of clubs.

To summarise: Strategy (a) requires both the king of clubs and the ace/king of diamonds to lie with West. Strategy (b) needs West to hold just one specific card: the ace of

**Teams**

|  |  |  |
|---|---|---|
|  | ♠ K 8 6 2 |  |
|  | ♥ A J 9 8 2 |  |
|  | ♦ Q J 8 |  |
|  | ♣ J |  |

| West | | East |
|---|---|---|
| ♠ Q J 10 5 4 3 | N | ♠ – |
| ♥ 10 | W E | ♥ 7 6 3 |
| ♦ A 9 2 | S | ♦ 7 6 4 3 |
| ♣ Q 4 3 | | ♣ A 10 9 8 6 2 |

|  |  |  |
|---|---|---|
|  | ♠ A 9 7 |  |
|  | ♥ K Q 5 4 |  |
|  | ♦ K 10 5 |  |
|  | ♣ K 7 5 |  |

| S | W | N | E |
|---|---|---|---|
| 1♥ | 1♠ | 4♣ (1) | PASS |
| 4♥ (2) | END | | |

(1) Splinter Bid, showing a raise to (at least) 4♥ with club shortage.
(2) A wasted ♣K and a barren shape makes it clear for South to sign off.

**Contract: 4♥**          **Opening lead: ♠Q**

diamonds. East pursued the defensive option that needed more from his partner, and was thus less likely.

# Insoluble Dilemma

West leads the queen of diamonds against your Three Notrump contract. You win your king and count eight tricks. You need to guess which opponent holds the queen of clubs in order to score your ninth. You have a two-way finesse position – which way should you go?

At the table declarer deliberated for some minutes. Eventually he elected to play East for the queen of clubs on the grounds that West had shown a weak hand with long diamonds in the auction, making East more likely to have greater club length (and the queen).

At Trick Two declarer crossed to dummy's king of clubs and at Trick Three he led and passed the ten of the suit. He was right in the sense that East did hold more clubs than West. But, crucially, it was West who held the queen. West won with that card and promptly cashed five winning diamonds. Down two.

*Question:* Was declarer simply unlucky or was there more to the situation than meets the eye?

*Answer:* Declarer misplayed the hand at Trick One. He should duck West's queen of diamonds lead (key play).

This puts West in an insoluble dilemma. If he switches to a major-suit at Trick Two, declarer can finesse clubs safely into West's hand (leading to the king and running the ten), knowing that West cannot profitably attack diamonds from his side. If West presses on with diamonds (cashing the ace and leading a third round to declarer's king), then it is safe to finesse the clubs into East (running the jack), because East has no more diamonds.

What it boils down to is this: if declarer wins the king of diamonds at Trick One, both his opponents are danger hands (and a misguess in clubs will doom the contract).

But if declarer ducks the queen of diamonds lead, then West can only make one defender into the danger hand (East if he switches suits at Trick Two, West if he continues diamonds). Declarer can then finesse clubs into the safe hand and so ensure his contract.

A fascinating lesson in Avoidance Play.

**Dealer: South**  **Vulnerability: Both**

**Rubber**

|  | ♠ A Q 5 |  |
|---|---|---|
|  | ♥ K 5 4 3 2 |  |
|  | ♦ 6 2 |  |
|  | ♣ K 10 4 |  |
| ♠ 9 6 3 | | ♠ J 10 8 7 |
| ♥ J 9 | N | ♥ Q 10 8 7 |
| ♦ A Q J 10 4 3 | W E | ♦ 9 8 |
| ♣ Q 8 | S | ♣ 7 6 2 |
|  | ♠ K 4 2 |  |
|  | ♥ A 6 |  |
|  | ♦ K 7 5 |  |
|  | ♣ A J 9 5 3 |  |

| S | W | N | E |
|---|---|---|---|
| 1♣ | 2♦ (1) | 2♥ | PASS |
| 2NT | PASS | 3NT | END |

(1) Weak Jump overcall, showing a good six-card suit and less than opening bid values.

**Contract: 3NT**     **Opening lead: ♦Q**

# Show Up

On our last deal of the chapter, it was unfortunate that a Five Club contract had only ten top tricks. Oh, for a third heart in either hand! The contract seemed to depend purely on the diamond finesse.

West led out his three top spades. East discarded a heart on the third round, and declarer ruffed. He drew trumps in three rounds, then played diamonds in the normal fashion. He cashed the ace then led to dummy's jack. East won the queen and the contract was down.

Somewhat irritatingly, East was quick to point out that his queen of diamonds had been doubleton and that declarer could have picked it up by rising with the king on the second round.

'How on earth was I supposed to know?' retorted a slightly ruffled declarer. 'The odds massively favour taking the second round finesse,' he continued.

True, but declarer could have given himself an extra chance by delaying broaching diamonds until the very end. At Trick Ten (after cashing hearts and trumps) he leads his last trump (his other three cards are his diamonds). Dummy, yet to discard, holds the eight of spades and the three diamonds. West has to retain the ten of spades to prevent dummy's eight of spades becoming a winner. And that is the crux.

Dummy's spade is now discarded, declarer cashes the ace of diamonds and, at Trick Twelve, leads the four towards dummy's king-knave. West follows with the ten and dummy...

West's last card is known to be the ten of spades, so there is no point in finessing the jack of diamonds. Declarer must rise with the king in the hope that East's queen is dropping (he knows it will be if he is counting).

If West had held the queen of diamonds it

would have shown up on the penultimate trick, because his last card is a spade winner.

West is the victim of a 'show-up squeeze'.

Teams

|  | ♠ 8 6 5 3 |  |
|---|---|---|
|  | ♥ K J |  |
|  | ♦ K J 2 |  |
|  | ♣ J 9 8 6 |  |

| ♠ A K Q 10 9 |  | ♠ 7 2 |
|---|---|---|
| ♥ 10 7 4 | N | ♥ 9 8 7 5 3 2 |
| ♦ 10 8 7 6 3 | W   E | ♦ Q 9 |
| ♣ – | S | ♣ 5 3 2 |

|  | ♠ J 4 |  |
|---|---|---|
|  | ♥ A Q |  |
|  | ♦ A 5 4 |  |
|  | ♣ A K Q 10 7 4 |  |

| S | W | N | E |
|---|---|---|---|
| 1♣ | 1♠ | 2♣ | PASS |
| 5♣ (1) | END | | |

(1) A trifle precipitate. Although it would have made no difference here, a Two Spade bid to ask for a stopper would have been a wiser choice.

**Contract: 5♣**          **Opening lead: ♠A**

# CHAPTER 9

# Spot Cards

Spot cards – the lowly deuce (two) up to the nine (the ten is an honour) – get short shrift. Unfairly so. Although the glamorous honours receive most of the attention, ignore spot cards at your peril.

Compare ♦J10987 and ♦J10432, both holdings facing a void. J10987 will score two tricks, after forcing out the ace, king and queen. J10432 will rarely be worth anything, unless the suit splits 4-4.

Contrast the following pair of One Notrump openers:

(i)   ♠A Q 3 2    (ii) ♠A Q 9 7
      ♥K 10 4       ♥K 10 9
      ♦K J 4 2      ♦K J 8 7
      ♣5 3         ♣9 8

Say your partner raises to Two Notrumps, inviting you to game. You have a close decision, which might be affected by the form of scoring (more likely to try for the game bonus at Teams/Rubber than Duplicate, especially when vulnerable and you can win the rubber/a 500 bonus). However look at the eights and nines. Hand (ii) has far better such fillers than Hand (i) and that should tip the balance.

Making use of all of your assets is one secret of the winning player. I say it again – ignore spot cards at your peril.

# Small Please

'Small please'. These words were haunting South, weeks after the deal occurred. You'll soon see why...

After opening Five Clubs and hearing North-South power into slam, East came forth with a special double.

Invented by US player Theodore Lightner, an out-of-the-blue double of a slam contract asks partner to put back the lead he was about to make, and try something unusual instead. If dummy has bid another suit apart from the trump suit, the double calls for dummy's first bid suit. Otherwise the opening leader has to use common-sense – bearing in mind that the double will typically be based on a void somewhere.

So what should West have led against Six Hearts? In truth he has nothing to go on at all. He might just as well shuffle his ten cards in spades and diamonds and pick one out at random. Unfortunately West had not come across the Lightner Slam Double and out popped the singleton six of his partner's clubs.

'Small please,' said declarer to dummy.

Can you see what happened next? After close scrutiny of the club 'pips', East followed with the four. West's six had won the trick! There followed a protracted pause...

Eventually West asked whose lead it was. After recovering from the shock of finding out that it was *his* lead, West stopped to think.

West belatedly realised his partner was void somewhere (why else had he been left on lead?). On the grounds that declarer was more likely to have a second suit of diamonds headed by the king-queen-jack rather than a second suit of spades headed by the ten, in order to justify his Five Heart overcall, West switched to a diamond at Trick Two. East trumped. One down.

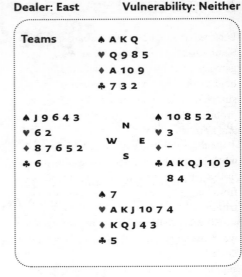

Teams

|  | |
| --- | --- |
| ♠ A K Q | |
| ♥ Q 9 8 5 | |
| ♦ A 10 9 | |
| ♣ 7 3 2 | |

West: ♠ J 9 6 4 3 ♥ 6 2 ♦ 8 7 6 5 2 ♣ 6

East: ♠ 10 8 5 2 ♥ 3 ♦ – ♣ A K Q J 10 9 8 4

South: ♠ 7 ♥ A K J 10 7 4 ♦ K Q J 4 3 ♣ 5

| S | W | N | E |
| --- | --- | --- | --- |
| | | | 5♣ |
| 5♥ | PASS | 6♥ | DOUBLE (1) |
| END | | | |

(1) Lightner – a request for an unusual lead. East would love a diamond – which he can ruff.

**Contract: 6♥ doubled  Opening lead: ♣6 (?)**

If only declarer had bothered to cover the six of clubs opening lead with dummy's seven...

# Singleton Lead

Benito Garozzo, Italian Blue Team hero of the Sixties and Seventies and still playing a gritty game as he approaches 80, says that if you hold a side-suit singleton defending against a suit slam, you do not have an opening lead problem. You put your singleton on the table and hope.

Leading the singleton will result in a ruff when partner has the ace of the singleton suit or the ace of trumps; it also prevents declarer from losing the lead to partner before your trumps are drawn.

However there are occasions – particularly when the singleton suit has been bid by declarer – when you would be well advised to seek an alternative. Take this deal from the Brighton Pairs.

West chose to lead his singleton nine of hearts against the Six Diamond slam. Declarer won dummy's king, drew trumps in three rounds finishing in dummy, then led and passed the seven of hearts (reading West's lead to be a singleton – the only explanation for leading declarer's other bid suit as opposed to an unbid black suit).

A third heart to the ace-queen-eight enabled declarer to discard two clubs from dummy. He cashed the black aces, crossruffed, and gave the defence the last trick. Twelve tricks and slam made.

On any other lead, declarer would have been bound to draw trumps and play hearts from the top. The four-one split would render him one trick short (he needed five heart tricks to go with his five trumps and two black aces).

**Pairs**

|  | North |
|---|---|
| ♠ | 10 8 5 |
| ♥ | K 7 6 |
| ♦ | A K 7 6 |
| ♣ | A 7 4 |

| West | East |
|---|---|
| ♠ K 9 7 3 2 | ♠ Q J 6 4 |
| ♥ 9 | ♥ J 10 5 4 |
| ♦ J 4 3 | ♦ 10 2 |
| ♣ Q 5 3 2 | ♣ K 10 8 |

|  | South |
|---|---|
| ♠ | A |
| ♥ | A Q 8 3 2 |
| ♦ | Q 9 8 5 |
| ♣ | J 9 6 |

| S | W | N | E |
|---|---|---|---|
|  |  | 1 NT | PASS |
| 2♦ (1) | PASS | 2♥ (2) | PASS |
| 3♦ (3) | PASS | 4♦ | PASS |
| 4♠ (4) | PASS | 5♣ (4) | PASS |
| 6♦ (5) | PASS | PASS (6) | END |

(1) Transfer bid, showing five (+) hearts.
(2) Duly completing the transfer.
(3) Natural and forcing, showing five hearts and four (+) diamonds.
(4) Ace-showing cue-bids.
(5) After hearing partner has the precious ♣A.
(6) North knows that there are two eight-card fits, 5-3 hearts and 4-4 diamonds. But a 4-4 fit generally plays better, because there is a source of discards on the long cards of the 5-3 suit if a side-suit. As you can see, 6♥ has no play, whilst 6♦ only requires 3-2 splits in each red suit.

**Contract: 6♦**          **Opening lead: ♥9**

# One in a Hundred

Nine times out of ten rash bidding will get punished. Perhaps even ninety-nine times out of hundred if the bidding is as rash as this North-South. But this was that one time!

A sensible auction would go 1♠ from South, 2♣ from North, 3NT from South, Pass from North. West would lead his fourth highest diamond, the four and East would win the king and return a second diamond. Declarer would play low, West would win the jack, cash the ace (felling declarer's queen), and follow with the six and two. One down – unlucky, but normal.

Against the absurdly over-optimistic 6NT contract, West was understandably loath to lead from his strong diamond holding. Swap the queen and king of the suit and a lead away from his strength would be the only way that declarer would be able to score a trick with his king.

Instead West settled on the eight of hearts, the other unbid suit. Let us see what happened. Noticing the potential power of his seven, declarer covered the eight with dummy's jack, East covering with the queen and declarer winning with the king. At Trick Two declarer crossed to dummy's ten of spades and then led a low heart. When East followed low, declarer paused. Placing the nine with East (West having led the eight), declarer eventually inserted the seven. Success!

With the seven of hearts having won the trick, he cashed the ten, then turned his attentions to clubs. He cashed the king and then followed by taking the finesse, leading low to the jack. More success! The jack winning, he now cashed the ace of hearts discarding a diamond, crossed to the ace-king-queen of spades (discarding diamonds from dummy), then led his third club to dummy's ace.

**Teams**

```
              ♠ J 10
              ♥ A J 4 2
              ♦ 10 9 8
              ♣ A J 6 3

♠ 8 6 3              N          ♠ 9 7 5 4
♥ 8 3          W         E      ♥ Q 9 6 5
♦ A J 6 4 2          S          ♦ K 7
♣ Q 10 8                        ♣ 9 5 2

              ♠ A K Q 2
              ♥ K 10 7
              ♦ Q 5 3
              ♣ K 7 4
```

| S | W | N | E |
|---|---|---|---|
| 1♠ | PASS | 2♣ | PASS |
| 3NT | PASS | 4NT (?) | PASS |
| 6NT (??) | END | | |

Note: Bidding not recommended!

**Contract: 6NT (!)**    **Opening lead: ♥8**

With both opponents following, declarer was able to score a trick with dummy's thirteenth club and the slam had actually made. What incredible luck (but I doubt you'll hear much about the other ninety-nine hands)!

# Magic Nine

A good declarer is like a magician. Watch him make one of his four seemingly certain losers disappear; he is in Four Hearts on the ace of diamonds opening lead, West continuing with the king of diamonds, then switching to the queen of clubs.

If you find yourself staring at the deal, unable to see a way of avoiding a spade and a club loser, the clue is: use the nine of spades.

At the table declarer found the solution. He won dummy's ace of clubs, then led a low spade (key play). There was no defence.

Say East had played low on the spade. West would have beaten the jack with the queen, and led the jack of clubs. Declarer would have won the king, crossed to the ace of spades (felling East's ten), ruffed a low spade (felling East's king), drawn trumps in three rounds finishing in dummy, then he would have discarded the losing third club on the master nine of spades.

In fact East rose with the king of spades at Trick Four, and led a second club. Declarer won his king and led the jack of spades, covered by West's queen, and won by dummy's ace. He ruffed a low spade (bringing down East's ten), drew trumps in three rounds finishing in dummy, then cashed the promoted nine of spades discarding his club loser. Ten tricks and game made.

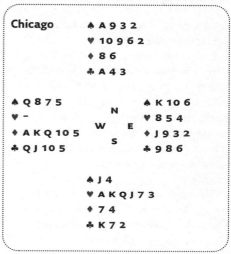

| S | W | N | E |
|---|---|---|---|
|  | 1♦ | PASS | PASS (1) |
| 2♥ (2) | PASS | 4♥ (3) | END |

(1) Strong case for scraping up a Two Diamond raise, which would in all probability, have led to West bidding on to Five Diamonds, just down one. Passing gave partner no assistance, and ceded the momentum to the opposition.

(2) Protective jump overcall, showing opening values and a good six-card suit.

(3) Two aces and four-card support are ample for a game bid.

**Contract: 4♥**          **Opening lead: ♦A**

# Giving Little Away?

What would you lead against a Four Spade contract with the West hand?

Defensive prospects seem hopeful. North-South's auction to Four Spades was hardly confident and your strong holdings in hearts and clubs will surely take tricks – especially if declarer has to lead the suit to you. There is a strong case for the passive opening lead of a low diamond, letting declarer do the work, and giving little away. Little... but not nothing.

Though it appears as though declarer is staring at two heart losers and two club losers, that is without noticing the potential of the spot cards in diamonds.

South African international declarer Neville Moses did not ignore such subtleties. He won the diamond lead (to East's queen) with his king. He cashed just two rounds of trumps (leaving the third trump outstanding), cashed the ace of diamonds, then led the ten (key play). West covered with the jack, dummy trumped, and declarer noted with delight the fall of East's nine.

Declarer crossed back to hand with a third trump and triumphantly cashed the promoted seven of diamonds discarding a heart from dummy. He drove out the ace-king of clubs to establish his third round club winner. Ten tricks made.

West was left to rue that his choice of a diamond was the only opening lead that enabled declarer to succeed (provided he guessed to lead the ten of diamonds on the third round to pin East's nine).

One final point – note the importance of declarer not drawing the third trump immediately. Had he done so, he would have had to cross back to hand with a fourth trump in order to cash the promoted seven of diamonds. He would have only held one

trump remaining in dummy and so been a tempo behind to establish the third round of clubs.

**Dealer: South**  **Vulnerability: East-West**

|  | Teams |  | ♠ J 10 6 4 3 2 |
|---|---|---|---|
|  |  |  | ♥ J 6 |
|  |  |  | ♦ 8 2 |
|  |  |  | ♣ Q 10 4 |

| ♠ – |  | ♠ 9 7 5 |
|---|---|---|
| ♥ A Q 9 7 3 | N | ♥ K 8 5 2 |
| ♦ J 6 5 4 | W E | ♦ Q 9 3 |
| ♣ K 9 7 6 | S | ♣ A 3 2 |

|  | ♠ A K Q 8 |
|---|---|
|  | ♥ 10 4 |
|  | ♦ A K 10 7 |
|  | ♣ J 8 5 |

| S | W | N | E |
|---|---|---|---|
| 1♠ | PASS | 2♠ | PASS |
| 3♠ | PASS | 4♠ | END |

**Contract: 4♠**  **Opening lead: ♦4**

# Two Small

A Dummy Reversal is a declarer-play technique which involves making dummy into the master hand. Though not normally advantageous for declarer to trump in his own hand (assumed to be the one with longer trumps), if he trumps enough times in his hand to make dummy into the long trump hand, the process can gain trick(s).

This deal was declared over fifty years ago by the Swedish wizard Jan Wohlin, but it has lost none of its appeal. West led the ace of diamonds against Four Hearts, and declarer ruffed. Now look away (really) and answer the following question: what, precisely, are dummy's trumps?

Did you simply answer 'two small'? Or did you specify 'the eight and the seven'? The relevance of those trumps will shortly be seen – in one of the most amazing Dummy Reversals I have ever seen.

Declarer ruffed the diamond, and proceeded to use dummy's four black suit entries to ruff all the four remaining diamonds. At Trick Two he crossed to the king of spades, and ruffed a second diamond; he then crossed to the ace of spades, ruffed a third diamond, over to the king of clubs, ruffed a fourth diamond and finally back to the king of clubs and ruffed his last diamond.

Declarer scored the first nine tricks and now dummy's trumps came into their own. The eight-seven were equals against the outstanding nine and had to make one more trick. Five trumps in hand and one in dummy meant that declarer had conjured up a sixth trump trick. Game made.

It was a brilliantly conceived plan: so simple yet effective – only a bad black suit split would beat declarer. However any other opening lead and he would be one entry short to pull off his Dummy Reversal. For

there was no point in ruffing four diamonds in hand – it was the fifth and final ruff that generated the extra trick.

---

**Dealer: North**       **Vulnerability: Neither**

**Teams**

|  | ♠ A K 3 |  |
|---|---|---|
|  | ♥ 8 7 |  |
|  | ♦ 7 6 5 4 2 |  |
|  | ♣ A K 8 |  |

| ♠ J 9 7 4 |  | ♠ Q 10 |
|---|---|---|
| ♥ 6 3 | **N** | ♥ 9 5 4 2 |
| ♦ A K J | **W    E** | ♦ Q 10 9 8 3 |
| ♣ Q 10 6 2 | **S** | ♣ J 9 |

|  | ♠ 8 6 5 2 |  |
|---|---|---|
|  | ♥ A K Q J 10 |  |
|  | ♦ – |  |
|  | ♣ 7 5 4 3 |  |

| S | W | N | E |
|---|---|---|---|
|  |  | 1 ♦ (1) | PASS |
| 1 ♥ | PASS | 1 NT (1) | PASS |
| 4 ♥ (2) | END |  |  |

(1) Playing a Strong Notrump, North opens a suit and rebids One Notrump to show 12-14 points.

(2) A trifle optimistic – only a five-card suit (albeit one that looks like six), and no high-cards outside. But opening bids were much sounder in those days, so he could rely on more opposite.

**Contract: 4♥**       **Opening lead: ♦A**

# The Other Trump

Dealer: South     Vulnerability: East-West

There are those who would have passed Three Spades with North's hand, arguing that they held a minimum for their bidding to date. This North hoped that his ace of trumps would be worth more than one trick. I doubt he attached much value to the size of his other trump.

To make Four Spades, declarer had to negotiate trumps and hearts without loss, as he had three certain minor suit losers. Do you think he can succeed against best defence?

West led the jack of clubs, which held the trick, and continued with a club to East's king. Declarer trumped East's ace of clubs continuation with his two of trumps. He led the jack of trumps and ran it successfully (paucity of dummy entries making it more convenient to play West for the queen). He next played a trump to the ace (both following), then led a heart to his jack, that finesse also working. He cashed the king of trumps felling West's queen, then looked around for a dummy entry to repeat the heart finesse.

There was none. Declarer led out his trumps in the hope that East would bare his king of hearts. East did not. He forlornly cashed the ace of hearts and had to concede one down when the king did not appear.

Lady Luck had been on declarer's side and he had not taken full advantage. He should have trumped the third club with the eight of trumps (not the two). He then leads the two of trumps to dummy's seven (key play). He uses the entry to finesse the jack of hearts. He returns to the ace of trumps and plays a heart to the queen. He cashes the king of trumps felling West's queen, and has six trump tricks, three hearts and a diamond. 10 tricks and game made.

So the contract can always be made? Actually, no: what if West inserts the queen

**Rubber**

|  | ♠ A 7 |  |
|  | ♥ 7 4 3 |  |
|  | ♦ 10 7 6 3 2 |  |
|  | ♣ Q 5 2 |  |

| ♠ Q 5 3 | | ♠ 6 4 |
| ♥ 9 8 6 | N | ♥ K 10 5 2 |
| ♦ K 8 5 | W   E | ♦ Q 9 4 |
| ♣ J 10 9 7 | S | ♣ A K 8 6 |

|  | ♠ K J 10 9 8 2 |  |
|  | ♥ A Q J |  |
|  | ♦ A J |  |
|  | ♣ 4 3 |  |

| S | W | N | E |
|---|---|---|---|
| 1♠ | PASS | 1 NT | PASS |
| 3♠ | PASS | 4♠ (1) | END |

(1) Optimistic.

**Contract: 4♠**     **Opening lead: ♣J**

of spades on the first round of trumps (pretty tough play – close to impossible I'd say)? Dummy's seven now ceases to be an entry to allow the heart finesse to be repeated and declarer must fail.

# Golden Card

A 'Golden Card' is a top honour in partner's suit. The presence of such a card can be a tremendous asset in the play, and its value must be anticipated in the auction.

This South looked at the king of diamonds, his partner's response, and the card grew so large in his hand that he felt compelled to jump straight to game in his self-supporting spade suit. Encouraged by his partner's leap, North bid on to slam.

West led the king of clubs against Six Spades and declarer surveyed the dummy. How right he had been to upgrade his hand in the light of holding that golden king of diamonds! On normal splits (diamonds three-two and trumps no worse than four-two) he would make twelve tricks via six trumps, five diamonds and the ace of clubs. Could he make the slam if the suits split less well?

Declarer won dummy's ace of clubs at Trick One, then crossed to his ace-king-queen of trumps, observing the even split and discarding two clubs from dummy. It was time to begin the diamonds. Which card should he begin with on the first round?

Say declarer led the five to dummy's queen, East following with the jack. He would then cross back to his king, East discarding, and lead the nine. But West would follow low and, after also following low from dummy, declarer would be unable to reach dummy's ace-eight. No good.

Say declarer began with the king. East would follow with the jack, but declarer would not know whether this was singleton, from jack-ten doubleton, or even from jack-ten-small. He would probably play to dummy's queen (East discarding) then be unable to cash out the suit. Also no good.

Declarer worked out that he would be able to run five diamond tricks when East held a singleton honour (in addition to all the three-

**Pairs**

|  | North |
|---|---|
| ♠ | 3 |
| ♥ | Q 8 4 3 |
| ♦ | A Q 8 4 3 |
| ♣ | A 7 4 |

West
♠ 10 8 2
♥ K J 6
♦ J 7 6 2
♣ K Q J

East
♠ 9 7 5
♥ A 10 9 5 2
♦ 10
♣ 10 9 5 2

South
♠ A K Q J 6 4
♥ 7
♦ K 9 5
♣ 8 6 3

| S | W | N | E |
|---|---|---|---|
| 1♠ | PASS | 2♦ | PASS |
| 4♠ (1) | PASS | 4NT (2) | PASS |
| 5♠ (3) | PASS | 6♠ | END |

(1) Excited by that golden king in partner's suit.
(2) Roman Key Card Blackwood.
(3) Two of 'five aces' (including the king of trumps), plus the queen of trumps.

**Contract: 6♠**          **Opening lead: ♣K**

two splits) only if he led the nine of diamonds to dummy's queen on the first round of the suit (key play). East did follow with the jack, so declarer led the three back to his king (East discarding), then took the marked finesse against West's jack, leading to dummy's eight on the third round. He cashed dummy's ace (felling West's jack), then cashed the fifth diamond. Slam made.

# Once in a Lifetime

South, Dutch former World Champion Berry Westra will have been delighted that he made a highly dubious weak jump overcall of Three Clubs: not because his result on the deal – two down in Five Clubs doubled sacrificing against an iffy Four Hearts (which indeed failed in the other room) – was a good one; rather because he had the opportunity to pull off a once-in-a-lifetime coup in the play.

Declarer received the jack of hearts lead. East won the ace and switched neutrally to his singleton trump. Declarer rose with the ace and led a spade, ducking West's jack. West cashed his master trump (not best) and then had to switch to a diamond – or declarer could set up a long spade to discard his diamond loser. He duly switched to the nine of diamonds.

Declarer covered with dummy's ten, and beat East's jack with the ace. He next led back the seven of diamonds, covered by West's eight (correctly, or the seven would have been run), dummy's queen, and East's king. East then switched to his queen of spades, taken by dummy's ace.

The current diamond position was this:

```
                 Dummy
                 ♦5 3
        West             East
        ♦4               ♦6 2
                 Declarer
                 ♦ -
```

Reading the precise layout, declarer led dummy's five (key play). East had to cover with the six (or the five would be run, declarer throwing his losing spade), but can you see what is about to happen?

Declarer ruffed East's six, noting with pleasure the fall of West's four. He crossed to dummy in trumps (if West had not cashed his

**Teams**

|   |   |   |
|---|---|---|
| | ♠ A 10 8 6 3 | |
| | ♥ K | |
| | ♦ Q 10 5 3 | |
| | ♣ J 10 5 | |

| ♠ K J 2 | | ♠ Q 4 |
|---|---|---|
| ♥ J 10 8 6 3 | | ♥ A Q 9 7 4 2 |
| ♦ 9 8 4 | W E | ♦ K J 6 2 |
| ♣ K Q | | ♣ 8 |

|   |
|---|
| ♠ 9 7 5 |
| ♥ 5 |
| ♦ A 7 |
| ♣ A 9 7 6 4 3 2 |

| S | W | N | E |
|---|---|---|---|
| | | | 1♥ |
| 3♣ (1) | 4♥ | 5♣ | PASS (2) |
| PASS | DOUBLE (3) | END | |

(1) Not my cup of tea. Ace-empty holdings are better suited to defence. If partner holds a singleton club, then ace-of-clubs-club ruff (with the ace of diamonds to come) will get the defence off to a good start, whilst declaring a club contract will see the defence make at least two trump tricks.
(2) Does well not to bid Five Hearts – with his powerful playing hand.
(3) Clear – with a sure trump trick.

**Contract: 5♣ doubled     Opening lead: ♥J**

master trump earlier, declarer would have had no quick route back to dummy) and triumphantly cashed the promoted three of diamonds, East helplessly following with the two. Away went the long spade, and the doubled game was 'only' down two.

# Deep Finesse

Bidding and play are such different disciplines in Bridge. And yet they are so inextricably connected.

Take this fabulous deal from a Hubert Phillips match (the British knock-out event for mixed teams). The contract was Seven Spades (doubled). East-West had bid to the easy-to-make Seven Hearts using the Grand Slam Force, and, believing their bidding, North-South had very sensibly taken the 'sacrifice'.

West led a low heart – morally certain that his partner held the queen of the suit and wishing to put him on lead to cash diamonds. It was a clever move but one destined not to work (although nor would anything else). Declarer, Kent's Phil Bailey, in partnership with London's Richard Fleet, had a void and ruffed. It was now time for him to make some deductions from the bidding.

*Question*: How could East be inviting a grand slam should partner have two of the top three trump honours, given that he was missing the aces of both black suits?

*Answer*: Unless he was making a huge bluff, East had to hold a void in both spades and clubs.

Declarer now knew his way ahead. He crossed to dummy's king of trumps (East duly discarding), returned to his ace-queen (discarding a diamond), then led a club, West playing low. Normally one would not even consider taking such a deep finesse as the seven. But knowing that East was void, declarer did precisely that (key play).

The seven won the trick (East discarding), so declarer next ruffed a heart, finessed dummy's nine of clubs, ruffed the last heart, and finessed the jack of clubs. He was able to shed his two losing diamonds on dummy's ace-king of clubs and the sacrifice actually turned out to be a make. Doubled grand slam made – incredible.

**Teams**

|              | ♠ K 4        |              |
|              | ♥ 8 7 3      |              |
|              | ♦ 9 5 2      |              |
|              | ♣ A K J 9 7  |              |

| ♠ J 10 3        |       N       | ♠ –              |
| ♥ A K J 6 4     |   W       E   | ♥ Q 10 9 5 2     |
| ♦ –             |       S       | ♦ A K Q 8 7 6    |
| ♣ Q 10 8 4 3    |               | 4 3              |
|                 |               | ♣ –              |

|              | ♠ A Q 9 8 7 6 5 2 |
|              | ♥ –               |
|              | ♦ J 10            |
|              | ♣ 6 5 2           |

| S      | W      | N      | E        |
|--------|--------|--------|----------|
|        | 1♥     | 2♣     | 5NT (1)  |
| 6♠     | 7♥     | 7♠     | DOUBLE   |
| END    |        |        |          |

(1) A bid of 5NT when not preceded by 4NT is the Grand Slam Force (or 'Josephine' after Ely Culbertson's wife). It asks partner to bid Seven with two of the top three trump honours (trumps presumed to be the last bid suit), otherwise to bid Six.

**Contract: 7♠ doubled     Opening lead: ♥4**

# CHAPTER 10

# Bluff and Deception

First and foremost, Bridge is a partnership game, a cooperative game of truth-telling. That is why the chapter headed 'Partnership' came first. Those players who believe that the way to win at Bridge is through continual bluffs have left Bridge for a game more tailored to their approach: Poker.

However when your partner is out of the equation, and that will primarily be when you are declarer, you have the opportunity to induce your opponents down a false trail. These will range from outrageous bluffs, such as 'developing a suit' of two small cards facing three small cards in notrumps, in the hope that the opponents will not realise their combined assets are so strong, to routine signal-scrambling manoeuvres. Take this suit:

Dummy

♠9 4 2

West          East

♠A K J 6          ♠10 8 5

Declarer (you)

♠Q 7 3

West leads the ace, and East follows with the five. If you follow with the three, West knows that his partner's signal is a discouraging 'throw low means no'. Instead play the seven, suggesting to West that his partner's spades may be Q53, and that he is encouraging.

Showing weakness when you have strength, showing strength when you have weakness, and much, much more to make your jaw drop: there are some truly wonderful, creative deceptions in this chapter.

# Feigning a Stopper

'When you have shown a stopper in the bidding, you do not need one in the play'.

These pithy words of wisdom – originating from that prolific Scottish Bridge writer Hugh Kelsey – were rarely more appropriate than on our first deal of the chapter, from the Open European Championships.

South's Two Notrump bid feigned a heart stopper (the opponents' bid-and-supported suit) and West believed him, kicking off with a spade lead against the Three Notrump contract. An opening heart lead would have seen the defence score the first six tricks – five hearts and the ace of spades. It was rather different on a spade lead.

Declarer won the spade with his king and crossed to the king of clubs. The fall of the jack from East suggested that the queen was with West (using the Principle of Restricted Choice – which states that when an opponent has turned up with a critical card in a suit, his partner is almost twice as likely to have the adjacent card in that suit).

Declarer next cashed dummy's queen of diamonds and crossed to his ace-king of the suit. When West discarded on the second round, it was clear to play him for both missing clubs (and thus having started with nine major-suit cards). East holding queen-jack doubleton club and West two small cards would leave West with ten major-suit cards. He would surely have done more bidding with such a shapely hand.

Declarer led his second club and, when West followed low, confidently finessed dummy's ten. East did indeed discard, so declarer cashed dummy's ace, felling West's queen, and ran the four remaining clubs. He emerged with eleven tricks – a spade, three diamonds and seven clubs. Game made.

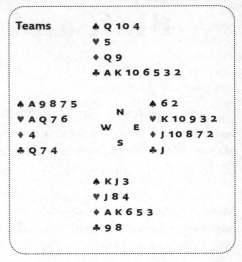

**Teams**

|  | North |
|---|---|
| ♠ | Q 10 4 |
| ♥ | 5 |
| ♦ | Q 9 |
| ♣ | A K 10 6 5 3 2 |

West:
♠ A 9 8 7 5
♥ A Q 7 6
♦ 4
♣ Q 7 4

East:
♠ 6 2
♥ K 10 9 3 2
♦ J 10 8 7 2
♣ J

South:
♠ K J 3
♥ J 8 4
♦ A K 6 5 3
♣ 9 8

| S | W | N | E |
|---|---|---|---|
|  |  | 1♣ | PASS |
| 1♦ | DOUBLE (1) | 2♣ | 2♥ (2) |
| 2NT (3) | PASS | 3NT (4) | END |

(1) Take-out – for the majors.
(2) Rather timid. Despite the low point-count, East has a very shapely hand and a known nine-card heart fit. 3♥ (even 4♥) is indicated.
(3) See Hugh Kelsey's aphorism.
(4) Hoping the clubs will run.

**Contract: 3NT**       **Opening lead: ♠7**

# Red Faces

Bare-faced robbery was the name of the game on this deal. It goes a long way to demonstrate why most people these days consider Josephine Culbertson (the declarer and perpetrator of the crime) to be a better player than her famous husband Ely, the great marketeer of Bridge in the 1920s and 1930s.

West led the three of spades against the near-hopeless Three Notrumps. The technical line is to duck two spades and win the third; then to follow by running dummy clubs and playing to bring East under pressure should he hold both red aces. All rather unlikely and Josephine preferred a swindle. But what a swindle she found...

Declarer immediately took East's queen of spades with the ace, looking like someone with plenty of further strength in the suit. At Trick Two she laid down the ace of clubs (key play). She had no intention of following with the jack, but wanted to create the impression that she had a singleton ace – rebidding notrumps did not strictly guarantee a balanced hand in those days, so the defenders might just fall for the ploy.

At Trick Three declarer found the bold and imaginative shot of leading the king of diamonds. She hoped that the ace and queen were in separate hands and that the player with the ace would be loath to take the trick, for fear of creating a dummy entry with dummy's jack. It worked – West ducked his ace.

At Trick Four declarer led her other red king. For the same reason as his partner had ducked the king of diamonds, East ducked the king of hearts. He was not going to let declarer reach dummy via the queen of hearts.

The defenders faces were about to turn red. For at Trick Five declarer led the jack of

**Rubber**

|  | ♠ 10 9 |
| | ♥ Q 3 2 |
| | ♦ J 7 |
| | ♣ K Q 10 4 3 2 |

| ♠ J 5 4 3 2 | | ♠ K Q 8 |
| ♥ J 8 5 | N | ♥ A 10 6 4 |
| ♦ A 6 5 | W E | ♦ Q 10 8 |
| ♣ 9 8 | S | ♣ 7 6 5 |

|  | ♠ A 7 6 |
| | ♥ K 9 7 |
| | ♦ K 9 4 3 2 |
| | ♣ A J |

| S (JOSEPHINE) | W | N | E |
|---|---|---|---|
| 1♦ | PASS | 2♣ | PASS |
| 2NT | PASS | 3♣ | PASS |
| 3NT (1) | END | | |

(1) Only a tad optimistic, partner having shown about eight or nine points with six clubs.

**Contract: 3NT**          **Opening lead: ♠3**

clubs. She overtook with dummy's queen, rattled off dummy's remaining winners in the suit, and was soon writing down 100 points below the line under 'We'.

Have you ever seen such brazen piracy?

# Trade Secrets

In case you ever find yourself playing against jigsaw maker and Bridge professional, Yorkshireman Simon Stocken, let me divulge two of his 'specials'.

When declaring a notrump contract, he loves to play on his danger suit – to lay a false trail. Give Simon three small cards in dummy facing jack doubleton in hand and he will cross to dummy to lead confidently to his jack. It often puts the opponents off leading the suit for themselves at a later stage, preferring to attack the suits in which he is relatively loaded. Occasionally the jack even wins the trick when a defender chooses the wrong moment to make a 'clever' duck.

Simon's second special occurs when defending a contract in which dummy has shown a long, strong suit. Give Simon a doubleton king of that suit and he loves to lead the low card at trick one.

Take this deal – from the US Nationals. On lead to Four Spades with dummy having advertised long, strong diamonds, Simon tried the effect of the two of diamonds lead! Now put yourself in declarer's shoes. Why has West not led his partner's suit? He must have a good reason – and that can only mean that his diamond is singleton.

So reasoning declarer rose with dummy's ace of diamonds. His next shot was a trump to his queen. Simon won the king, cashed the king of diamonds (declarer fuming), and switched to a heart. East beat dummy's king with the ace and, judging correctly that declarer held no more hearts, led his third diamond. Whether or not declarer ruffed high, West's nine of trumps was promoted into a trick – the fourth defensive trick. Declarer actually ruffed with the seven so West overruffed with his nine. Down one – in a contract that would have made an

overtrick (losing just a heart and a trump) on a more normal defence.

Apologies, Simon, for giving away your trade secrets, but I cannot resist sharing them: for the simple reason that they're very, very good!

| | | | |
|---|---|---|---|
| **Dealer: North** | | **Vulnerability: Both** | |

**Pairs**

|  | ♠ 8 |
|---|---|
| | ♥ K 5 3 |
| | ♦ A Q 8 7 5 4 |
| | ♣ A K 7 |

| ♠ K 9 6 | | ♠ J 4 |
|---|---|---|
| ♥ 9 7 4 2 | N | ♥ A Q 10 8 6 |
| ♦ K 2 | W E | ♦ J 9 6 |
| ♣ Q 8 3 2 | S | ♣ 9 5 4 |

|  | ♠ A Q 10 7 5 3 2 |
|---|---|
| | ♥ J |
| | ♦ 10 3 |
| | ♣ J 10 6 |

| S | W | N | E |
|---|---|---|---|
| | | 1♦ | 1♥ |
| 1♠ | 2♥ | 3♦ | PASS |
| 4♠ | END | | |

**Contract: 4♠**    **Opening lead: ♦2 (!)**

# Jazz Club

Have you had the experience of bumping into someone in a most unexpected place and finding that your friendship increases immeasurably as a result?

Though we had not seen each other much since our junior Bridge days, Parisian Jean-Christophe Quantin and I chanced upon one another a couple of years ago through the smoke of Chelsea's 606 Jazz Club. Since that unlikely encounter, we now welcome each other like bosom buddies (although our conversations are never very long, as his English is nearly as poor as my French).

Jean-Christophe, sitting East, outwitted declarer on this deal – from Juan Les Pins. West led the queen of clubs against the Six Spade slam and declarer won dummy's ace. Needing to set up diamonds using dummy's trumps, declarer correctly broached the suit immediately. At Trick Two he crossed to his king of diamonds, and followed by cashing the ace.

At every other table in the large field, both defenders played low on the top diamonds. Declarer led a third diamond and ruffed with dummy's four. There was no point in ruffing with the ace because to do so would only gain when East had a doubleton diamond, in which case another diamond would have to be ruffed.

When East followed to the third diamond with the queen, rendering the suit established, declarer could cash the ace of trumps, cross to his king-queen-jack (drawing trumps), cash his diamonds, and flush out the ace of hearts. Slam made.

But Jean-Christophe as East deviously dropped the queen of diamonds under the second top diamond (key play). Naturally believing that East held no more diamonds, declarer then ruffed a low diamond with the ace of trumps (wouldn't you?). When he led

to his king-queen-jack of trumps and West discarded on the second round, he found that he could not make his slam anymore, with the promoted ten of trumps and ace of hearts to lose. Down one.

**Dealer: South   Vulnerability: North-South**

| Pairs | ♠ A 4 2 |
|       | ♥ 9 7 2 |
|       | ♦ 4 3 |
|       | ♣ A 10 4 3 2 |

| ♠ 7 | | ♠ 10 8 5 3 |
| ♥ A 10 8 3 | N | ♥ J 6 5 4 |
| ♦ 9 8 5 | W   E | ♦ Q 10 7 |
| ♣ Q J 9 7 6 | S | ♣ K 8 |

| | ♠ K Q J 9 6 |
| | ♥ K Q |
| | ♦ A K J 6 2 |
| | ♣ 5 |

| S | W | N | E |
|------|------|------|------|
| 1♠ | PASS | 2♠ | PASS |
| 3♦ | PASS | 4♠ | PASS |
| 4NT (1) | PASS | 5♥ (2) | PASS |
| 6♠ | END | | |

(1) An optimistic Roman Key Card Blackwood.
(2) Two 'aces' (including ♠K), but no ♠Q.

**Contract: 6♠**          **Opening lead: ♣Q**

# The Modest Forrester

Dealer: North　　　Vulnerability: Both

Though the scene was a Las Vegas casino after an evening Bridge session, none of us felt like gambling. We retired to the peace of a suite to discuss the hands. Several had been dissected to pieces before one of the assembled, Tony Forrester, said 'Oh, Board Eleven was fun'.

This was a huge understatement. Board Eleven was not merely fun. It saw an outstanding piece of deception from the modest Forrester. Most people would not have managed to last a minute after the session before divulging the details. Tony had lasted fully one hour before sharing his brilliance.

West, James Mates, led the five of spades and East, Tony, played his ace on dummy's nine, and watched it get trumped. Declarer naturally sought to establish his clubs whilst dummy still held trumps. At Trick Two he cashed the ace of clubs, and at Trick Three he continued with the king of clubs.

Had East followed with his two low clubs, declarer's natural line would be to ruff a third club with dummy's queen of trumps, bringing down East's queen. He would follow by cashing the ace of trumps, East's king fortuitously dropping, and now it would be a simple matter to trump a spade, cash the jack-ten of trumps and, leaving West's master trump outstanding, play established clubs. Slam made.

But Tony did not follow with two low clubs on declarer's top honours. On the second round of the suit he dropped the queen (key play)! This created an entirely different scenario for declarer. With no need to ruff the third club in dummy, declarer was able to take the trump finesse at Trick Four. Disaster!

East took the queen of trumps with his singleton king, and led a second spade. Declarer ruffed and crossed to the ace of

**Pairs**

|  |  |  |  |
|---|---|---|---|
| | ♠ Q J 10 9 | | |
| | ♥ A Q J 7 4 | | |
| | ♦ A Q | | |
| | ♣ 10 3 | | |

| ♠ K 7 6 5 2 | | ♠ A 8 4 3 |
|---|---|---|
| ♥ 8 6 | N | ♥ K 10 9 5 2 |
| ♦ 9 8 3 2 | W　　E | ♦ K |
| ♣ 9 2 | S | ♣ Q 8 4 |

|  |  |  |  |
|---|---|---|---|
| | ♠ – | | |
| | ♥ 3 | | |
| | ♦ J 10 7 6 5 4 | | |
| | ♣ A K J 7 6 5 | | |

| S | W | N | E |
|---|---|---|---|
| | | 1♥ | PASS |
| 2♦ | PASS | 2♠ | PASS |
| 3♣ | PASS | 3♦ | PASS |
| 6♦ (1) | END | | |

(1) Six-six shapes are hard to bid scientifically.

**Contract: 6♦**　　　　**Opening lead: ♠5**

trumps, but East discarded. With trump control now lost, declarer ruffed a third spade with the ten of trumps, cashed the jack, then led a winning club. West ruffed, cashed the king-seven of spades, then switched to a heart to East's king. When the dust had settled, declarer was four down in his slam!

What a difference dropping the queen of clubs had made. Humble to the end, all Tony did was praise his partner for the opening spade lead, without which the slam would always succeed.

# Manchester United

Football-mad regular of the England team along with his twin brother Jason, Justin Hackett made a fabulous psychological play as declarer on this deal from a match against Japan.

West led a trump and declarer tried dummy's ten. One can only speculate that if it had won the trick, declarer would have been tempted to use this first and last time he would be in dummy to play a club to the jack. This would have led to an easy down one. But East covered dummy's ten with the jack and declarer won in hand and drew a second round of trumps.

Lacking any other attractive alternative, and seeking more information, declarer wisely played out four more trumps. West threw all his four hearts and East threw two clubs and two hearts. What do you think the club layout is likely to be in the light of West clinging on to all his clubs and East discarding two of them painlessly?

Because it was looking very much as though West held the guarded queen of clubs, declarer realised that he had no legitimate play for his game. Instead he found a brilliant creative psychological shot. He advanced the jack of clubs (key play).

West studied this card for some time – and perhaps he should not have fallen for the ruse. But he eventually played low, and declarer's gambit had won the day. He could now cash the ace-king of clubs and merely concede three red-suit tricks at the end. Ten tricks and game made.

**Dealer: North**   **Vulnerability: Neither**

```
Teams          ♠ 10 4
               ♥ 10 9 6
               ♦ K 8 6 5
               ♣ 10 9 3 2

♠ 8 3              N          ♠ J 6
♥ Q 5 3 2      W     E        ♥ A K J 7 4
♦ J 7 4 2          S          ♦ A Q 10
♣ Q 8 7                       ♣ 6 5 4

               ♠ A K Q 9 7 5 2
               ♥ 8
               ♦ 9 3
               ♣ A K J
```

| S | W | N | E |
|---|---|---|---|
|   |   | PASS | 1♥ |
| DOUBLE | 3♥ (1) | PASS | PASS |
| 4♠ | END |   |   |

(1) Preemptive.

**Contract: 4♠**          **Opening lead: ♠3**

# Ramadan

There is a subtlety about the deception in declarer's play of this slam deal that is most ingenious: and all the more impressive given that it was an afternoon match during the Bridge Olympics and declarer, Egyptian Walid el Ahmady, was observing Ramadan.

Through rose-tinted spectacles, South drove to slam on a hand that seems barely worth it. Dummy had a perfectly normal hand for his bidding yet the slam seems completely hopeless with two diamonds to lose.

Declarer won West's king of hearts lead with the ace, cashed the ace of trumps, then led the jack of trumps to dummy's king (perhaps creating a false impression to East that his partner held the queen of trumps). Now came the real brilliancy.

At Trick Four declarer led dummy's two of diamonds. By not leading the queen, jack, ten or nine, declarer was taking the risk of losing three diamond tricks – to the eight as well as to the ace-king. But it was a risk well worth taking, for East reasoned that declarer had to hold the king of the suit, or he would have led a high diamond from dummy as opposed to the two. Can you see what was about to happen?

East grabbed his ace of diamonds, perhaps expecting West to have the queen of trumps to defeat the slam, but in any event certain that declarer held the king of diamonds, possibly singleton. He was soon a sadder and wiser man. West's singleton king fell under East's ace and suddenly the slam was on.

East continued with a second diamond, but, with diamonds good and trumps drawn, the slam was home.

I bet Walid enjoyed his meal that night.

**Dealer: North**  **Vulnerability: Neither**

**Teams**

|  | ♠ K 5 3 |
|  | ♥ 8 |
|  | ♦ Q J 10 9 7 2 |
|  | ♣ A Q 9 |

| ♠ 9 8 | | ♠ 6 |
| ♥ K Q 5 4 3 2 | **N** | ♥ J 9 7 6 |
| ♦ K | **W E** | ♦ A 8 4 |
| ♣ 10 7 6 4 | **S** | ♣ K J 5 3 2 |

|  | ♠ A Q J 10 7 4 2 |
|  | ♥ A 10 |
|  | ♦ 6 5 3 |
|  | ♣ 8 |

| S | W | N | E |
|---|---|---|---|
|  |  | 1♦ | PASS |
| 1♠ | 2♥ | 2♠ | 4♣ (1) |
| 4NT (2) | PASS | 5♥ (3) | PASS |
| 6♠ (4) | END | | |

(1) Fit-showing jump, promising heart support and a club suit on the side.
(2) Roman Key Card Blackwood – an optimistic assessment of his six-loser hand with three small cards in partner's suit.
(3) Two of the 'five aces' (including the king of trumps), but not the queen of trumps.
(4) Being consistent with his decision to bid Blackwood, South is right to bid slam given that just one keycard is missing.

**Contract: 6♠**          **Opening lead: ♥K**

# Val de Lobo

Every season the Duplicate Ladder in my Bridge Club reaches its climax. Who will win the delicious food hamper kindly donated by club member Luigi Molinaro?

One Autumn, Luigi decided to offer a special prize – a week at his villa in the Val de Lobo in Portugal. In the event the winner of the Autumn Ladder, Liz Taylor, was unable to take advantage of her prize. So she sweetly donated it to the owner of the Bridge Club. And so it came to pass that your author found himself playing at the Val de Lobo Bridge club, during a lovely week's stay at Luigi's villa.

The standard of the club, brilliantly run by Nahid Ghani, was unexpectedly high, as is evidenced by the most interesting hand of the evening.

West led the king of clubs against the Six Spade contract, but a sight of dummy revealed that the contract was almost completely hopeless (with a heart loser and at least one club loser). Both hands holding a singleton in the same suit is never good news. Can you see any way for declarer to emerge victorious?

There is no genuine way of winning the slam, but there is a swindle that might – indeed did at the table – succeed. Declarer smoothly ducked the king of clubs lead!

With East – unfortunately for his side – holding no club lower than the nine, West believed that his partner was encouraging the club lead and held the ace. West continued blithely with his queen of clubs. He soon saw the error of his ways.

East followed with the jack under West's queen, and declarer won the ace. He cashed the ace of trumps (both opponents following), continued with the king (felling West's queen), and then returned to clubs. He cashed three further rounds of the suit, and

**Dealer: South**     **Vulnerability: Neither**

Pairs

|  |  |
|---|---|
| ♠ | J 10 9 5 3 |
| ♥ | K |
| ♦ | J 3 |
| ♣ | 10 7 6 5 2 |

West:
- ♠ Q 8
- ♥ Q 10 8 6 4
- ♦ 10 8 6 4
- ♣ K Q

East:
- ♠ 6
- ♥ A J 9 7 3 2
- ♦ Q 9 5 2
- ♣ J 9

South:
- ♠ A K 7 4 2
- ♥ 5
- ♦ A K 7
- ♣ A 8 4 3

| S | W | N | E |
|---|---|---|---|
| 1♠ | PASS | 4♠ (1) | PASS |
| 6♠ (2) | END | | |

(1) Do you play a jump to 4♠ as preemptive, or as showing a decent hand expecting to make? North evidently played it as preemptive.

(2) Bid in the hope that his partner belonged to the other school!

**Contract: 6♠**     **Opening lead: ♣K**

was able to discard his singleton heart on dummy's fifth card in the suit. All that remained to do was to cash the ace-king of diamonds and ruff his third diamond in dummy. The slam was made.

# Conceal the Threat

Defending is rarely easy, and the earlier a defender is forced to make the crunch decision, the more likely he is to err (knowing less about the hand).

Declarer's performance on this deal was uninspired. He won the queen of clubs lead with the ace, drew the opposing trumps in three rounds, then, correctly seeing that his only chance of a tenth trick lay in a 3-3 diamond split, played ace, king and a third diamond. West won his queen but, with the discard from dummy's fourth diamond immediately threatening, it was clear to switch to spades. East won his five of spades with the ace and returned the four. West won two further spades and the contract was down one.

Declarer does better to conceal the threat of the discard on dummy's fourth diamond. After winning the ace of clubs, he leads a low diamond from his hand at Trick Two. Caught unaware, the defence are likely to win and woodenly play a second round of clubs. Now declarer can win the king, draw two rounds of trumps, cash the ace and king of diamonds, cross to dummy's third trump, then lead the thirteenth diamond and discard a spade loser.

But can you spot the best line of all? Remember – the earlier you force to the defence to make the critical decision, the more likely they are to get it wrong.

Try ducking the opening queen of clubs lead completely! West will doubtless continue with a second club (although perhaps he shouldn't, given that East will have signalled with a discouraging two).

Win the second club with the ace, cash the ace and king of diamonds, cross to the ten of trumps, cash the king of clubs discarding the two of diamonds, ruff a third diamond; then draw the opposing trumps finishing in

**Dealer: South**     **Vulnerability: Neither**

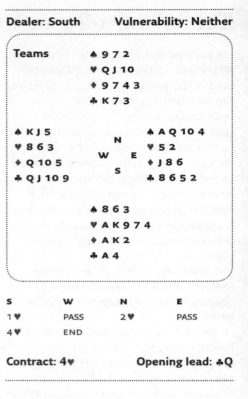

**Teams**

|  | ♠ 9 7 2 |  |
|  | ♥ Q J 10 |  |
|  | ♦ 9 7 4 3 |  |
|  | ♣ K 7 3 |  |

| ♠ K J 5 | | ♠ A Q 10 4 |
| ♥ 8 6 3 | N | ♥ 5 2 |
| ♦ Q 10 5 | W   E | ♦ J 8 6 |
| ♣ Q J 10 9 | S | ♣ 8 6 5 2 |

|  | ♠ 8 6 3 |  |
|  | ♥ A K 9 7 4 |  |
|  | ♦ A K 2 |  |
|  | ♣ A 4 |  |

| S | W | N | E |
|---|---|---|---|
| 1♥ | PASS | 2♥ | PASS |
| 4♥ | END | | |

**Contract: 4♥**          **Opening lead: ♣Q**

dummy on the third round; finally lead dummy's established diamond and discard a spade loser. Ten tricks and game made.

# Preferring a Swindle

As I stressed in the introduction to this chapter, Bridge is not primarily a game of bluff, rather one of communication. Partners do not usually appreciate being deceived – either in the bidding or in the defence. Having said that – it's different when they are dummy...

West leads the three of clubs – the unbid suit – to Three Notrumps and dummy reveals a mediocre mesh. East plays the jack and it is over to declarer. Put yourself in his shoes, and plan your campaign.

With the club lead having taken out the only entry to his hand, declarer's genuine chance is to hope that one opponent holds a doubleton queen of hearts, and that West holds the ace of diamonds. If that layout exists, declarer can succeed by taking the three top clubs, leading to the ace-king of hearts and, assuming the queen drops, crossing to the jack-ten of hearts, then leading towards dummy's king of diamonds. All rather unlikely.

At the table declarer preferred a swindle. He smoothly ducked East's jack of clubs at Trick One (key play)! And, furthermore, he played the four from his hand to make it look as though West had led fourth highest from five cards including the two.

East continued unsuspectingly with the nine of clubs, and declarer (trying not to smirk) won the queen, then cashed the ace-king and master two. He next led the jack of hearts and West did the best he could by refusing to cover with the queen (had he covered declarer would have had the communications to score four heart tricks).

Left in hand with the jack of hearts, declarer then led a diamond. West played low, declarer tried dummy's king, and when it held the trick, he quickly cashed the ace-king of hearts and the ace of spades. Nine tricks and game made.

**Dealer: North**  **Vulnerability: Both**

**Pairs**

|  | ♠ A 7 6 4 |  |
|  | ♥ A K 8 |  |
|  | ♦ K 8 7 4 2 |  |
|  | ♣ 6 |  |

|  |  |  |
| ♠ K 9 | N | ♠ Q J 8 5 2 |
| ♥ Q 7 2 | W    E | ♥ 6 5 3 |
| ♦ A K 6 5 | S | ♦ Q 10 |
| ♣ 10 8 5 3 |  | ♣ J 9 7 |

|  | ♠ 10 3 |  |
|  | ♥ J 10 9 4 |  |
|  | ♦ 9 3 |  |
|  | ♣ A K Q 4 2 |  |

| S | W | N | E |
| --- | --- | --- | --- |
|  |  | 1 ♦ | PASS |
| 1 ♥ (1) | PASS | 1 ♠ | PASS |
| 2 NT | PASS | 3 ♥ | PASS |
| 3 NT | END |  |  |

(1) Normal to respond Two Clubs, but declarer later uses his absence of a club bid to full advantage...

**Contract: 3NT**      **Opening lead:** ♣3

# Never say Never

*'Don't use no double negatives.'*
One of William Safire's top fifteen Never say Neverisms c.1970

Rarely are words such as 'never' or 'always' applicable at the Bridge table. Although 'rules' can be helpful to the learning player, Bridge is not painting by numbers.

'Second hand low', 'third hand high', 'cover an honour with an honour': these ditties can undoubtedly help you in the heat of battle. However it is important to stress that they are general guidelines, not hard-and-fast rules. And as mere guidelines, they should all, on occasion, be broken.

This chapter considers those situations where motto-adhering autopilot plays are not best, and why.

To give you a taster, take this suit layout, with dummy entry-less:

```
                 Dummy
               ♣A J 10 9 3
   West (you)              East
     ♣Q 6 2                ♣K 8 4
               Declarer
               ♣7 5
```

Declarer leads a club from hand, and of course you as second hand play low... I hope not. If you play low, then East will have to duck dummy's nine to prevent the whole suit from running. However you can prevent declarer from scoring even a second trick in this suit by inserting your queen.

# Reflex Covering

'Cover an honour with an honour' is certainly a useful maxim for defenders. But it is important to understand the reason for doing so: by drawing two opposing honours for one of yours, you promote lower cards for your side.

Our opening deal of the chapter illustrates the danger of covering an honour with an honour as a reflex. Defending Six Spades, West led a club. Winning dummy's ace, declarer tried dummy's jack of trumps at Trick Two, covered by East's queen and taken by declarer's ace. Trumps were drawn and then the queen of hearts was led. West covered with the king, so declarer won dummy's ace, cashed the promoted jack, discarding a club, and claimed the remainder in top tricks. Thirteen tricks and slam made (plus one).

At Table Two – same contract on the same club lead – declarer won dummy's ace and led the jack of trumps (again – tempting a cover). This time East played low (smoothly) so declarer played the odds missing four cards including the queen, rising with the king then cashing the ace. With West discarding (a club) to expose a trump loser, declarer needed to avoid a club loser.

One possibility for declarer was to take the heart finesse (running the queen), discarding his club on dummy's second-round heart winner. But when he led the queen of hearts and West played low, he saw a superior plan. He rose with the ace and started cashing diamonds.

If East followed to three diamonds, declarer could have thrown both dummy's clubs on the third and fourth rounds. He would not mind East ruffing the fourth diamond – dummy's clubs having gone – as he could then ruff his club in dummy.

**Dealer: South**　　　　**Vulnerability: Both**

**Teams**

|  | ♠ J 4 2 |  |
|---|---|---|
|  | ♥ A J 9 8 3 |  |
|  | ♦ J 4 |  |
|  | ♣ A J 3 |  |

| ♠ 3 | | ♠ Q 8 7 |
|---|---|---|
| ♥ K 7 5 | **N** | ♥ 10 6 4 2 |
| ♦ 10 9 7 5 3 | **W　　E** | ♦ 8 2 |
| ♣ Q 9 5 4 | **S** | ♣ K 10 7 2 |

|  | ♠ A K 10 9 6 5 |  |
|---|---|---|
|  | ♥ Q |  |
|  | ♦ A K Q 6 |  |
|  | ♣ 8 6 |  |

| S | W | N | E |
|---|---|---|---|
| 1♠ | PASS | 2♥ | PASS |
| 3♦ | PASS | 4♠ | PASS |
| 5♠ (1) | PASS | 6♣ (2) | DOUBLE (3) |
| 6♠ | END | | |

(1) When one suit is unbid, a raise to Five of the Major shows two losers in that suit (here clubs).

(2) In response, partner looks at his holding in that unbid suit: Pass = Two (+) losers; 5NT = the king; Six of the suit = the ace (as here); Six of the Trump suit = a singleton.

(3) Lead directing.

**Contract: 6♠**　　　　**Opening lead: ♣4**

However this plan failed when East ruffed the third diamond and promptly cashed the king of clubs. Down one.

# Third Hand High?

I am sure that you have heard the motto for defenders: 'Third Player plays high'.

There are certain situations where it is reasonably clear to break the motto: e.g.

```
              Dummy
               Q 5 3
   West                 East (you)
leads the two          K 10 4
```

If West leads low and dummy also plays low, it will almost certainly be best for you (East) to insert the ten (not the king). Consider two likely holdings for declarer:

(i) He has Axx. Your ten forces out the ace and dummy's queen never scores.

(ii) He has AJx. He takes the ten with the jack, scores his ace, but never scores the queen. Playing the king would see him score all three tricks in the suit.

Then there are situations where it is far from clear: e.g.

```
              Dummy
               9 8 7 5
   West                 East (you)
leads the three        J 6 2
```

Look at the heart suit on this deal from the English Trials. After West had led the three and dummy had played the seven, East did not make the reflex play of the jack – 'Third Player Plays High'. Had he done so the defence would only have made two heart tricks and the favourable club layout would in all probability have seen declarer home.

Instead East played a low heart at Trick One (key play). Declarer won his queen and ran the queen of diamonds. East won the king and led back a low heart (again withholding his jack). West took declarer's king with the ace, returned a low heart to

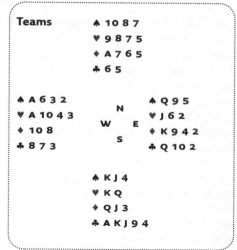

| S | W | N | E |
|---|---|---|---|
| 2NT | PASS | 3♣ (1) | PASS |
| 3♦ (2) | PASS | 3NT | END |

(1) Stayman – asking for four-card majors.
(2) None to offer.

**Contract: 3NT**          **Opening lead: ♥3**

East's jack and East fired through a spade. Declarer had to try the king – his only chance of avoiding five losers (three hearts, the king of diamonds and the ace of spades) was to hope that West had no entry to his promoted ten of hearts. West beat declarer's king with the ace, cashed the ten of hearts and returned a second spade to East's queen. Down two.

It was a thoughtful play at Trick One by East. The only layout of the heart suit that would have seen his play backfire is West leading from ♥KQxx.

# One Out of Two

In order to defeat Three Notrumps – on this deal from the World Championships – the Swedish defenders had to break both the 'Third Player plays High' and 'Second Player plays Low' maxims. One out of two did not prove good enough.

West led the five of hearts (declarer having opened One Spade), dummy played low, and East...

When dummy has only low cards it is normally correct for the third player to play high (lower of touching highest cards). But when dummy has a high card that is not played, the third player should generally keep a high card to beat that card. Extending that principle, if dummy has two relevant cards that are not played – here the king and nine – the third player should keep a high card to beat each of those cards. East must insert the eight at Trick One (Key Play No. 1) to enable the defence to score three heart tricks.

The Swedish East made no mistake. His eight was beaten by declarer's queen and a low diamond was led at Trick Two. Now it was West's turn. At the table he was understandably afraid to play his queen – fearing declarer held the king and was guessing the location of the missing queen for his contract.

East played low and now the game could not be beaten. Declarer played dummy's jack and East ducked, but a low diamond was led to the next trick to maintain the necessary communications. All the defence could take were one diamond and three hearts, declarer claiming nine tricks via ace-king of spades, one heart, four diamonds and the ace-king of clubs.

However what if West inserts his queen of diamonds at Trick Two (Key Play No. 2 – breaking the 'Second Player plays Low' guide)? Without a dummy entry outside

**Dealer: South**     **Vulnerability: Both**

**Teams**

|  |  |
|---|---|
| ♠ 7 5 |  |
| ♥ K 9 3 |  |
| ♦ A J 10 8 2 |  |
| ♣ J 10 6 |  |

| ♠ J 10 3 2 | | ♠ Q 8 |
| ♥ 10 7 6 5 | N | ♥ A J 8 4 |
| ♦ Q 7 | W    E | ♦ K 5 4 |
| ♣ Q 7 4 | S | ♣ 9 8 5 2 |

|  |  |
|---|---|
| ♠ A K 9 6 4 |  |
| ♥ Q 2 |  |
| ♦ 9 6 3 |  |
| ♣ A K 3 |  |

| S | W | N | E |
|---|---|---|---|
| 1♠ | PASS | 2♦ | PASS |
| 2NT | PASS | 3NT | END |

**Contract: 3NT**     **Opening lead: ♥5**

diamonds, declarer cannot score four diamond tricks any longer. If he ducks the queen, he scores at most three diamond tricks (and in any event loses three hearts and two diamonds first); if he wins the queen of diamonds with ace, then returns the jack, provided East ducks the king, his diamond winners are restricted to two.

# Cardinal Sin?

Maxims such as 'Don't lead from an ace', 'Third hand high' and 'Cover an honour with an honour' are reasonable guides for a defender. But, in truth, there is no substitute for thinking through each individual situation.

On this hand you are West. Can you find the best way to ensure that your side takes the four tricks necessary to defeat the opposing Four Heart game?

At the table West found the fine, attacking lead of the queen of spades, and declarer ducked in dummy. His queen winning the first trick, West continued with his second spade to East's jack. East then led the ace of spades and it was West's turn. How can he ensure that his ace of clubs does not run away?

West considered discarding the three of clubs (unfortunately his highest club spot), but in the end he discarded the discouraging two of diamonds ('throw low means No'). Now perhaps (probably) East should have switched to a club, but he actually tried a fourth spade, hoping to create a trump winner for West should he hold the jack and two small cards. It appears as though West will still get his ace of clubs – but watch what happened.

Declarer ruffed high and ran all his trumps. On the last trump West was forced to discard down to three diamonds in order for him to keep his ace of clubs. Dummy's last four cards were all diamonds. Declarer led the king of diamonds, finessed dummy's jack, cashed the ace felling West's queen, and tabled the master nine of diamonds.

West had been squeezed and suffered the ignomony of 'going to bed' with his ace. Can you see what he should have done?

West should have trumped his partner's ace of spades at Trick Three and simply

cashed the ace of clubs.

Perhaps the maxim 'Don't trump your partner's ace' deflected him?

Did you get it right? You will have to do a bit more trumping of partner's ace later in the chapter.

**Pairs**

|  | ♠ K 7 3 |  |
|---|---|---|
|  | ♥ 6 4 2 |  |
|  | ♦ A J 9 4 |  |
|  | ♣ K Q 4 |  |

| ♠ Q 4 |  | ♠ A J 10 8 2 |
|---|---|---|
| ♥ 9 8 5 | N | ♥ 7 |
| ♦ Q 10 7 5 2 | W    E | ♦ 8 6 |
| ♣ A 3 2 | S | ♣ 10 8 7 6 5 |

|  | ♠ 9 6 5 |  |
|---|---|---|
|  | ♥ A K Q J 10 3 |  |
|  | ♦ K 3 |  |
|  | ♣ J 9 |  |

| S | W | N | E |
|---|---|---|---|
| 1♥ | PASS | 2♦ | PASS |
| 2♥ | PASS | 4♥ | END |

**Contract: 4♥**          **Opening lead: ♠Q**

# Active or Passive?

Although Bridge is not a game for the lazy-minded, there are many occasions where a defender should simply do nothing. Unless there is the danger of declarer ruffing a suit in dummy (in which case the defence should lead trumps), or of discarding losers from his hand on established winners in dummy (in which case the defence must attack the other suits), a passive approach is a winning one.

A look at dummy generally reveals whether the defence can sit back and wait, or whether there is a threat that calls for immediate action. But sometimes the last chance for the defence occurs before dummy is tabled: with the opening lead.

The opening leader therefore has a dilemma. Does he attack (e.g. leading from a suit with broken honours), risking costing a trick in the suit led? Or does he do nothing (e.g. leading from only small cards or a trump) and perhaps see declarer discard his losers in a suit in which you held cashable winners?

On this deal from the Open European Championships West decided that the opponents would not bid Five-over-Five unless there was a trick source. He elected to do something meaningful with his opening lead. Indeed he played for the exact layout – partner holding the king of hearts and declarer the king of clubs. He found the only lead to defeat the game – he led a low heart.

Whilst it is normally a very risky policy to underlead an ace, West hit the jackpot this time. East won Trick One with the king of hearts and was not hard pressed (now able to view dummy with his two small clubs) to switch to a club. West's ace beat declarer's king and the queen of the suit took the setting trick. Down one.

**Dealer: West          Vulnerability: Neither**

Teams
- ♠ J 9 8 5
- ♥ 2
- ♦ K J 9 6 5 4
- ♣ 10 6

♠ 6 3
♥ A 10 7 3
♦ 10 7 3 2
♣ A Q 2

♠ 4
♥ K J 8 6 5
♦ Q 8
♣ J 9 8 7 3

♠ A K Q 10 7 2
♥ Q 9 4
♦ A
♣ K 5 4

| S | W | N | E |
|---|---|---|---|
|  | PASS | PASS | PASS |
| 1♠ | DOUBLE (1) | 3♠ | 4♥ |
| 4♠ | PASS | PASS | 5♥ (2) |
| 5♠ (3) | END |  |  |

(1) As a passed hand, East will not expect more.
(2) Marginal decision. He hopes South will...
(3) ...bid one more. Another close call. South might have heeded the motto, 'The five-level belongs to the opponents', and doubled 5♥.

**Contract: 5♠          Opening lead: ♥3**

Had West done nothing with his opening lead – say a trump – declarer would have set up dummy's diamonds and breezed home with an overtrick.

# Bold Stroke

Look at the auction and decide what to lead against Five Clubs as West.

Apart from the normal six of diamonds (partner's suit), a case could be made for the queen of diamonds (to retain the lead) or the ten of trumps (to cut down possible ruffing in dummy). But what about the jack of spades?

Even considering such a bold stroke (leading from an ace is a highly risky strategy at the best of times, but when partner has bid a different suit twice...) shows admirable insight, but actually to place the card face up on the table is, well, let English International Tony Forrester (West at the table) take over:

'I read declarer for a long, solid club suit and precious few diamonds (probably none). Dummy's heart bid implied that his suit could be established for spade discards, so it seemed imperative to attack spades as soon as possible. Admittedly my lead could backfire if partner held the queen and declarer the king, but if partner held the king (provided he played it at Trick One), or no honour (with declarer holding the king and queen), then the jack of spades lead would work well.'

Very well. Declarer won the jack of spades lead with the queen, drew trumps, then led the king of hearts. East won the ace and a second spade return from him was clear (knowing from the bidding that no diamonds were cashing). West's ace-ten of spades beat declarer's king-four and the game was down one.

Consider what would have happened on a more mundane diamond (or trump) lead. Declarer ruffs the diamond, draws trumps, then leads the king of hearts. East wins the ace and shoots through a spade, declarer's queen losing to West's ace; but declarer can win the jack of spades return with the king and discard his third spade on a long heart. Game made.

**Teams**

|  | North |  |
|---|---|---|
|  | ♠ 7 6 3 2 |  |
|  | ♥ Q 9 6 4 2 |  |
|  | ♦ J 5 2 |  |
|  | ♣ 6 |  |

| West | | East |
|---|---|---|
| ♠ A J 10 | | ♠ 9 8 5 |
| ♥ 8 7 3 | N | ♥ A 10 |
| ♦ Q 9 6 | W     E | ♦ A K 10 8 7 4 3 |
| ♣ 10 9 8 5 | S | ♣ 3 |

|  | South |  |
|---|---|---|
|  | ♠ K Q 4 |  |
|  | ♥ K J 5 |  |
|  | ♦ – |  |
|  | ♣ A K Q J 7 4 2 |  |

| S | W | N | E |
|---|---|---|---|
|  |  |  | 1♦ |
| DOUBLE (1) | 2♦ (2) | 2♥ (3) | 3♦ |
| 5♣ | END |  |  |

(1) Too strong for any immediate club bid.
(2) West would have bid 1NT without South's take-out double, but it pays to support after a double. Quick fit finding is crucial in the competitive auction.
(3) Expecting majors and short diamonds opposite, North's mediocre hand has skyrocketed.

**Contract: 5♣**          **Opening lead: ♠J**

# Distressing Suit Quality

Flexibility of mindset is crucial at the bridge table. It is no use sticking hard-and-fast to axioms such as 'Never trump your partner's ace'. There is a time for everything...

This deal comes from a home game of Rubber Bridge. And lest you are thinking, 'How does he manage to deal such freaky hands?', I have to confess that it was a goulash (cards dealt in piles of five, five and three).

West leads the ace of hearts against the redoubled Five Diamond contract. You as East see the depressingly powerful dummy tabled. But there is one possible chink in declarer's armoury. Cover up the South and West cards and see if you can find it.

At the table East took one look at dummy and gave up. There seemed no way to take more than the two major-suit aces. He discarded a club on partner's ace of hearts and West led a second heart. Declarer simply ruffed in dummy, drew the opposing trumps, and flushed out the ace of spades. Dummy's hand was quickly high and the redoubled contract claimed.

Have you spotted the winning defence? It requires West to have two features:
(a) A void spade.
(b) The six of trumps.

OK, clues over. You must ruff partner's ace of hearts lead, cash the ace of spades (hoping declarer has the one missing card in the suit) and then lead a second spade. Declarer ruffs but partner is able to score his singleton six of trumps via an overruff. Down one.

Rubber
(Goulash)

|  | North |
|---|---|
| ♠ | K Q J 10 9 8 |
| ♥ | 5 |
| ♦ | A K Q J 10 9 |
| ♣ | - |

West:
♠ -
♥ A J 10 8 4 3 2
♦ 6
♣ K Q 9 7 6

East:
♠ A 7 6 4 3 2
♥ -
♦ 8 7
♣ 10 8 5 4 3

South:
♠ 6
♥ K Q 9 7 6
♦ 5 4 3 2
♣ A J 2

| S | W | N | E |
|---|---|---|---|
|  | 1♥ | DOUBLE (1) | 1♠ |
| 2♦ (2) | 2♥ | 5♦ | DOUBLE |
| PASS | PASS | REDOUBLE (3) | END |

(1) Making take-out doubles of opening bids with two-suited hands is quite dangerous. What if partner bids the third suit? I would bid a quiet 1♠ with North's hand, expecting further bidding given that I hold such a shapely collection.

(2) South wants to enter the auction, but all actions are flawed. The options are 1NT (relying on partner to hold the spades for his take-out double of 1♥), or his actual choice, 2♦, (in spite of the rather distressing suit quality).

(3) I would probably not redouble here, but more out of the fear that E-W would run to 5♥ (or 6♣) than that my partner would go down.

**Contract: 5♦ redoubled   Opening lead: ♥A**

# Lords – Commons

Ruffing partner's ace might be considered a careless crime of the highest order, but there are hands where it is vital. Take this deal from the annual Lords v Commons Bridge match.

Defending Three Hearts West led his singleton diamond. East won the jack and continued with the ace. West discarded an encouraging seven of clubs, but when, at Trick Three, East switched to the queen of clubs, declarer cleverly ducked (key play).

It was all over. East tried a third diamond, but declarer ruffed in dummy, cashed the king of trumps, overtook the jack with his queen, then ran his three remaining trumps. West was caught in a black suit squeeze, and elected to come down to ♠Q108 and ♣A (best), dummy retaining all his spades. Declarer finessed dummy's jack of spades and took the last three tricks with the ace, king, and promoted six. He ended up with an unlikely overtrick.

East had to resist the temptation to cash a top diamond at Trick Two, instead switching to the queen of clubs a trick earlier. Declarer does best to duck (if he covers with the king West will win the ace, cash the jack, give his partner a third-round ruff and East will cash a diamond). However ducking the queen of clubs does not save the day this time. It gives West not one but two winning options, both involving the same 'crime': he must later ruff his partner's ace of diamonds.

West can either overtake the queen of clubs with the ace, lead back a second club, East ruffing, ruff East's ace of diamonds continuation, and lead a third club, East ruffing again. Alternatively (perhaps less stylishly) he can let East's queen of clubs win, ruff the ace of diamonds continuation, cash the ace of clubs, then lead a third club for East to ruff. Down one.

**Dealer: North**      **Vulnerability: Both**

|  | Teams |  |
|---|---|---|
|  | ♠ A K J 6 |  |
|  | ♥ K J 8 |  |
|  | ♦ Q 2 |  |
|  | ♣ 10 8 6 3 |  |

| ♠ Q 10 8 4 | N | ♠ 7 3 2 |
|---|---|---|
| ♥ 7 4 3 | W   E | ♥ 10 5 |
| ♦ 9 | S | ♦ A K J 8 6 5 3 |
| ♣ A K 7 5 2 |  | ♣ Q |

|  |
|---|
| ♠ 9 5 |
| ♥ A Q 9 6 2 |
| ♦ 10 7 4 |
| ♣ K 9 4 |

| S | W | N | E |
|---|---|---|---|
|  |  | 1 NT | 2♦ |
| 2♥ | PASS | PASS | 3♦ |
| PASS | PASS | 3♥ | END |

**Contract: 3♥**      **Opening lead: ♦9**

The nub of the defence – the reason why East cannot cash a top diamond at Trick Two – is that the second round of diamonds is a ruffing entry to West's hand to ensure that East receives a (second) club ruff.

# Pepsi Crossruff

I have heard of quite a few 'Nevers' in Bridge:

'Never underlead an ace at trick one in a suit contract.'

'Never bid a Grand Slam in an inexperienced Duplicate event.'

'Never lead a singleton trump at Trick One.'

It's time to look at our last deal of the chapter.

Two of the world's strongest Bridge nations over the past couple of decades have been Brazil and Poland. Here they are pitted against one another in the World Championships.

The bidding at both tables was identical – leading to a contract of Five Diamonds doubled. The swing was entirely created by West's choice of opening lead.

The Brazilian West led a club (his partner's suit) and the Polish declarer, Pszczola ('Pepsi'), soon made him regret it. He ruffed in dummy, ruffed a heart, ruffed a club, ruffed a heart, ruffed a club, ruffed a heart, cashed the ace of spades, then continued the crossruff. He made all his ten trumps separately. Add to that the ace of spades, and you can see that he chalked up his doubled game.

At the other table the West player argued as follows:

'The opponents have contracted for eleven tricks, yet clearly do not have the high-card strength to make that number. They will have to score tricks with trumps. Although it is not normally a good idea to lead a singleton trump (in case partner's trump holding is exposed), here it could be vital, in order to draw two of the opposing trumps on one trick.'

West for Poland duly led the three of trumps. The Brazilian declarer played the Five Diamond contract along identical crossruff

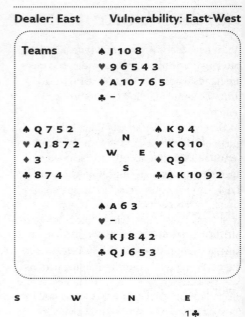

**Teams**

|  | ♠ J 10 8 |  |
|---|---|---|
|  | ♥ 9 6 5 4 3 |  |
|  | ♦ A 10 7 6 5 |  |
|  | ♣ – |  |
| ♠ Q 7 5 2 |  | ♠ K 9 4 |
| ♥ A J 8 7 2 | N | ♥ K Q 10 |
| ♦ 3 | W  E | ♦ Q 9 |
| ♣ 8 7 4 | S | ♣ A K 10 9 2 |
|  | ♠ A 6 3 |  |
|  | ♥ – |  |
|  | ♦ K J 8 4 2 |  |
|  | ♣ Q J 6 5 3 |  |

| S | W | N | E |
|---|---|---|---|
|  |  |  | 1♣ |
| 1♦ | 1♥ | 5♦ | DOUBLE |
| END |  |  |  |

**Contract: 5♦ doubled**

**Opening lead: ♣7/♦3**

lines to the Polish declarer – but with one critical difference. He could only score nine trump tricks instead of all ten. The doubled game was down one.

'Never lead a singleton trump at Trick One...'?

'Never say Never': a fitting way to end the chapter.

# CHAPTER 12

# The Mind of an Expert

'How did you know?', the Bridge expert is often asked, after getting yet another decision right.

There is a special elusive quality to the Bridge expert, one that goes beyond the long hours of rigorous practice that all have endured on their path upwards. It is the ability to harness the multivariate factors, some deductive, some inferential, some creative, and some psychological, that each decision at the table entails. And then to output the right bid or play.

This chapter opens up the expert's mind, like a surgeon, to reveal the secret workings inside.

Take this expert at work as a defender (East) to a Two Notrump contract, after the (unopposed) auction: One Notrump – Two Clubs (Stayman) – Two Spades – Two Notrumps – Pass. Let us delve into their mind:

'In the bidding, declarer (South) has revealed four spades, and not four hearts. My partner led the two of diamonds, so must have precisely four of them (assuming a fourth highest lead), leaving declarer also with four. My partner cannot have five clubs, or he would have preferred a club lead; so declarer has at least three clubs. But declarer cannot have four clubs, or that would leave room for just one heart (not a One Notrump opener); declarer's precise shape must therefore be four-two-four-three (in ranking order, spades down to clubs); therefore partner's shape must be three-three-four-three. Declarer has shown twelve to fourteen points, but quickly rejected his partner's game-invite. It looks like he has precisely twelve points. I have eleven points and dummy has twelve; therefore partner has six points.'

Things aren't always as conclusive, but thinking the right thoughts, and drawing the right inferences, both positive and negative, has told the expert East the precise shapes (most importantly) and point-counts of the hidden hands. At Trick One.

# Clearer Picture

Let us learn from a master craftsman at work: Zia Mahmood, who divides his time between his young family in Clapham, the Sunningdale golf course, the New York Rubber Bridge table, and his native Pakistan. The deal comes from the US Nationals.

West led the ace of hearts, and continued with the king. Declarer, Zia, ruffed, and it was immediately clear that his contract depended on losing no spade tricks.

To seek a clearer picture of the opposing hands at no real cost (barring a seven-one split in the suit), declarer made the first key move of eliminating diamonds. He cashed the king at trick three, followed by leading to dummy's ace, and then ruffed a third diamond (not with the two).

When West discarded on the third diamond, declarer reflected on East's hand pattern. He started with six diamonds and presumably four hearts (not five – with a six-five shape he would probably have bid on to Five Hearts). Because West would surely have bid on to Five Hearts with a 5♠6♥2♦0♣ pattern (leaving East with 1♠4♥6♦2♣), it was likely that East was 2♠4♥6♦1♣. With West not overruffing, declarer placed the ace of trumps with East, and therefore the king of spades (but not necessarily the jack) where he needed it for a successful finesse, with West.

Backing his judgement, Zia did not lead a trump at this point. Had he done so, East would have won, and exited with a low spade (best). Beating West's king with dummy's ace, declarer would be left guessing the location of the jack. Unless he next cashed the queen to drop East's jack (an unlikely move) he would fail.

No – instead Zia made the key move of stripping East of his spades, finessing dummy's queen of the suit, and cashing the ace (felling East's jack). Only then did he lead a trump.

**Teams**

|              | ♠ A Q 10 5        |                  |
|--------------|-------------------|------------------|
|              | ♥ 7 4             |                  |
|              | ♦ A 8 3           |                  |
|              | ♣ J 9 6 5         |                  |

| ♠ K 8 7 3        |           | ♠ J 6              |
|------------------|-----------|-------------------|
| ♥ A K Q 9 6 3    |     N     | ♥ J 10 5 2        |
| ♦ Q 4            |   W   E   | ♦ J 10 9 6 5 2    |
| ♣ 3              |     S     | ♣ A               |

|              | ♠ 9 4 2           |                  |
|--------------|-------------------|------------------|
|              | ♥ 8               |                  |
|              | ♦ K 7             |                  |
|              | ♣ K Q 10 8 7 4 2  |                  |

| S    | W         | N            | E    |
|------|-----------|--------------|------|
|      | 1♥        | DOUBLE (1)   | 4♥   |
| 5♣   | END       |              |      |

(1) Almost sub-minimum, however North is non-vulnerable and has good cards in the other major.

**Contract: 5♣**          **Opening lead: ♥A**

East won his bare ace and, as Zia planned, held only red cards. Zia was able to ruff his return in dummy, and discard his losing spade from hand.

Game made. What vision!

# Benji

'Benji Acol' is perhaps the most popular bidding system in English Club Bridge. It combines Weak Two openers (2♥ and 2♠ showing 5-10 points and a six-card suit) with Strong Twos (which all open 2♣ before revealing the suit next time). 2♦ becomes the equivalent of the normal 2♣ opener (23+ points and/or any game-force). But who is this mysterious 'Benji' – some Eastern mystic?

'Benji' was Glaswegian Albert Benjamin, who died recently, aged 95. Reputedly not a fan of his own Benjaminised Acol ('I invented it to have my opponents play it against me'), Albert was one of the great characters of the game, with a constant supply of side-splitting stories.

Here he is from a Scottish Cup match some years ago, teaching West a salutary lesson. At the other table (by a quirk of fate) the declarer was Albert's wife Judy. Here West demurely passed Six Spades and Judy naturally played out a top trump at some early stage. West now had to score his two trump tricks – down one.

Tipped off by the double – which could be based on nothing but all four missing trumps, Albert planned a trump endplay. Winning the ace-king of hearts, declarer cashed the thee top clubs throwing a diamond. He cashed the ace-king of diamonds, ruffed a third diamond, and cashed the queen of hearts.

Very conveniently West had followed to all three rounds of each side-suit, and we have reached this four-card ending:

```
              ♠ K 9 6 3
♠ Q J 10 8                  Irrelevant
              ♠ A 7 5 4
              (leading)
```

**Teams**

```
              ♠ K 9 6 3
              ♥ A K
              ♦ A K 10 5
              ♣ A K Q

♠ Q J 10 8           N         ♠ -
♥ J 10 6                       ♥ 9 7 5 3 2
♦ 8 6 2        W     E         ♦ Q 7 3
♣ 9 4 2              S         ♣ 10 7 6 5 3

              ♠ A 7 5 4 2
              ♥ Q 8 4
              ♦ J 9 4
              ♣ J 8
```

| S | W | N | E |
|---|---|---|---|
| | | 2♣ (1) | PASS |
| 2♠ (2) | PASS | 4NT (3) | PASS |
| 5♦ (4) | PASS | 5♥ (5) | PASS |
| 5♠ (6) | PASS | 6♠ (7) | PASS |
| PASS | DOUBLE (8) | END | |

(1) 23+ or any game-force. Benji was not playing 'Benji' (or he would have opened 2♦).
(2) Positive (only just) with five spades.
(3) Roman Key Card Blackwood agreeing spades.
(4) One of the 'five aces' (including ♠K).
(5) Do you have ♠Q?
(6) No.
(7) Rejecting the grand – as ♠Q is missing.
(8) Looks like he has two trump tricks...
Indeed he does – until he opens his big mouth.

**Contract: 6♠ doubled     Opening lead: ♥J**

Declarer led the four of trumps and let West hold the ten. West was poleaxed, declarer winning his return of the queen with his ace, then finessing dummy's nine.

Slam made – brilliant. Albert will be sorely missed.

# Forcing Defence

Congratulations to Brighton's Gunnar Hallberg on becoming the first Englishman to win the prestigious US Vanderbilt Trophy. A last-minute team cobbled together by fellow TGR Rubber player Zia Mahmood (who was eliminated early, in a much more fancied team), Gunnar's squad of five players was seeded 45th (the lowest seed to win in living memory). It contained just one regular partnership (Chinese – Fu and Jack).

Their victory is further evidence that simple bidding methods can suffice, even at the top level. Gunnar played almost no conventions with his two partners, Texan textile millionaire Seymon Deutsch, and New York Rubber player Fred Chang.

Here is Gunnar (as West) on defence to a part-score – turning minus into plus by using his limited assets to best advantage.

Defending the quiet Two Hearts, West's first decision came at Trick One. Although it is normal (these days) to lead low from three-to-an-honour, even in partner's suit, West chose to lead the jack of his partner's diamonds. This might be necessary if dummy held the length and strength. It was to prove the first key move – declarer can duck a low diamond lead to East, who cannot profitably continue the forcing defence. Not so the jack.

Letting West's jack of diamonds win, declarer saw West lead a second diamond. He ruffed and led a low club, correctly seeking to set up tricks in that suit before drawing trumps.

West now made his second key move, rising sharply with the ace of clubs in order to lead a third diamond, crucially through dummy's king. Declarer ruffed, led a second club to dummy's queen and East's ace, and now East could lead a fourth diamond (the ace over dummy's king). Declarer ruffed, but away went West's third club.

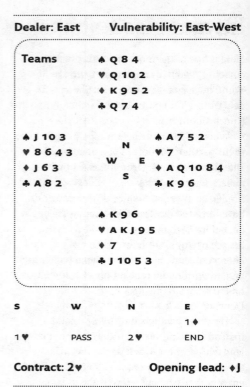

**Dealer: East     Vulnerability: East-West**

Teams

♠ Q 8 4
♥ Q 10 2
♦ K 9 5 2
♣ Q 7 4

♠ J 10 3
♥ 8 6 4 3
♦ J 6 3
♣ A 8 2

♠ A 7 5 2
♥ 7
♦ A Q 10 8 4
♣ K 9 6

♠ K 9 6
♥ A K J 9 5
♦ 7
♣ J 10 5 3

| S | W | N | E |
|---|---|---|---|
|  |  |  | 1♦ |
| 1♥ | PASS | 2♥ | END |

**Contract: 2♥**          **Opening lead: ♦J**

At Trick Seven declarer led a spade, to the ten, queen and ace, thus setting up his king. East returned a second spade to the king, and declarer tried his last chance, a sneaky ten of clubs, hoping West would be caught napping. Not Gunnar. He ruffed the club, and cashed the promoted jack of spades. Down one.

Lead a low diamond at Trick One, or play low on the club at Trick Three (both normal defensive plays), and declarer would make his part-score.

# Inward Head-shaking

Dealer: South        Vulnerability: Both

Here is one of the most promising of the current English international team, London's Tom Townsend, showing his technique on a deal from a Young Chelsea Bridge Club Knock-out match.

West led the two of diamonds in response to his partner's double of North's Five Diamonds. If declarer had finessed the queen, East would have won the king and fired back a second diamond. This would have removed dummy's ace prematurely – i.e. before declarer has been able to cash his ace of clubs. Declarer would then have been unable to enjoy dummy's king of clubs, and, in dummy for the last time, would have had to resort to the (losing) spade finesse. Down one.

However Townsend made no mistake, instead covering West's two of diamonds lead with dummy's eight (key play). East won the nine, but was unable to kill the diamond entry without giving declarer two tricks in the suit (and a spade discard from hand). In practice East switched at Trick Two to a spade, but declarer rose with the ace (no temptation to finesse), cashed the ace-king of trumps (felling the queen); he unblocked the ace of clubs, crossed to the ace of diamonds, and disposed of his spade loser on the king of clubs. Slam made.

By this point West was inwardly shaking his head. Can you see why? If he led not the two of diamonds but the jack, declarer would not have been able to duck the trick to East. The ace would be flushed out before the ace of clubs had been played and the slam would have to fail. As things proved, this was to prove the difference between winning and losing the match.

**Teams**

|  | ♠ Q J 10 |  |
|---|---|---|
|  | ♥ 7 4 |  |
|  | ♦ A Q 8 |  |
|  | ♣ K 8 6 3 2 |  |

| ♠ K 9 6 4 3 2 |  | ♠ 8 5 |
|---|---|---|
| ♥ 9 | N | ♥ Q 5 |
| ♦ J 4 2 | W   E | ♦ K 10 9 7 5 |
| ♣ Q 5 4 | S | ♣ J 10 9 7 |

|  | ♠ A 7 |  |
|---|---|---|
|  | ♥ A K J 10 8 6 3 2 |  |
|  | ♦ 6 3 |  |
|  | ♣ A |  |

| S (TOWNSEND) | W | N | E |
|---|---|---|---|
| 2♣ (1) | PASS | 2NT (2) | PASS |
| 4♥ (3) | PASS | 5♦ (4) | DOUBLE (5) |
| 6♥ | END |  |  |

(1) 23+ points or, as here, a hand expecting to make game opposite nothing.
(2) Positive without a good five-card suit.
(3) Implying a light 2♣ opener with a self-supporting heart suit.
(4) Ace-showing cue-bid agreeing hearts.
(5) Lead-directing.

**Contract: 6♥**        **Opening lead: ♦2**

# If They Don't Cover

Some declarers like to play the best technical line – they assume the defence will be perfect. Others are happy to adopt a clearly inferior technical line on the grounds of its practical chances of success. Take this deal, featuring Californian World Champion Lew Stansby as South. West leads the six of hearts to East's nine and declarer's jack.

The best technical line – assuming perfect defence – is to combine chances in the minors. Play to the ace-king of diamonds. If the queen drops doubleton, cash the remaining diamonds and claim ten tricks. If the queen does not drop, cross to the ace-king of spades, then run the jack of clubs, making whenever West holds ♣Kx or ♣Kxx. As you can see, this strategy would not have been a success on the actual layout, the queen of diamonds not dropping nor West holding the king of clubs.

Stansby adopted a very different approach. He led the jack of clubs at Trick Two. When West played low, he took the winning view that the king rated to be with East (recalling Zia Mahmood's maxim, 'If they don't cover, they don't have it').

Declarer rose with dummy's ace of clubs, cashed the ace of diamonds, crossed to the ace-king of spades, and led his second diamond to dummy's jack (the correct percentage play taking the suit in isolation). The finesse was successful, so he could cash the king of the suit felling West's queen, and run the remaining diamonds. Ten tricks and game made (plus one).

Stansby's line is based on the premise that West will probably cover the jack of clubs if he holds the king – which would indeed be necessary if declarer held, say ♣Jx. Maybe – although perhaps looking at the six-card diamond suit in dummy, West should consider the possibility that declarer is

**Dealer: West   Vulnerability: North-South**

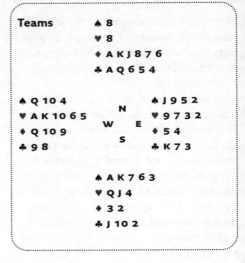

Teams

|  | |
|---|---|
| ♠ | 8 |
| ♥ | 8 |
| ♦ | A K J 8 7 6 |
| ♣ | A Q 6 5 4 |

West:
♠ Q 10 4
♥ A K 10 6 5
♦ Q 10 9
♣ 9 8

East:
♠ J 9 5 2
♥ 9 7 3 2
♦ 5 4
♣ K 7 3

South:
♠ A K 7 6 3
♥ Q J 4
♦ 3 2
♣ J 10 2

| S | W | N | E |
|---|---|---|---|
|  | PASS | 1♦ | PASS |
| 1♠ | 2♥ | 3♣ | PASS |
| 3NT | END | | |

**Contract: 3NT**          **Opening lead: ♥6**

leading the jack to tempt a cover, with no intention of letting it ride, rather switching his attentions to diamonds.

It interested me that one of the best players in the world would be prepared to base his whole line of play on an opposing misdefence (West covering the jack of clubs when holding the king).

# Trump Lead

Here is a fabulous piece of declarer play from London and England's David Price, en route to a narrow win against the fancied Greek team in the European Championships.

With six points facing a partner who has opened the bidding, West knew that North-South were light on strength for a game. In such situations a trump lead – to cut down ruffs – is usually best. West duly led a trump to East's jack, declarer ducking his ace (best).

East would have done best to follow his partner's lead and continue trumps at Trick Two, but, worried about dummy's diamonds, he elected to switch to hearts to try to score some quick tricks in the suit. Declarer made the first key move of rising with his king, playing opener for the ace. He cashed the ace of trumps and then played four rounds of clubs, discarding both dummy's remaining hearts (West discarding a diamond on the last round).

At Trick Eight declarer led his singleton diamond towards dummy's king-jack. West smoothly ducked his ace but declarer had no choice but to rise with the king. If East held the ace, declarer had no chance even if he played the jack and it drew the ace – for East could cash his last trump and draw dummy's last trump.

With dummy's king of diamonds winning the trick, declarer could ruff a second diamond, ruff a heart with dummy's last trump, and wait to score further trump tricks with his ♠109. Ten tricks and game made.

**Dealer: East**     **Vulnerability: North-South**

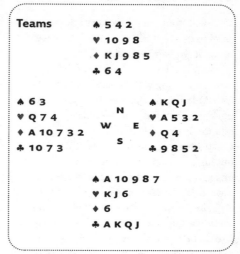

Teams

North: ♠ 5 4 2  ♥ 10 9 8  ♦ K J 9 8 5  ♣ 6 4

West: ♠ 6 3  ♥ Q 7 4  ♦ A 10 7 3 2  ♣ 10 7 3

East: ♠ K Q J  ♥ A 5 3 2  ♦ Q 4  ♣ 9 8 5 2

South: ♠ A 10 9 8 7  ♥ K J 6  ♦ 6  ♣ A K Q J

| S | W | N | E |
|---|---|---|---|
|  |  |  | 1♣ (1) |
| 1♠ (2) | PASS | 2♠ (3) | PASS |
| 4♠ (4) | END |  |  |

(1) Playing Five-card Majors and Strong Notrump.
(2) Many would consider this too strong for a simple overcall, but the modern style is to show a decent five-card major immediately, in preference to doubling.
(3) With pre-emption in mind...
(4) ...but South can hardly do less.

**Contract: 4♠**          **Opening lead: ♠3**

# Most Talented

This deal from the Bridge Olympics saw a combination of brilliant English defence and brilliant Norwegian declarer play.

West led the jack of hearts and declarer beat East's king with his ace. At Trick Two he led to dummy's jack of diamonds (East ducking), then followed with the queen of diamonds to East's ace.

Though it seems obvious for him to lead out his three top clubs (hoping that declarer has no more than three cards in the suit), East, Brian Callaghan, looked more deeply.

With declarer almost marked with no more than three hearts (West having shown five in the bidding) and precisely two diamonds (West having signalled upwards in the suit to show an odd number), he was very likely to have (at least) four clubs. At Trick Four East switched to a small club – which would unblock the suit if West held ♣Jx.

In fact West held ♣10x, leaving declarer with a most awkward guess. Normal play would be to insert the nine, in the hope that East held the ten. The jack was unlikely to be the right play – surely no East would underlead ace-king-queen…?

Declarer naturally remembered that East's One Notrump overcall showed fifteen to nineteen points. But it was still possible that West held the queen or king of clubs. However after much soul-searching, declarer did rise with the jack. Perhaps he was influenced by the time and manner in which East had made his small club switch. Getting such decisions right is what marks out the Norwegian, Geir Helgemo, many people's vote for Most Talented Bridge Player in the World.

Good decision – the jack won! Declarer crossed to the ace of spades, ran dummy's diamonds, and emerged with twelve tricks.

**Dealer: North**　　**Vulnerability: Both**

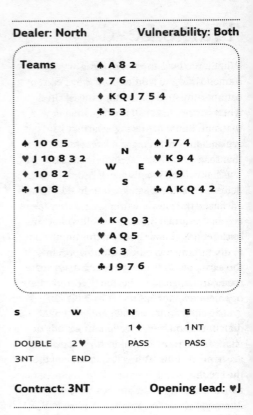

| Teams | ♠ A 8 2 |
| | ♥ 7 6 |
| | ♦ K Q J 7 5 4 |
| | ♣ 5 3 |

♠ 10 6 5　　　　♠ J 7 4
♥ J 10 8 3 2　　♥ K 9 4
♦ 10 8 2　　　　♦ A 9
♣ 10 8　　　　　♣ A K Q 4 2

♠ K Q 9 3
♥ A Q 5
♦ 6 3
♣ J 9 7 6

| S | W | N | E |
|---|---|---|---|
| | | 1♦ | 1NT |
| DOUBLE | 2♥ | PASS | PASS |
| 3NT | END | | |

**Contract: 3NT**　　**Opening lead: ♥J**

# 'Marked'

Whether to lead an unsupported ace against a small slam in a trump suit is a age-old conundrum. To do so certainly works well when partner has the king or a singleton in that suit. But sometimes declarer ruffs the ace and dummy's king is promoted – take this deal.

After ruffing West's ace of hearts lead, declarer, the late US star Norman Kay, advanced the king of trumps. East won the ace and returned the queen of hearts. A lesser declarer might have grabbed this opportunity to discard the two of clubs. But Norman foresaw a possible use of that card. He ruffed the heart, and cashed the ten of trumps (both opponents following).

The slam appears to depend on the diamond finesse, but declarer saw an extra chance. At Tricks Five and Six he cashed the ace-king of clubs. When East's queen fell on the second round, he could lead that precious two and take the 'marked' finesse of dummy's nine of clubs, then discard two diamonds on the king of hearts and jack of clubs. Twelve tricks and slam made.

Why did I put inverted commas around the word marked? Because an inspired East might falsecard with the queen on the second round of clubs when holding ♣Q10x. But Norman knew from experience that such defenders only exist in fantasies (or – from declarer's perspective – nightmares).

Could the slam have been made without that ace of hearts lead – giving you as declarer the second diamond discard? The answer is yes – if you play West for both the ace of hearts and queen of diamonds.

Say West leads a neutral trump and East wins and returns the suit. Win and cash the ace of diamonds plus ace-king of clubs. Then run all your trumps, reducing dummy down to ♥K, ♦10 and ♣J9. Take dummy's clubs

**Teams**

|  | ♠ J 8 6 |  |
|  | ♥ K 5 2 |  |
|  | ♦ 10 9 7 |  |
|  | ♣ J 9 5 3 |  |

| ♠ 5 3 | | ♠ A 7 |
| ♥ A 10 9 7 | N | ♥ Q J 8 6 4 3 |
| ♦ Q 6 3 | W   E | ♦ 8 4 2 |
| ♣ 10 8 7 4 | S | ♣ Q 6 |

|  | ♠ K Q 10 9 4 2 |  |
|  | ♥ – |  |
|  | ♦ A K J 5 |  |
|  | ♣ A K 2 |  |

| S | W | N | E |
|---|---|---|---|
| 2♣ (1) | PASS | 2♦ (2) | PASS |
| 2♠ | PASS | 3♠ | PASS |
| 6♠ (3) | END | | |

(1) 23+ points or any game-force.
(2) Negative – any hand of up to seven points.
(3) A reasonable punt – South may only need one minor-suit queen opposite to have a good play.

**Contract: 6♠**      **Opening lead: ♥A**

(finessing against West's ten if necessary) and reflect that West has had to bare his queen of diamonds in order to retain the ace of hearts. So lead a diamond to the king, felling his queen, and table the promoted jack. Twelve tricks – via a squeeze.

# Virtual Blueprint

Love it or hate it – the Gambling Three Notrump opener does present a virtual blueprint of the hand to the opponents. Watch this declarer – French World Champion Michel Perron – take advantage of East's descriptive bid.

Declarer ruffed West's opening club lead and cashed the ace-king of trumps (observing the even split with pleasure). But with West certain (on the bidding) to have the ace of diamonds, he was faced with three losers in the suit.

Declarer crossed to the ace of spades and ruffed a second club. He cashed the queen of spades, led to the king-jack (discarding a diamond from hand and watching East discard two clubs) and ruffed dummy's last club. He had eliminated the black suits and, if the lead was in dummy, could ensure his contract by leading a diamond and covering East's card (endplaying West to lead back a diamond – his last four cards were known to be diamonds – and so score a trick in the suit). But the lead was in his hand.

Declarer had a genuine choice. If West held ♦AQJx, the lead of the ten of diamonds would endplay him. Perron preferred to play East to hold either the queen or jack (the percentage choice). He exited with the king of diamonds (key play). West won the ace and, had East also followed low, West would have led a second diamond to East's bare queen, East then having to lead a club and enabling declarer to ruff in one hand and discard the last diamond from the other.

At the table East threw his queen of diamonds under West's ace (the correct play - in case West held the jack and ten). West cashed the jack (hoping East held queen-ten doubleton) but declarer's ten was promoted. Eleven tricks and game made.

**Dealer: East    Vulnerability: North-South**

**Teams**

|  | North |  |
|---|---|---|
|  | ♠ A K J 3 |  |
|  | ♥ J 6 4 |  |
|  | ♦ 7 5 3 |  |
|  | ♣ 9 6 2 |  |

| West | | East |
|---|---|---|
| ♠ 10 9 5 4 | | ♠ 8 6 |
| ♥ 10 7 | | ♥ Q 9 |
| ♦ A J 9 4 | | ♦ Q 8 |
| ♣ J 8 5 | | ♣ A K Q 10 7 4 3 |

|  | South |  |
|---|---|---|
|  | ♠ Q 7 2 |  |
|  | ♥ A K 8 5 3 2 |  |
|  | ♦ K 10 6 2 |  |
|  | ♣ – |  |

| S | W | N | E |
|---|---|---|---|
|  |  |  | 3NT (1) |
| 4♥ | 5♣ | 5♥ (2) | END |

(1) Gambling – showing a long (seven+ cards), solid minor and no ace or king outside.
(2) Doubling and 'taking the money' (300 points as it happens) is tempting. But North knows his partner's declarer-play skills and tries for game.

**Contract: 5♥**          **Opening lead: ♣5**

West was left to rue his opening club lead – which gave declarer the extra entry he needed to eliminate the suit. A major-suit lead and he would have no way to succeed.

# Battle of the Giants

The last few deals of the 2004 World Individual saw your author locked in a duel for the Gold Medal with Italy's Norberto Bocchi. It was soon dubbed the Battle of the Giants (we are both six foot six inches tall).

The good news on this final deal of the chapter from towards the end of the final session was that your columnist got a near-top for bidding and making Three Notrumps. The bad news was that his partner was Bocchi (each of the 52 competitors plays two boards with each other and this was our turn), who thus got the same near-top.

Declarer ran West's five of hearts lead around to his jack and at Trick Two led a low spade. Unable to rise with his ace (or declarer would have three spade tricks), West played low. Scoring dummy's queen, declarer next broached diamonds (a three-three split in mind). But when West followed with the ten and queen under the ace-king, the even split looked unlikely. Moving to clubs, declarer crossed to the king, successfully finessed the jack, and then cashed the ace (felling West's queen).

Declarer's trick tally was up to eight and he secured his ninth via an endplay. Reading West's shape, he cashed the ace of hearts and exited with a third heart. West won and cashed his two other hearts but, at Trick Twelve, was forced to lead from his ace-jack of spades around to declarer's king-nine. Nine tricks and game made.

Sad to report, I came second in the Battle of the Giants.

**Dealer: West    Vulnerability: East-West**

Pairs

|  | North |  |
|---|---|---|
|  | ♠ Q 7 6 3 | |
|  | ♥ A 7 3 | |
|  | ♦ A K 9 | |
|  | ♣ A J 8 | |

West
♠ A J 2
♥ K Q 8 5 4
♦ Q 10
♣ Q 6 3

East
♠ 10 5 4
♥ 10 9
♦ J 8 4 3
♣ 10 9 5 4

South
♠ K 9 8
♥ J 6 2
♦ 7 6 5 2
♣ K 7 2

| S | W | N | E |
|---|---|---|---|
|  | 1♥ (1) | DOUBLE (2) | PASS |
| 1NT (3) | PASS | 3NT | END |

(1) Playing Five-card Majors and 15-17 No-trump – the system used by all 'partnerships'.
(2) Cleverly chooses this in preference to 1NT because (a) he has four spades, and (b) his heart holding suggests that notrumps may play better from partner's side with the lead running around to his putative ♥J or ♥Q (as indeed it did).
(3) Seemingly an odd choice with no heart stopper, facing a partner who has advertised heart shortage, but hearts had not been supported, so I hoped for something opposite. Plus the scoring was matchpoints, where the advantage of playing notrumps rather than diamonds is accentuated. Responding 1♠ (the other viable alternative apart from 2♦) would all-too-likely see partner get over-excited with four-card 'support'.

**Contract: 3NT          Opening lead: 5♥**

# CHAPTER 13

# Experts Err

Bridge experts do get most decisions right. But not all.

They will not go wrong in standard situations, where there is a play that cannot cost, only gain. Thus they will always lead the jack from J8743 facing AQ965, although it is rarely right to lead a lone honour when finessing. (As an aside, can you see why leading the jack is better than leading low to the queen? Consider a 3=0 split onside.)

However, they sometimes misjudge (experts don't make mistakes, they 'misjudge'). Apart from being refreshing – and often rather amusing – these misjudgements can be very instructive. Like a scientist who learns more from deviant behaviour, so you can learn much from the near-perfectionist on those occasions they topple off their perch of perfection. And when those occasions take place at crucial stages of big tournaments (as they tend to, with pressure mounting), there can be much drama...

# Page 143

Zia Mahmood and I love to partner one another once or twice a year. But though we agree on many aspects of the game, we do not see eye to eye on one. I prefer a fairly simple freewheeling approach to the auction, with not too many obscure conventions. Zia does not (unless at the rubber table). He has nearly 200 pages of system with his regular partner, New Yorker Michael Rosenberg.

Nestling in small print on page 143 (he showed me afterwards) was the following sentence: 'Second-in-hand vulnerable Three Club and Three Diamond openers must contain one of the two top honours in the suit'. It is an eminently sensible agreement. The trouble was that I had only got as far as page three of his system before reaching saturation point, and attempting to persuade Zia to adopt a less complex approach with me.

Despite being successful on our two previous years together in the Cap Gemini Invitational, disasters had been waiting to happen. Sure enough, on our third year we came down to earth with a bump.

This deal was one of our more spectacular calamities from the event, borne of my failure to read page 143 (and Zia's expectation that I had read it!).

Instead of trying Four Notrumps in response to my preemptive Three Diamond opener (which we play as Roman Key Card Blackwood – asking about the king of trumps as well as the four aces), Zia leapt immediately to Six Diamonds. He 'knew' I had either the ace or king of diamonds – as per page 143.

A slam missing the ace and king of trumps is never a thing of beauty but I, as declarer, did have an outside chance. I ruffed West's queen of spades lead and led the queen of trumps at Trick Two. West, the legendary

**Dealer: East     Vulnerability: North-South**

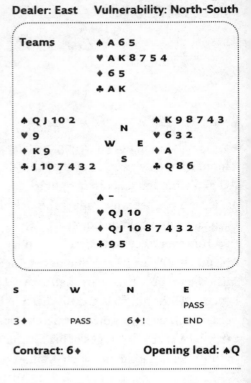

Teams

North: ♠ A 6 5  ♥ A K 8 7 5 4  ♦ 6 5  ♣ A K

West: ♠ Q J 10 2  ♥ 9  ♦ K 9  ♣ J 10 7 4 3 2

East: ♠ K 9 8 7 4 3  ♥ 6 3 2  ♦ A  ♣ Q 8 6

South: ♠ –  ♥ Q J 10  ♦ Q J 10 8 7 4 3 2  ♣ 9 5

| S | W | N | E |
|---|---|---|---|
|   |   |   | PASS |
| 3♦ | PASS | 6♦! | END |

**Contract: 6♦**          **Opening lead: ♠Q**

Benito Garozzo, was looking at the one trump holding that gave him a problem. Was I trying to pull a fast one on him with a suit headed by ace-queen-jack?

After some agonising, he correctly came to the conclusion that my play was completely illogical unless I was also missing the ace of trumps (with ace-queen-jack I would lead the suit from dummy and take a finesse). He played low, East won his singleton ace, and I conceded one down shortly after.

The odd disaster notwithstanding – roll on the next tournament with Zia. He is truly a pleasure to sit opposite.

# Nightmare

Imagine the worst possible Bridge nightmare – use your imagination and be as far-fetched as you like.

How about this... you, sitting West, are in the semifinals of the World Championships, and have a slight lead going into the last deal. All you have to do to reach the final is to defeat a Five Club contract that your partnership has doubled.

You lead the ace of hearts (see layout) and the paltry dummy goes down. You think for a while and then, to cut down trumping in dummy, switch to the ace of trumps... Oops! Partner's king crashes underneath.

With perspiration trickling down your forehead, you convince yourself that your partner's double must include the ace of spades. At Trick Three you switch to the five of spades. Declarer plays dummy's jack and you are devastated to see it win the trick.

Declarer crosses to his ace of spades, trumps a second heart, cashes dummy's ace of diamonds, trumps a diamond, trumps his last heart with dummy's last trump, trumps a spade, then cashes the queen of trumps to fell your jack. Contract made – 550 points to North-South. You blew your berth to the final.

Even cashing the ace of trumps was not fatal. All you needed to do was follow up with your second trump and declarer is still a trick short – unable to trump both his losing hearts for the lack of a second trump in the dummy.

You found the only sequence of plays to condense your four defensive tricks (king of spades, ace of hearts, and ace-king of trumps) into two. Nightmare!

**Dealer: East**  **Vulnerability: East-West**

Teams

|  | ♠ Q J 4 2 |  |
|  | ♥ 7 |  |
|  | ♦ A J 7 6 3 |  |
|  | ♣ 8 4 3 |  |

| ♠ K 10 8 5 | | ♠ 9 7 6 |
| ♥ A K 5 4 3 | **N** | ♥ Q 8 6 2 |
| ♦ Q 4 | **W        E** | ♦ K 10 9 5 2 |
| ♣ A J | **S** | ♣ K |

|  | ♠ A 3 |  |
|  | ♥ J 10 9 |  |
|  | ♦ 8 |  |
|  | ♣ Q 10 9 7 6 5 2 |  |

| S | W | N | E |
|---|---|---|---|
|  |  |  | PASS |
| 3♣ | DOUBLE | 5♣ | DOUBLE (1) |
| END |  |  |  |

(1) More of an expression of general values than pure penalties.

**Contract: 5♣ doubled    Opening lead: ♥A**

*Postscript*: This was no imaginary nightmare. It really happened: Norway defeating Brazil exactly as described in the 1993 World Championship Semi-Finals in Chile! Happy to report – the Brazilian West has not given up the game and, indeed, goes from strength to strength.

# Bad Commentary

On occasions I give a commentary for a Simultaneous Pairs event (same set of deals used around the country/world). On board 17 of one such commentary (this deal) I wrote, 'Five Diamonds makes because the diamond finesse is onside. Declarer crosses twice in clubs to take and repeat the finesse. He just loses two spades.'

Well they say that to err is human, and the flaw in my analysis was revealed by Hampshire's Julian Pottage (West) and David Bird (East), both authors and journalists of some renown. Can you spot how they defeated the contract, giving declarer no chance?

West led the ace of spades, continued with the king, and then followed with the jack. On this third trick East had the opportunity to make the killing discard. He threw a club (key play).

After ruffing declarer crossed to the queen of clubs to lead a trump to his jack, the finesse succeeding. But because of East's club discard, he was unable to cross to dummy's king of clubs to repeat the trump finesse (or East would ruff). He was left hoping that East's king of diamonds would fall on the second round. He led the ace of trumps, but the king did not fall and the contract was down one.

Oops. Nicely spotted, and nicely defended.

It is interesting that game in the 6-3 diamond fit cannot be made, whilst Five Clubs, the 5-3 fit, cannot be beaten. After ruffing the third spade, declarer crosses to the queen of trumps (clubs), and finesses the jack of diamonds. He then cashes the ace of trumps, crosses to the king (drawing West's trumps), finesses the queen of diamonds, cashes the ace (felling East's king) and runs his promoted winners in the suit. Eleven tricks and game made.

**Dealer: West**     **Vulnerability: Neither**

Pairs

|  |  |  |
|---|---|---|
| | ♠ 8 5 2 | |
| | ♥ A 10 7 5 | |
| | ♦ 7 6 5 | |
| | ♣ K Q 3 | |
| ♠ A K J 9 6 3 | N | ♠ Q 4 |
| ♥ K 8 6 | W   E | ♥ Q J 9 4 3 2 |
| ♦ 8 | S | ♦ K 10 3 |
| ♣ J 10 8 | | ♣ 7 4 |
| | ♠ 10 7 | |
| | ♥ – | |
| | ♦ A Q J 9 4 2 | |
| | ♣ A 9 6 5 2 | |

| S | W | N | E |
|---|---|---|---|
| | 1♠ | PASS | 2♥ (1) |
| 3♦ | 4♥ (2) | PASS | PASS |
| 5♣ | PASS | 5♦ | END |

(1) This response – uniquely – guarantees at least five cards in the suit bid.

(2) Pushy – but West is trying to bounce his opponents into a 'phantom sacrifice'.

**Contract: 5♦**     **Opening lead: ♠A**

# Sleepless Nights

Some losses are easier to bear than others.

'The opponents were luckier...'

'Even if we had played card-perfect Bridge, we would not have won...'

'My partner/teammates were off-colour...'

'Oh good – now I can go away with the family,' etc.

However some losses cannot easily be rationalised away. The 2003 World Championships fall into that category. I am sure that all six Italian losing finallists will have had sleepless nights for quite a while. Favourites for the title, and all brilliant players, they blew a number of opportunities in the final against the USA (including pulling the wrong card from dummy on the very last deal, whilst holding an eleven imp lead), and lost by just one imp (the equivalent of a mere overtrick).

The Italian declarer turned no less than 28 imps (for the worse) on this deal – undoubtedly the most exciting (if not dramatic – that was surely the last) of the whole Championships. How would you declare Six Spades redoubled, East having doubled both a diamond cue-bid (implying the king), and then the final contract?

Declarer won dummy's ace of diamonds and, without playing a top spade, led a heart. Instead of finessing the queen (doubtless worried about East holding a singleton), he rose with the ace and led a second heart. West won the jack and cleverly continued with the king of the suit.

Declarer almost found the winning play of ruffing with dummy's two (playing East to have doubled Six Spades with a void trump), but instead ruffed with dummy's jack. When he next led the ace of trumps and East discarded, he cursed. West's ten of trumps had to score a trick. Down one.

Had declarer cashed a top trump from dummy at Trick Two, he would have seen East discard, and known to ruff the third heart low. A sixteen imp gain turned into a twelve imp loss.

**Dealer: East**  **Vulnerability: East-West**

**Teams**

|  |  |  |  |
|---|---|---|---|
|  | ♠ A J 2 |  |  |
|  | ♥ 10 6 |  |  |
|  | ♦ A Q J 3 2 |  |  |
|  | ♣ Q 10 3 |  |  |

| ♠ 10 7 6 4 | | ♠ – |
| ♥ K J 2 | N | ♥ 8 3 |
| ♦ 10 6 | W      E | ♦ K 8 7 5 4 |
| ♣ K 9 6 5 | S | ♣ A J 8 7 4 2 |

|  |
|---|
| ♠ K Q 9 8 5 3 |
| ♥ A Q 9 7 5 4 |
| ♦ 9 |
| ♣ – |

| S | W | N | E |
|---|---|---|---|
|  |  |  | PASS |
| 1♠ | PASS | 2♦ | PASS |
| 2♥ | PASS | 4♠ | PASS |
| 5♣ (1) | PASS | 5♦ (1) | DOUBLE |
| 6♠ | PASS | PASS | DOUBLE |
| REDOUBLE | END |  |  |

(1) Control-showing cue-bids.

Note: The Italian auction was actually nine rounds long (no kidding), and contained some highly complex artificial bids. I have simplified it, whilst retaining all the key elements.

**Contract: 6♠ redoubled**

**Opening lead: ♦10**

# Easy to Overlook

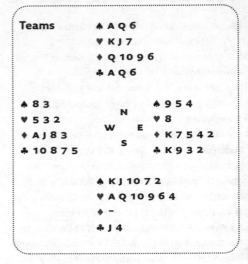

'Six-five come alive.'

Three South players certainly did that on this deal from the European Championships. But of those three declarers who drove the bidding all the way to Seven Hearts, only Spain's Andrea Buratti managed to make the Grand Slam.

West hopefully led the ace of diamonds and the two failing declarers ruffed and drew trumps. They hoped the split would be two-two, in which case they would be able to draw trumps in two rounds, play five rounds of spades discarding two clubs from dummy, cross to the ace of clubs, ruff a diamond, and ruff the jack of clubs with dummy's last trump. But the three-one trump split meant that dummy had no trumps left after the opposing cards in the suit had been drawn. After cashing the five spades declarer was forced to take the club finesse, failing when the jack ran to East's king. Down one.

Enter Buratti. After ruffing the ace of diamonds lead, declarer led the nine of trumps (key play – preserving his other low trump) to dummy's jack, observing the fall of the eight from East. He ruffed a second diamond (with the ten), then led the low trump to dummy's seven (East discarding). He ruffed a third diamond in hand, crossed to the queen of spades, then ruffed dummy's last diamond (with his last trump). He crossed to dummy's ace of clubs (no finesse necessary) then cashed the king of trumps, finally drawing West's last trump (discarding the jack of clubs from hand). All that remained was to cash dummy's ace of spades and lead to his king-jack-ten of the suit. Grand slam made.

West's ace of diamonds lead had made declarer's task a little easier, but he would have succeeded on a club lead too, by spurning the finesse and using the ace of

| S | W | N | E |
|---|---|---|---|
| | | 1♦ | PASS |
| 1♥ | PASS | 2NT | PASS |
| 3♠ | PASS | 4♥ | PASS |
| 4♠ (1) | PASS | 5♣ (2) | PASS |
| 5♦ (2) | PASS | 5♠ (2) | PASS |
| 7♥ | END | | |

(1) Showing a six-five shape and a slammy hand.
(2) Ace (void)-showing cue-bids agreeing hearts.

**Contract: 7♥**          **Opening lead: ♦A**

spades as the final dummy entry instead of the ace of clubs.

It was a perfect Dummy Reversal – trumping enough times in your hand (here four) to make your hand into the shorter trump length and using dummy's trumps to draw the opposing trumps. So satisfying, but so easy to overlook.

# Too Quick

Have you ever had one of those days when everything you touch turns to gold? I was lucky enough to have one during the 2004 World Individual Trophy, held in Verona, Italy. Sadly the following day was far from epic and gold turned to silver (quite literally – I was in the Gold Medal position until the very last deal of the event but had to settle for the Silver).

Overcalling Three Notrumps (as I did) over East's preemptive Three Clubs is far from gilt-edged: no club stopper nor source of tricks. Fortunately my partner's singleton jack of clubs bolstered the club situation and he tabled a source of tricks (diamonds). Three Notrumps was still destined to fail on the correct defence, but there was more luck for your author when East failed to spot the winning play.

West led the nine of clubs to dummy's jack. East won his queen and, realising declarer held a club stopper with his guarded ten, switched to a low heart. Rising with the ace, declarer led the king of diamonds (ducked), the queen (also ducked), and a third diamond won by West's ace. A second club to East's ace-king would have held declarer to nine tricks, but when West led a second heart, declarer could claim eleven tricks via three spades (overtaking the second round), three hearts and five diamonds.

East should read his partner's nine of clubs opening lead as top of a doubleton (he has little hope if it is a singleton). He should therefore make the key play of ducking the first trick (playing the eight to encourage). This way he retains communication with his partner so that when West wins the ace of diamonds, he can lead his second club. East now takes his ace-king-queen and follows with the six and three. Down two.

Did the expert East play too quickly and

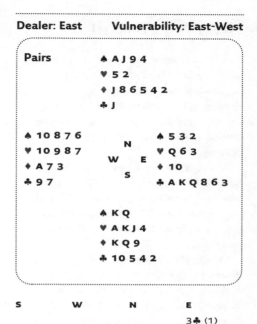

| Pairs | ♠ A J 9 4 |
| | ♥ 5 2 |
| | ♦ J 8 6 5 4 2 |
| | ♣ J |

| ♠ 10 8 7 6 | | ♠ 5 3 2 |
| ♥ 10 9 8 7 | N | ♥ Q 6 3 |
| ♦ A 7 3 | W E | ♦ 10 |
| ♣ 9 7 | S | ♣ A K Q 8 6 3 |

| | ♠ K Q |
| | ♥ A K J 4 |
| | ♦ K Q 9 |
| | ♣ 10 5 4 2 |

| S | W | N | E |
|---|---|---|---|
| | | | 3♣ (1) |
| 3NT (2) | END | | |

(1) A bold choice at the adverse vulnerability...
(2) ...but it certainly left South with a series of unappetising options. Double is for take-out and too many clubs (thus not enough cards outside) are held. Pass with 18 points seems overly timid, and overcalling 3♥ with just four cards is a real stab in the dark. In the end South followed the maxim seemingly attributed to many experts, 'If in doubt, bid 3NT.'

**Contract: 3NT          Opening lead: ♣9**

overlook the Trick One duck? Or did he consider it and reject it? My guess is the former, as it has so much going for it.

# Sorry, Partner

Dealer: South     Vulnerability: Both

Some expert errors are 'solos', some are partnership. This one falls somewhere between the two, and was to cost my team the prestigious Lederer Memorial Trophy a couple of years ago. Can you spot the winning defence to Four Spades after the king of hearts lead?

The defenders must switch to diamonds without West playing the ace. East can then win the first trump with the ace and lead his second diamond. West wins the ace this time, and a third diamond sees East ruff. Down one.

At the table East was on the right track, overtaking the king of hearts with the ace and switching to the ten of diamonds (he knew from West's overcall that just one heart was cashing). Unfortunately West read this as a singleton. He won the ace and tried to give East an immediate ruff. The communications were now severed between the defenders, so East lost his ruff. Game made.

The overtake and switch ploy superficially looks dramatic enough to be a singleton. But let us think deeper and see if West can work out that it is a doubleton.

Even assuming West gives his partner the diamond ruff, East still needs a black suit ace to beat the game. If East is switching to a doubleton diamond, that ace needs to be in trumps, enabling him to win the first trump and, assuming West ducked his ace of diamonds, lead his second diamond for the ruff.

So what should East do when he has the same hand with a diamond fewer? He must make a play that he cannot afford to make with a diamond more. He must cash the ace of trumps (the ace of clubs would carry the same message) before switching to his diamond. It follows that when East fails to cash his ace of trumps, he must, if West assumes that the contract is defeatable, hold a doubleton diamond.

Ducking the ace of diamonds at Trick Two was the indicated play. Sorry partner (for your author was West)!

**Teams**

```
                 ♠ 10 9 6 4
                 ♥ 8 7 3
                 ♦ K 9 4
                 ♣ K Q 5
 ♠ 2                          ♠ A 7
 ♥ K Q J 4 2        N         ♥ A 10 9 6
 ♦ A 7 3 2      W     E       ♦ 10 5
 ♣ 10 6 2          S          ♣ 9 8 7 4 3
                 ♠ K Q J 8 5 3
                 ♥ 5
                 ♦ Q J 8 6
                 ♣ A J
```

| S | W | N | E |
|---|---|---|---|
| 1♠ | 2♥ | 2♠ | 4♥ |
| 4♠ | END | | |

**Contract: 4♠**     **Opening lead: ♥K**

# Fraction Too Late

Look at East's hand (and cover up South and West), on a deal from the US Vanderbilt. Your highest card is the king of clubs and, in order to defeat South's Three Notrump contract, you must use it wisely. West leads the ten of spades to declarer's jack, and at Trick Two declarer runs the ten of diamonds. You win the jack and...

No – this is not the time to lead the king of clubs. Although it will remove dummy's entry to the fifth diamond (the dreaded Merrimac Coup), setting up partner's spades is the priority and leading back your second spade is the only defence to give you a chance. Partner beats declarer's queen of spades with the ace and leads the nine of spades. You must find a discard.

If you discarded the king of clubs, well done! You can now relax – the contract is bound to fail. But say you humanly threw a discouraging low heart. You are still in with a shout.

Declarer wins the king of spades and crosses to the ace-king of diamonds, looking disappointed as partner discards (an encouraging nine of hearts) on the third round (declarer also throwing a heart from hand). He then leads the ace of clubs.

Last chance. Did you jettison the king of clubs under dummy's ace? If you did, then declarer cannot set up the suit without letting partner on lead with his jack-ten. But if you hung on to your best asset one more time, then you are doomed.

Declarer leads a second club to your nine and his queen; he then shrugs and leads a third club, your king agonisingly beating partner's jack. Declarer wins your heart return with the ace and cashes his two promoted long clubs. Nine tricks and game made.

**Dealer: South**     **Vulnerability: Both**

| Teams | ♠ 5 4 2 |
| --- | --- |
| | ♥ J 10 3 |
| | ♦ A K 8 4 2 |
| | ♣ A 2 |

|  ♠ A 10 9 8 7 | N | ♠ 6 3 |
| --- | --- | --- |
| ♥ K 9 5 | W    E | ♥ 7 6 4 2 |
| ♦ 6 5 | S | ♦ Q J 7 3 |
| ♣ J 10 4 | | ♣ K 9 3 |

| | ♠ K Q J |
| --- | --- |
| | ♥ A Q 8 |
| | ♦ 10 9 |
| | ♣ Q 8 7 6 5 |

| S | W | N | E |
| --- | --- | --- | --- |
| 1 NT | PASS | 3NT (1) | END |

(1) Worth 3NT with the fine five-card suit plus the ♥J10 and ♦AK sequential honour combinations.

**Contract: 3NT**     **Opening lead: ♠10**

If you failed to dispose of that wretched king in time then you can perhaps take solace from the fact that neither did a tall English International player who runs a Bridge Club in South West London... and writes on Bridge for *The Times*...

Argghhh. I just didn't see it until a fraction too late.

# CHAPTER 14
# Freaks

No – I'm not talking about most Bridge players! This chapter considers those wild deals, where the power of shape comes to the fore, and those words of US champion Marty Bergen and others spring to mind: 'Points Schmoints'.

Most of these freaks, almost incredibly, occurred after a normal shuffle and deal. However they are interspersed with a few 'ghoulies', the result of dealing the cards in clumps of five, five, and three (or, generally leading to even crazier distributions, five, four and four). Some purists will claim that Goulash Bridge is an oxymoron. Perhaps, but such deals are often very instructive in the play, and are certainly very entertaining.

In a chapter to savour, we start with the deal we all dream about...

# Machine Malfunction

**Dealer: South**   **Vulnerability: Neither**

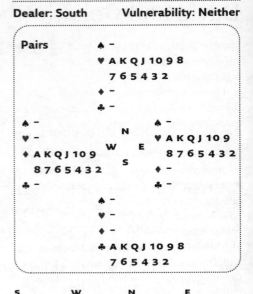

Pairs

♠ -
♥ A K Q J 10 9 8
   7 6 5 4 3 2
♦ -
♣ -

♠ -           N        ♠ -
♥ -        W     E     ♥ A K Q J 10 9
♦ A K Q J 10 9    S        8 7 6 5 4 3 2
   8 7 6 5 4 3 2           ♦ -
♣ -                        ♣ -

♠ -
♥ -
♦ -
♣ A K Q J 10 9 8
   7 6 5 4 3 2

| S | W | N | E |
|---|---|---|---|
| 7♣ (1) | PASS (2) | 7♠ | END |

(1) Showing something of a lack of imagination.
(2) Made up for by West.

**Contract: 7♠ by North    Opening lead: -**

In Tournament Bridge, the cards are 'dealt' by a Duplimate machine (using magnetic bar codes). Very occasionally, a malfunction might see a pack evade the machine. In that case the cards of the pack will be placed in the pockets of the wallets as they are. A new pack – with the cards separated into entire suits – will therefore be placed with one complete suit in each pocket.

Cut to our first 'deal', a real scenario from a recent tournament. South picked out his cards of the wallet and saw thirteen clubs. He could not be sure that things had gone astray – after all holding thirteen clubs is just as likely as any other specific hand (e.g. ♠AQ85, ♥K73, ♦Q2, ♣9762). Perhaps he cast a glance at the other players, but they were poker-faced. Despite the late Terence Reese advising you to open just Four Clubs with all thirteen of them in his classic book *Play These Hands With Me* (opening Seven Clubs gives a blueprint of your hand so the opponents are sure to bid over you), South did open a somewhat unoriginal Seven Clubs.

Over to West. He came up with the classiest call. He passed! Suspecting a machine breakdown with each player holding an entire suit, he realised that it was no use bidding Seven Diamonds – he might just as well bid Seven Hearts. For the player holding the spade suit was in the box seat and the final contract would be bound to be Seven Spades.

Unfortunately for West it was his opponent, North, who concluded the bidding – and the play – by bidding Seven Spades and showing his hand amidst much laughter by all four players.

Naturally it was presumed that this was as a result of a machine breakdown, and a proper deal was soon substituted. But no one could be sure. The odds may be

2,235,197,406,895,366,368,301,559,999 to one against all four players holding an entire suit. But they are not zero.

# David and Goliath

Imagine South picking up his hand. He sees a collection of red and black cards and just one high-card point. Yuk!

However closer inspection reveals that all the red cards are hearts and all the black cards are clubs. He is going to be able to have some fun on the deal after all. Just how much fun he could scarcely imagine...

Now move to East. Will he ever pick up a more powerful hand than this rock-crushing one-loser affair? I doubt it. His hopes will have been sky-high as the bidding commenced...

The David vs Goliath encounter began with David's partner opening One Notrump. Goliath doubled – East was rather sadistically looking forward to cashing the first twelve tricks and watching declarer agonise about which ace (heart or club) to retain at Trick 13.

South removed quietly to Two Hearts and the bidding returned to East. Taking the practical approach, he simply bid what he thought he could make: Six Spades (because it was Duplicate Pairs he went for the higher scoring slam between spades and diamonds). He could not believe it when South, who could only muster up a weakness take-out last time, came again with Seven Clubs.

East was unwilling to bid on to Seven Diamonds and go down one (though South needs to lead a club to defeat the grand slam – or declarer can draw trumps and discard dummy's singleton club on a long spade). He doubled.

Had West divined to lead a heart, East would have at least netted a small plus score from Seven Clubs doubled, able to ruff the opening lead. But when West led a spade, declarer could ruff, fell both the outstanding king and queen of trumps under dummy's ace, and run the hearts. Doubled grand slam made and Goliath was slain.

**Pairs**

|  | North |
| --- | --- |
| ♠ | 7 6 2 |
| ♥ | A K Q |
| ♦ | 8 5 |
| ♣ | A 10 8 6 5 |

| West | East |
| --- | --- |
| ♠ 10 9 4 3 | ♠ A K Q J 8 5 |
| ♥ J 9 8 | ♥ – |
| ♦ 7 6 4 3 2 | ♦ A K Q J 10 9 |
| ♣ Q | ♣ K |

| South |
| --- |
| ♠ – |
| ♥ 10 7 6 5 4 3 2 |
| ♦ – |
| ♣ J 9 7 4 3 2 |

| S (DAVID) | W | N | E (GOLIATH) |
| --- | --- | --- | --- |
|  |  | 1 NT | DOUBLE (1) |
| 2♥ | PASS | PASS | 6♠ |
| 7♣ | PASS | PASS | DOUBLE |
| END |  |  |  |

(1) 1NT doubled down six scores 1400, more than the value of a small slam. Should partner hold ♣A (dream on), the penalty will be 1700 (down seven), more than the value of a grand slam.

**Contract: 7♣ doubled   Opening lead: ♠10**

# Fewest Possible

Last deal was a making grand slam with just fourteen points between the partnership. This one – from a home game in North London – is a grand slam made (although not bid) with just five points (the fewest possible). I have a feeling that the deal may have been rigged, because the scenario is so unlikely, but it's highly amusing nonetheless.

West led a diamond against Six Spades doubled. He knew that the ace of hearts would be ruffed – although in fact the ruff-and-discard heart lead makes life a tiny bit more awkward for declarer as it uses up a trump, but does not advance the establishment of either minor.

After ruffing the lead, declarer ruffed a club, ruffed a second diamond, then led a trump to dummy's ace. Delighted to see both the missing honours crash, he ruffed a third diamond and was soon claiming all thirteen tricks when the suit split 3-3. Doubled small slam made – with an overtrick.

The traveller would make interesting reading if the deal occurred in a duplicate – I suspect many North-Souths (the point-counters) would not even enter the bidding.

*Question*: what is the 'par' result on the deal (i.e. if both partnerships take the best possible action for their side)?

*Answer*: North-South would bid up to Seven Spades, but East-West would not defend (losing 1510 points – chicago/duplicate scoring). Instead they would sacrifice in Seven Notrumps. North-South would then double and lead a spade, setting the contract six tricks. The par result is thus 1400 points to North-South.

All North-South scored at the table was a 'measly' 1310 (Six Spades doubled plus one) – a moral victory for East-West!

**Rubber**

|  |  |
|---|---|
| ♠ | A 10 8 6 4 2 |
| ♥ | – |
| ♦ | 10 9 8 7 6 5 2 |
| ♣ | – |

|  |  |  |  |
|---|---|---|---|
| ♠ K | | ♠ Q | |
| ♥ A J 10 9 4 3 | N | ♥ K Q 8 7 6 5 2 | |
| ♦ K 4 2 | W   E | ♦ A Q J | |
| ♣ A J 2 | S | ♣ K Q | |

|  |  |
|---|---|
| ♠ | J 9 7 5 3 |
| ♥ | – |
| ♦ | – |
| ♣ | 10 9 8 7 6 5 4 |

| S | W | N | E |
|---|---|---|---|
| | | | 2♥ (1) |
| 3♣ (2) | 4NT (3) | PASS | 5♦ (4) |
| 5♠ (2) | 6♥ | 6♠ | DOUBLE |
| END | | | |

(1) Five years ago one would not annotate a Strong Two, but now one needs to do so in order to separate it from the increasingly common Weak Two. A sign of changing times.

(2) Points schmoints.

(3) Scarcely able to believe his partner's opening, he trots out (simple Four-Ace) Blackwood.

(4) One ace.

**Contract: 6♠ doubled     Opening lead: ♦2**

# Law of Symmetry

Ely Culbertson's Law of Symmetry – purporting that there is a correlation between suit-patterns and hand-patterns – has no mathematical basis, and has now been discredited. A shame in a way, for he writes so alluringly on the subject. Take the 4-3-3-3 (West's shape on this – otherwise freaky – deal from my Club). Ely writes (from his 1934 *Red Book*):

'The pattern 4333, while it usually indicates a number of 4432s, 4333s and 5332s around the table, is sometimes the most deceiving symptom of all. It may be the tail-end of violent distributional storms which are raging in the other hands. It is the peculiarity of the 4333 that it often serves as a joiner between the freakish and normal distributions.' The 4333 has never known it so good.

Defending Five Hearts doubled, West led a spade, his side's suit. Had declarer ruffed in dummy, a tempting way to score dummy's singleton trump, he would have failed. He cannot then conveniently reach his hand to draw trumps, and will probably play ace of diamonds – diamond ruff. After drawing trumps he leads his club, but West wins his ace, exits passively with a third diamond, and East must score two spades when declarer, as he must, leads away from his king. Down one.

However declarer made no mistake, discarding from dummy on West's spade lead (key play). East won the ace and needed to do two things: lead a trump to remove dummy's singleton (his actual choice), or switch to a diamond, to remove the entry to the soon-to-be-promoted king of clubs.

Leading a diamond would allow declarer to win the ace, ruff a diamond, ruff a spade, ruff a diamond, draw trumps, and concede a club. Switching to a trump worked no better –

**Dealer: North          Vulnerability: Neither**

| | | | |
|---|---|---|---|
| **Pairs** | ♠ – | | |
| | ♥ 3 | | |
| | ♦ A 8 5 4 2 | | |
| | ♣ K 10 9 7 6 5 4 | | |

| | | |
|---|---|---|
| ♠ Q 8 6 | **N** | ♠ A J 10 5 4 3 2 |
| ♥ 10 5 2 | **W   E** | ♥ 4 |
| ♦ Q J 9 | **S** | ♦ K 10 7 6 |
| ♣ A Q 8 2 | | ♣ J |

| | |
|---|---|
| | ♠ K 9 7 |
| | ♥ A K Q J 9 8 7 6 |
| | ♦ 3 |
| | ♣ 3 |

| S | W | N | E |
|---|---|---|---|
| | | 3♣ | 3♠ |
| 4♥ | 4♠ | PASS | PASS |
| 5♥ | DOUBLE (1) | END | |

(1) 'The Five-Level is for the opponents.'

**Contract: 5♥ doubled     Opening lead: ♠6**

declarer drew trumps and led a club towards the king. West won the ace and led a second spade, but declarer could win the king, cross to the ace of diamonds, then throw his losing spade on the promoted king of clubs. Eleven tricks and doubled game made.

Perhaps West should have led a trump. Now see if you can make Five Hearts (don't try too hard – you can't).

# Spicy Mixture

Goulash is a version of Bridge in which the pack is not shuffled, and the thirteen cards are dealt in piles of five, five and three. The name apparently comes from Hungarian goulash, a spicy mixture of meat and vegetables, Goulash Bridge deals invariably being spicy too.

Typically a 'ghoulie' is played when the bidding of a normal deal dies out at the one-level (the contract being conceded). The potential swings are enormous, so many contracts end up at the seven-level, no one being prepared to let the opponents declare. Take this deal – from a home game.

With the spade suit winning the auction – as so often in ghoulies – at the inevitable seven-level, West led the three of trumps. It was scarcely possible that a heart would stand up – indeed it might have even given a 'ruff-and-discard' (if declarer and dummy were both void rather than declarer and partner).

Relieved to have escaped a club lead, declarer won the trump (East discarding) and assessed his prospects. He had twelve top tricks – nine trumps and three diamonds. The thirteenth could come from a favourable diamond position (enabling dummy's ten to score a fourth trick in the suit). But the bidding (and trump split) made it clear that East was stashed full of minor-suit cards. Can you see what can be done?

Declarer simply rattled off all nine trumps. On the last round East was squeezed. Dummy's last four cards were his diamonds, so East needed to keep four diamonds. That meant discarding his last club. This promoted declarer's clubs (the only ones left in the pack) and the grand slam was made.

East-West were left regretting that they had pushed North-South from game into small slam, and then from small slam into grand slam.

**Dealer: South**  **Vulnerability: Both**

Rubber (Goulash)

North:
♠ 8 2
♥ 5 2
♦ K Q 10 8
♣ Q 10 8 5 2

West:
♠ Q 3
♥ A K Q J 10 9 8 7 6 4 3
♦ –
♣ –

East:
♠ –
♥ –
♦ J 9 7 6 5 3
♣ A K J 7 6 3

South:
♠ A K J 10 9 7 6 5 4
♥ –
♦ A 4
♣ 9 4

| S | W | N | E |
|---|---|---|---|
| 1♠ | 5♥ | PASS | PASS |
| 5♠ | 6♥ | PASS | PASS |
| 6♠ | PASS | PASS | 7♥ (1) |
| PASS | PASS | 7♠ (2) | END |

(1) It appears strange to bid 7♥ with a void, but if partner has, say, eleven hearts and two clubs, both sides could be making a (grand) slam.

(2) Bidding one more on the principle of 'who knows who can make what, but there are far more points to gain than lose by declaring.'

**Contract: 7♠**  **Opening lead: ♠3**

# Hoary Jest

This deal – from the prestigious US Blue Ribbon Pairs – reminded me of an old hoary jest: what would you lead against Two Notrumps with?

♠ A K 10 8 6 4 3
♥ K Q 10 9 3 2
♦ –
♣ –

Ridiculous of course, as you would hardly let the opponents play Two Notrumps with that once-in-a-lifetime distributional monster!

Less spectacularly, but you would think it unlikely that you would table this hand as dummy:

♠ 8 3
♥ A K J 10 8 7 5 2
♦ –
♣ A 10 9

Yet US Women's World Champion Jill Meyers did precisely that as North, raising partner Zia Mahmood to slam in his suit, clubs. It was to prove a brilliant decision.

Elsewhere round the room, all the selfish Norths (including a tall author from Putney) were declaring heart contracts, normally Five or Six), invariably losing two spades and the queen of trumps to go down. Watch Zia demonstrate the superiority of playing in clubs.

West led out the ace-king of spades. Whilst both honours would survive against a heart contract (South having no hearts with which to ruff), Zia could ruff the second in his club slam. At Trick Three, he led the queen of trumps, and West played low. Should he finesse or rise with the ace?

The a priori odds favour the finesse – it is

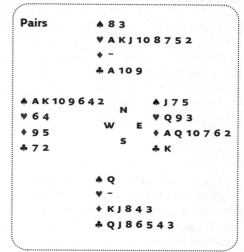

**Pairs**

♠ 8 3
♥ A K J 10 8 7 5 2
♦ –
♣ A 10 9

♠ A K 10 9 6 4 2
♥ 6 4
♦ 9 5
♣ 7 2

♠ J 7 5
♥ Q 9 3
♦ A Q 10 7 6 2
♣ K

♠ Q
♥ –
♦ K J 8 4 3
♣ Q J 8 6 5 4 3

| S (MAHMOOD) | W | N (MEYERS) | E |
|---|---|---|---|
| | 3♠ | 4♥ | 4♠ |
| 5♣ | PASS | 6♣ (1) | END |

(1) The masterstroke.

**Contract: 6♣**          **Opening lead: ♠A**

relatively unlikely that the king will be singleton. But West had opened preemptively and had already revealed the ace-king of spades. Surely he would have opened at the One-Level if he also held another king. Plus, in a motto attributed to Zia himself, 'If they don't cover, they don't have it.'

Declarer rose with the ace and to his delight, East's singleton king was felled. He ruffed a low heart (high), crossed to the nine of trumps, then cashed dummy's top hearts (the queen falling – thanks to ruffing a round), and followed with three of the remaining promoted hearts. Away went his five diamonds, and the slam was made.

# Wait, Listen and Learn

I think that you will find this freak most insightful. You (as South) hold:

♠ A Q 9 7 6 5 4 3
♥ K Q 8 5 2
♦ –
♣ –

You are fourth to speak, vulnerable vs not. Your left-hand opponent opens One Club (playing Strong Notrump and Five-card Majors), partner passes, and right-hand opponent responds One Heart. How many spades do you bid?

Your distributional monster appears to have improved in value, in the light of the heart bid on your right. Not only do your hearts now look well-placed, but you can deduce that partner, likely to be short in hearts, probably has some spades. You can ruff your losing hearts with these trumps, overruffing your left-hand opponent if necessary. Is settling for 'a mere' Four Spades even a tad conservative?

Okay, okay, I'll stop leading you up the garden path. The Austrian expert sitting South bid Four Spades, full of hope. He was soon to be disappointed. Very. Four Spades was doubled (in the metaphorical – bidding boxes were being used – 'voice of thunder'), and, worse, partner ran to Five Clubs. He reverted to Five Spades and, when the dust had settled, was writing down -1100.

Enter South at the other table, Israel's David Birman. He bid no spades at all at his first turn. He passed. This may at first sight seem incredible, when three low spades 'and a bust' opposite would give play for game. However, there is no rush.

East's One Heart bid is 100% forcing, so

**Dealer: West    Vulnerability: North-South**

Teams

|  | ♠ – |  |
|  | ♥ 7 |  |
|  | ♦ Q J 8 7 6 3 |  |
|  | ♣ Q J 10 8 7 6 |  |

| ♠ K 10 8 2 |  | ♠ J |
| ♥ A 10 | N | ♥ J 9 6 4 3 |
| ♦ K 10 5 | W    E | ♦ A 9 4 2 |
| ♣ A 5 3 2 | S | ♣ K 9 4 |

|  | ♠ A Q 9 7 6 5 4 3 |  |
|  | ♥ K Q 8 5 2 |  |
|  | ♦ – |  |
|  | ♣ – |  |

| S | W | N | E |
|---|---|---|---|
|  | 1♣ (1) | PASS | 1♥ |
| PASS (2) | 1♠ | PASS | 1NT |
| 2♠ (3) | END |  |  |

(1) Strong Notrump and Five-card Majors.
(2) 'Let's wait and see.' This was the key bid (or lack of).
(3) 'Hmmm. I heard you bid Spades, West. I'd better be conservative.'

**Contract: 2♠          Opening lead: ♥A**

West will bid again. When you have gleaned as much information as possible, only then need you decide how many spades to bid. When South heard West bid spades, he knew to take the low road.

Two Spades failed by one trick (losing three tricks in each major), but this represented a huge gain for the Israeli team.

The point is this: Normally you enter an auction early to give information to partner. Here partner is basically irrelevant, as he will never play you for this freak. So don't involve him; rather wait, listen and learn.

# Hush at the Table

Goulash Bridge is fun and exciting; but is it really Bridge? Perhaps not... But who cares when hands as rich as this – a Moroccan holiday goulash – are 'dealt'?

Each hand (following a deal in which the bidding died at the one-level) is sorted into suits, added to one another (starting with the dealer and progressing anticlockwise), and then cut once. The cards are dealt out in piles of five, five and three.

East was to regret his double of Six Diamonds at the end of the play – but it was hardly obvious that Seven Clubs would make. When his partner led the normal king of spades, however, there was no defence to beat the grand slam.

Declarer ruffed in hand and needed a minor miracle (or two). He ruffed a low diamond and ruffed a heart (bringing down East's ace – an irrelevancy). He ruffed a second low diamond and noted the fall of the queen from East with interest. He ruffed a second heart and now needed two slices of luck.

Firstly declarer needed the ace of trumps to drop a singleton king. He cashed his ace and – lo and behold – the king appeared from West. He quickly drew East's remaining trumps.

Secondly he needed the king of diamonds to fall under his ace (presumably from East given the fall of his queen of the suit on the second round). Amazingly the ace did fell East's king and now it was a simple matter to cash the jack, catching West's ten, and lead out his two long diamonds. Thirteen tricks and grand slam made.

As the play was concluded there was a hush at the table – all the players knew that they had just partaken in the most extraordinary deal of the week's holiday. The silence was only broken when a kibitzer

(spectator) pointed out that there was one opening lead that would have broken the grand slam. Just one. West needed to lead his singleton king of trumps – impossible!

---

**Dealer: East**       **Vulnerability: Both**

**Rubber (Goulash)**

|            |  |
|------------|--|
| ♠ A 2 | |
| ♥ K J 9 8 6 5 4 3 2 | |
| ♦ – | |
| ♣ 10 3 | |

West:
- ♠ K Q 9 4 3
- ♥ Q 10 7
- ♦ 10 8 6 3
- ♣ K

East:
- ♠ J 10 8 7 6 5
- ♥ A
- ♦ K Q 4
- ♣ 9 5 2

South:
- ♠ –
- ♥ –
- ♦ A J 9 7 5 2
- ♣ A Q J 8 7 6 4

| S | W | N | E |
|------|------|------|------|
|  |  |  | 2♠ (1) |
| 3♣ | 4♠ | 5♥ | PASS |
| 6♦ | PASS | PASS | DOUBLE (2) |
| PASS | PASS | 7♣ (3) | END |

(1) Weak Two – 5-10 points and a six-card suit.
(2) Unwise – as events were to prove.
(3) What he should have bid a round earlier.

**Contract: 7♣**       **Opening lead: ♠K**

# Coup Without a Name

Being part of a game that is still evolving is most exciting. Twenty or so years ago, the manoeuvre necessary to land this Four Spade contract (from a Gala evening at London's Carlton Towers Hotel in aid of The Duke of Edinburgh's Awards) was called, somewhat unhelpfully, 'The Coup Without a Name'. To avoid giving away the point of the deal to those who are familiar with the modern term, I shall only divulge it at the end.

Here is Ely Culbertson (again), on the subject, quoted from his wonderful *Red Book* (published 1934, now sadly out of print), an inspiration to your columnist when a teenager (it was in the school library).

'A group of entry-killing plays that is so superhumanly obvious and yet profound that not more than half a dozen world's masters (including one woman) have seen it and grasped it, while only the rankest of dubs may stumble upon it, has not even a name.'

Can you prevent an enemy diamond ruff after West leads ace and another diamond against your Four Spades?

Say you win the second diamond and lead dummy's queen of trumps. West will win the ace, lead a heart over to his partner's ace, then receive a diamond ruff. Down one.

The solution is to snip the line of communication between the defensive hands by leading the king of clubs from the dummy and, because East does not possess the ace, discarding your singleton heart (key play). You have swapped a heart loser for a club loser but, crucially, prevented West from reaching his partner's hand via the ace of hearts (you can now ruff West's heart switch). On regaining the lead, you then lead a trump and, because West holds the ace (and the jack falls in two rounds), restrict yourself to the loss of West's three aces. Game made.

Because the technique involves snipping

**Pairs**

|  |  |
|---|---|
| | ♠ Q |
| | ♥ K J 8 4 2 |
| | ♦ Q 9 7 |
| | ♣ K J 7 3 |

| ♠ A 3 | | ♠ J 4 |
|---|---|---|
| ♥ Q 10 9 6 3 | N | ♥ A 5 |
| ♦ A 2 | W    E | ♦ 8 5 4 3 |
| ♣ A 10 4 2 | S | ♣ Q 9 8 6 5 |

| |
|---|
| ♠ K 10 9 8 7 6 5 2 |
| ♥ 7 |
| ♦ K J 10 6 |
| ♣ - |

| S | W | N | E |
|---|---|---|---|
| | | 1♥ | PASS |
| 4♠ (1) | END | | |

(1) Not a hand for approach bidding. You know you want to play 4♠; and you wish to prevent the opponents from getting together.

**Contract: 4♠**          **Opening lead: ♦A**

the line of communication between the two defensive hands, it is now termed the 'Scissors Coup'.

# Spread Bet

How can Goulash Bridge be Bridge when the cards are dealt in clumps of five, five and three? That's as maybe, but nonetheless many 'ghoulies' create situations as instructive as they are exciting.

Take this deal from a rubber at London's Portland Club (where ghoulies are played after the bidding has died out at the one-level). South, spread betting maestro and Conservative party benefactor Stuart Wheeler, demonstrated why he has been the leading Portland Club player for some five decades.

A spade opening lead and a trump/club return and all you as declarer can make are your ten top tricks. But on the ace of clubs lead your ruff and...

Did you ruff with the two of trumps? If so, your slam will be defeated by an alert East.

Provided you ruff the club with a higher trump, then lead out two top trumps (both following), you can cash a top spade to strip East of any spades (East does best to discard), but when he proves to have none, you exit with the precious two of trumps (key play).

This sacrifices an unnecessary trump trick to East, but three tricks come back because East now has to give access to the stranded dummy via a minor suit. The ace-king of diamonds and king of clubs provide discards for your three losing spades and the slam is made.

Ruff with the two of trumps at Trick One, however, and East can get rid of his nine and seven of trumps on the first two rounds, and then underplay your third trump with the three. With no way to dummy, you have to give West a couple of spade tricks and so fail in your slam.

Wheeler took the recommended time to plan at Trick One, found the key play of retaining his two of trumps, and so emerged victorious.

**Dealer: West        Vulnerability: Neither**

| Rubber (Goulash) | ♠ – |
| | ♥ – |
| | ♦ A K J 7 4 2 |
| | ♣ K 10 9 8 7 6 5 |

|  |  |  |
|---|---|---|
| ♠ Q 10 9 8 6 | | ♠ – |
| 4 3 2 | N | ♥ 9 7 3 |
| ♥ 6 4 | W    E | ♦ 10 9 8 6 5 3 |
| ♦ Q | S | ♣ J 4 3 2 |
| ♣ A Q | | |

| | ♠ A K J 7 5 |
| | ♥ A K Q J 10 8 5 2 |
| | ♦ – |
| | ♣ – |

| S | W | N | E |
|---|---|---|---|
| | 1♠ | 2♣ (1) | PASS |
| 6♥ (2) | END | | |

(1) You cannot play Stayman or Blackwood at the Portland Club, let alone the Unusual Two Notrump for the minors.

(2) Optimistic – especially at Goulash: the odds of partner having a void in both majors is hugely increased.

**Contract: 6♥            Opening lead: ♣A**

# Twenty Tricks

One of my Bridge club members handed me a crumpled piece of paper, on which was scrawled the inevitable Bridge deal.

At first I thought the hand was fantasy (it was so outrageously freaky). He assured me that it was normally dealt.

On the rare occasions that such wild deals occur, the final contract tends to be a grand slam, often in the highest ranking suit, spades. This was no exception.

It appears as though North-South can make a million tricks with either spades or hearts as trumps. Well – twenty at any rate (if such a thing were possible)!

In a spade contract declarer can trump, say, a diamond lead, trump a club (just for fun), trump a diamond, then score eight more trump tricks and lead the singleton heart to dummy to make the nine heart tricks. Total twenty.

In a heart contract declarer can trump, say, a club lead, trump a diamond (for fun), trump another club, then score seven more trumps and ten spades. Again – total twenty.

However in fact North-South did not make their Seven Spade contract at all, let alone chalk up those seven 'overtricks'. Can you see why not?

It was West's brilliantly conceived opening lead that did the job. Resisting the natural temptation to lead either of his aces, he found the devastating opening lead of his singleton heart. This killed declarer's contract stone dead, by completely severing declarer from dummy's hearts.

Declarer won the heart lead in dummy and did the best he could. He trumped a diamond, trumped a club with dummy's singleton trump, then led a winning heart discarding his remaining club loser. No good – West trumped and the contract was down one.

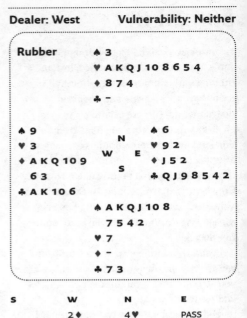

**Rubber**

North
- ♠ 3
- ♥ A K Q J 10 8 6 5 4
- ♦ 8 7 4
- ♣ —

West
- ♠ 9
- ♥ 3
- ♦ A K Q 10 9 6 3
- ♣ A K 10 6

East
- ♠ 6
- ♥ 9 2
- ♦ J 5 2
- ♣ Q J 9 8 5 4 2

South
- ♠ A K Q J 10 8 7 5 4 2
- ♥ 7
- ♦ —
- ♣ 7 3

| S | W | N | E |
|---|---|---|---|
|  | 2♦ | 4♥ | PASS |
| 4♠ | 5♣ | 5♥ | 7♣ |
| 7♠ | END |  |  |

**Contract: 7♠**      **Opening lead: ♥3**

Interestingly Seven Hearts by North would be defeated in a similar manner – by an opening spade lead.

# 434 Days

Assume one deal of Bridge lasts ten minutes, and you play round the clock. By my calculation you will pick up a ten-card suit once every 434 days (on average).

So imagine David Bakhshi's surprise as he picked up South's hand in a Pairs tournament in Norway (which he ultimately won).

Consulting partner with such a hand was certain to be unproductive, so David sensibly jumped to Six Clubs over East's preemptive opening. West toyed with doubling, also with sacrificing in Six Hearts (which would only mean one down). But eventually he opted out, and led the seven of his partner's suit.

Declarer trumped East's king of hearts and rattled off all ten trumps. He knew from the bidding that West was almost certain to have three hearts and both the king of spades and ace of diamonds (giving East the weak hand with seven hearts that his bid suggests).

What would you like West's last three cards to be? He has no winning option. All declarer has to do is keep track of how many hearts West discards.

If West keeps a heart, declarer cashes the ace of spades in the three-card ending (to drop West's king – his last three cards must be the king of spades, a heart and the ace of diamonds).

If West throws all his hearts (as he did in practice) declarer is safe to exit with the jack of diamonds to West's ace. West's last two cards will either be a losing diamond and the king of spades or (more likely and in actuality) the king and another spade. West had to lead into declarer's ace-queen of spades and the slam was made.

It would have been a different story if West had led the ace of diamonds at trick one, and switched to (say) a heart. With

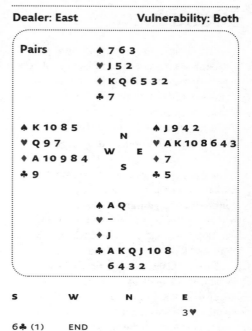

**Dealer: East          Vulnerability: Both**

```
Pairs          ♠ 7 6 3
               ♥ J 5 2
               ♦ K Q 6 5 3 2
               ♣ 7

♠ K 10 8 5              ♠ J 9 4 2
♥ Q 9 7          N      ♥ A K 10 8 6 4 3
♦ A 10 9 8 4   W   E    ♦ 7
♣ 9                S    ♣ 5

               ♠ A Q
               ♥ –
               ♦ J
               ♣ A K Q J 10 8
                 6 4 3 2
```

| S | W | N | E |
|---|---|---|---|
|   |   |   | 3♥ |
| 6♣ (1) | END | | |

(1) Not the time for subtlety.

**Contract: 6♣          Opening lead: ♥7**

declarer's diamond exit card gone, all West would have to do is keep two spades and wait patiently until Trick 13 to win his king.

# Brand New

This was Board Nine of a duplicate at London's Young Chelsea Bridge Club. After it had been played no less than ten times, one of the players summoned the Director – can you see why? More later.

At the table in question, South declared Two Hearts on a trump lead. Playing low from dummy, declarer beat East's jack with the ace and returned a second trump. West took the king and passively returned his third trump. Winning dummy's queen, a low club was led, East playing low and the queen winning. A second club was ducked to East's nine, and East led a low spade.

Declarer played low on the spade and West won the queen and returned a second spade to East's ace. Declarer won a third spade and reflected that East, a passed hand, had turned up with the ace of spades, the jack of trumps and the king of clubs: no room for the ace of diamonds.

At Trick Nine declarer led a low diamond towards dummy's king. West played low so he won dummy's king, cashed the ace of clubs felling the king and jack, and followed with the promoted ten, discarding a diamond. He lost a diamond but took the last trick, his eighth, with the remaining trump. Contract made.

Amongst those other nine results, there were two One Notrump contracts by South (perhaps playing the Mini – i.e. ten to twelve point One Notrump opener), a One Notrump by West, another Two Hearts by South, and two Two Spade contracts by East. Lead away from an ace or a queen and all these contracts fail (by one). Lead away from a king or a jack and they succeed (exactly).

Now, why was the director called? Because the brand new pack had not been shuffled! With North dealing, East received the ace of spades, South the king, West the queen, North the jack etc.

**Pairs**

|  | ♠ J 7 3 |  |
|---|---|---|
|  | ♥ Q 8 4 |  |
|  | ♦ K 9 5 |  |
|  | ♣ A 10 6 2 |  |

| ♠ Q 8 4 | | ♠ A 10 6 2 |
|---|---|---|
| ♥ K 9 5 | N | ♥ J 7 3 |
| ♦ A 10 6 2 | W  E | ♦ Q 8 4 |
| ♣ J 7 3 | S | ♣ K 9 5 |

|  | ♠ K 9 5 |  |
|---|---|---|
|  | ♥ A 10 6 2 |  |
|  | ♦ J 7 3 |  |
|  | ♣ Q 8 4 |  |

| S | W | N | E |
|---|---|---|---|
|  |  | PASS | PASS |
| 1♥ (1) | PASS | 2♥ (2) | END |

(1) Light third-in-hand openers have several advantages. You may steal the bidding or indicate a lead to partner. Plus you do not have to have a planned rebid – able to pass the response.

(2) North would bid 2♣ facing a first or second-hand opener, but, for fear of being left there, sensibly opts for a heavy single raise.

**Contract: 2♥**    **Opening lead: ♥5**

Apart from the fact that no one spotted this until near the end of the evening, what was interesting was the scarcity of pass outs. For everybody had a dead average hand.

I hope you agree – an irresistible way to end a chapter featuring some of the wildest deals you'll ever see!

# It All Goes Wrong

This chapter features some disasters. Not just run-of-the-mill disasters, but truly spectacular calamities: both for declarer – conceding huge 'telephone number' scores (i.e. four figures), and for defenders – seeing their double be redoubled, then the contract make with overtricks.

We will be featuring such characters as my Great Uncle John, who played for a penny-a-hundred all his life; and George, a limousine owner who saw his professional partner pull the wrong card to destroy one of his greatest moments; and a left-handed Welsh international who put the wrong bid on the table (right-handed bidding boxes), only to emerge with one of the most unlikely slam successes ever.

There is one common theme. Contrary to Mrs Bennett, who shot her husband (in 1929) after things had gone wrong (incidentally nowhere near as badly wrong as the calamities in this chapter), all disasters were taken gracefully, with humour. The players remembered the most important thing of all: Bridge may be a wonderful game, but a game is all it is. Not life and death.

# Drifting Off

**Dealer: West**      **Vulnerability: Neither**

Chicago limousine owner George Jacobs suffered all gamut of emotions on this extraordinary deal – from the US Nationals.

Opening a quiet One Club as West, George cannot for a second have dared even hope that his opponents would fetch up in Notrumps. But they did – and at the Six-Level to boot. He was even on lead – what could possibly go wrong?

George led a slightly unorthodox queen of clubs – doubtless to amuse himself – and you would think that North-South's eccentric bidding was about to get its just desserts, losing the first six club tricks and going down five. In fact the slam made. Can you work out how?

East, jazz pianist and San Francisco Bridge professional Ron Smith, was not paying the deal his full attention (after all he did not have much to get excited about). The queen of clubs lead looked for all the world like a boring top a of a queen-jack-ten sequence and he took his eye off the ball. He inadvertently dropped a spade on the table.

Declarer exerted his rights – as per the Rulebook – and requested West to play a spade at Trick Two. George's face fell. It was like having a winning lottery ticket stolen from under his nose. Declarer won his spade switch, and was soon claiming the remainder – with a plethora of spade and diamond winners. Twelve tricks and slam made.

George is a good-humoured man (as well as being a pretty decent Bridge player) and laughed wryly, saying to his partner, 'My fault. If I hadn't been so clever-clever and led the queen of clubs, instead preferring the normal top-of-a-sequence ace, you would not have drifted off.'

**Teams**

|  | North |
|---|---|
| ♠ | K J 9 7 5 4 3 |
| ♥ | A K |
| ♦ | A 3 |
| ♣ | 9 8 |

| West | | East |
|---|---|---|
| ♠ 8 2 | N | ♠ 10 6 |
| ♥ J 6 2 | W   E | ♥ 10 8 7 5 4 |
| ♦ 9 6 | S | ♦ 10 8 7 4 |
| ♣ A K Q J 4 3 | | ♣ 6 2 |

|  | South |
|---|---|
| ♠ | A Q |
| ♥ | Q 9 3 |
| ♦ | K Q J 5 2 |
| ♣ | 10 7 5 |

| S | W (JACOBS) | N | E |
|---|---|---|---|
| | 1♣ | 1♠ | PASS |
| 3NT (1) | PASS | 6NT (2) | PASS |
| PASS | PASS (3) | | |

(1) Very strange effort – with not the vestige of a club stopper. Perhaps he recalled the words of the late Scottish writer Hugh Kelsey, 'When you have shown a stopper in the bidding, you do not need one for the play.'

(2) Not the wild gamble it looks. Give partner a fitting spade honour plus a club stopper, and the slam will not be too far away.

(3) Wisely refrains from doubling – in case North runs to Seven Spades and East finds the wrong opening lead. How bad can 6NT down five be...?

**Contract: 6NT**      **Opening lead: ♣Q**

# Beat That

On this deal, overcalling Three or Four Hearts over East's preempt was too mundane for South. West doubled his choice of Three Notrumps, and South gave his gamble the vote of confidence by redoubling. Everybody stood their ground (though North twitched a little), and West led the ace of clubs.

That was a clever lead, keeping the defensive options open. When dummy appeared, West was able to work out to switch to a low spade. How? Dummy held a club stopper – making a club continuation unappealing; and a diamond lead would more profitably come from his partner. So a spade it was, West selecting a low card because it was likely either his partner or declarer had a singleton ace/king.

East won Trick Two with the ace of spades, felling declarer's king, and switched to the queen of diamonds. Declarer would have done a little better to duck his king. Had he done so, the queen would win, West would win the second diamond with the ace, cash the king of clubs (East discarding a heart), then lead a low spade to East's ten. East would cash his six remaining diamonds and give declarer the last (heart) trick.

Understandably, however, declarer played the king of diamonds on the queen, his heart sinking when West won the ace. West cashed the queen-jack of spades and the king of clubs (East discarding his two hearts). then led his second diamond. East simply tabled his last seven cards – all diamonds – and declarer had not scored a single trick!

A massive +5200 points to East-West. Beat that!

**Dealer: East** **Vulnerability: Game All**

Rubber

|  | ♠ 9 8 5 4 2 |  |
|---|---|---|
|  | ♥ 9 5 4 |  |
|  | ♦ 2 |  |
|  | ♣ J 10 6 4 |  |

| ♠ Q J 7 6 3 | N | ♠ A 10 |
| ♥ 7 | W E | ♥ 10 3 |
| ♦ A 6 | S | ♦ Q J 10 9 8 |
| ♣ A K 9 5 3 |  | ♣ 2 |
|  |  | 5 4 3 |

|  | ♠ K |
|  | ♥ A K Q J 8 6 2 |
|  | ♦ K 7 |
|  | ♣ Q 8 7 |

| S | W | N | E |
|---|---|---|---|
|  |  |  | 3♦ (1) |
| 3NT (2) | DOUBLE | PASS | PASS |
| REDOUBLE (3) | END |  |  |

(1) Many would open Four Diamonds – holding a sequential eight-card suit.
(2) Seven running hearts, the king of diamonds, and a trick 'in the wash'. Here's hoping...
(3) ...and backing his judgement.

**Contract: 3NT redoubled**

**Opening lead: ♣A**

# Arbitration

**Teams**

|  | ♠ 8 5 4 2 |  |
|---|---|---|
|  | ♥ 4 |  |
|  | ♦ 8 5 |  |
|  | ♣ J 7 6 4 3 2 |  |

| ♠ 6 3 | | ♠ A K 10 9 7 |
|---|---|---|
| ♥ A K 9 8 5 | N | ♥ 10 |
| ♦ 10 9 7 6 4 | W       E | ♦ A Q J 3 2 |
| ♣ 8 | S | ♣ A 5 |

|  | ♠ Q J |  |
|---|---|---|
|  | ♥ Q J 7 6 3 2 |  |
|  | ♦ K |  |
|  | ♣ K Q 10 9 |  |

Some huge penalties resulted from this deal from the London Easter Festival Teams. So much so, that the couple we were playing in the next match were still talking about it. As usual, I was called in to arbitrate.

*Man (North)*: 'You shouldn't have over-called Two Hearts.'

*Woman (South)*: 'Come on, it's a normal bid. I'm sorry it went for such a large number (1100), but it's just one of those things.'

Normally I refrain from entering such discussions, but I couldn't resist supporting the hapless South, who had clearly suffered enough in the play to her Two Hearts doubled, to hear further from her partner:

'Actually, I reckon Two Hearts doubled can go down five – for minus 1400; you (South) saved a trick in the play.'

I ventured to continue, 'Perhaps you (North) should have rescued your partner into Three Clubs. That's just two down doubled – not bad given that East-West can make a diamond slam.'

Equilibrium restored, we could begin the new match. However let us return to the deal and see how declarer can be held to three tricks in Two Hearts doubled.

West leads the six of spades, and East wins the king, cashes the ace, then switches to his trump (key play). West covers declarer's jack with the king, and switches to the ten of diamonds to East's ace, felling declarer's king.

East leads the ten of spades, ruffed and overruffed, and West's second diamond is ruffed by declarer, who advances the king of clubs. Winning his ace, East leads the nine of spades, ruffed and overruffed, and West leads a third diamond. Declarer ruffs with his penultimate trump, and when he leads a master club, West can ruff, cash the ace of

| S | W | N | E |
|---|---|---|---|
|  |  |  | 1♠ |
| 2♥ (1) | PASS (2) | PASS | DOUBLE (3) |
| PASS | PASS (4) | PASS (5) |  |

(1) Acceptable in spite of (a) the vulnerability, (b) the acelessness, and (c) the result!

(2) Double would be negative, so West must wait for his partner's reopening take-out double.

(3) Playing Negative Doubles, it is compulsory to reopen with double, when holding shortage in their suit.

(4) Converting it into penalties.

(5) Trickless for hearts, North should run to 3♣ (just down two).

**Contract: 2♥ doubled    Opening lead: ♠6**

trumps felling the queen, and follow with two winning diamonds. Down five and East-West +1400.

# Names Withheld

Dealer: West          Vulnerability: Both

Teams

```
                   ♠ K Q J 9
                   ♥ 8 3
                   ♦ K J 10 9 5 2
                   ♣ 4
    ♠ -                          ♠ 10 8 5 3
    ♥ A J 10 7 4        N        ♥ Q 9 6 2
    ♦ 7 4 3        W       E     ♦ A
    ♣ A K J 10 6       S         ♣ 8 7 5 3
                   ♠ A 7 6 4 2
                   ♥ K 5
                   ♦ Q 8 6
                   ♣ Q 9 2
```

What is the biggest penalty you have ever lost? I have lost 2000 points when making precisely no tricks in One Notrump doubled. But that was comfortably exceeded when a bidding misunderstanding (no kidding!) saw me lose 3400 points in Three Spades redoubled (one member of the 'partnership' thought that the redouble was for rescue; the other did not).

In the US Nationals, my team-mates (names withheld to avoid a mauling next time I see them) went for 2300 points. Here's how...

West led the ace of clubs against the Four Notrump doubled contract, East discouraging with the three. Reading declarer with the king of hearts for his notrump bidding, West sought to put his partner on play for a club lead through declarer's presumed queen of the suit. He duly found the diamond shift.

East won his ace of diamonds and fired through a club. Declarer forlornly played the nine, but West won the ten and cashed the king, felling declarer's queen. At Trick Five, West astutely led the six of clubs across to his partner's eight, enabling a heart lead to come from the right quarter.

East switched to the queen of hearts, covered by declarer's king and West's ace and four more heart winners followed shortly after. When the dust had settled, the defence had taken the first eleven tricks. Declarer was eight down: -2300.

| S | W | N | E |
|---|---|---|---|
|  | 1♥ | 2♦ | 2♥ (1) |
| 3NT (2) | 4♥ | PASS | PASS |
| 4NT (3) | DOUBLE | PASS (4) | PASS |
| PASS (5) |  |  |  |

(1) A 3♥ bid on the Losing Trick Count.
(2) Expecting a heart trick (with ♥K) on the lead, ♠A, six diamond tricks for the vulnerable overcall, and a 'trick in the wash'.
(3) When I asked South if, on reflection, he should have done something different at some stage in the auction or whether it was 'just one of those things', he said that he might have tried 4♠ at this juncture - to offer a choice.
(4) Is there a case for North to remove to 5♦? Though his partner has not really involved him, he knows he is highly unsuitable for Notrumps.
(5) Last chance to run to the safer haven of 5♦.

**Contract: 4NT doubled   Opening lead: ♣A**

# Then East Smiled

Dealer: South      Vulnerability: Neither

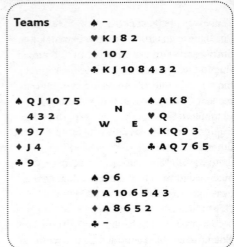

More than almost any game, Bridge is full of surprises. Some happy, some not.

Take East on this deal from the US Vanderbilt. With his 20 points facing a partner who had bid up to the five-level, East must have felt pretty confident that he would shortly be writing down at least a medium-sized penalty from the opponents' Six Hearts sacrifice. He was to be surprised – and not the happy variety.

West led the nine of clubs and declarer, after due reflection, made the excellent play of ducking in dummy. He deduced that the nine was singleton (or West would probably have led a spade), and did not want to release one of dummy's honours. East naturally played low too, and declarer ruffed.

At Trick Two declarer cashed the ace of trumps, felling East's queen, then crossed to dummy's king, drawing West's second trump. He next led the king of clubs. East covered with the ace and he ruffed. He ruffed a spade and then led the jack of clubs for a second ruffing finesse. East covered with the queen and declarer ruffed again. He ruffed his second spade with dummy's last trump and then cashed the four established club winners in dummy, discarding his four diamond losers. At Trick Twelve he led to his ace of diamonds and finally took the last trick with his remaining trump.

Declarer had made his doubled slam with an overtrick, leaving East astounded. He had not taken one single trick with his power-house! His first reaction was to lash out: at his partner for not removing his final double to Six Spades (just one or two down, depending on whether the defence find their club ruff); and at his opponents for their luck. Then he smiled. What an incredible game Bridge is, he mused, when such an

unexpected turn of events can take place. He made a mental note to be on the right side next time.

| S | W | N | E |
|---|---|---|---|
| 2♥ (1) | PASS | 4♥ | DOUBLE (2) |
| PASS | 4♠ | 5♥ | DOUBLE (3) |
| PASS | 5♠ | 6♥ | DOUBLE (4) |
| END | | | |

(1) Weak Two. Six-card suit and six to ten points.

(2) The first of East's three doubles was for take-out.

(3) East's second double was optional. Partner was expected to remove to Five Spades with a hand better suited to play than defence (the actuality). Otherwise to pass.

(4) East's third double was basically penalty.

**Contract: 6♥ doubled    Opening lead: ♣9**

# Portuguese Calamity

Dealer: South     Vulnerability: Neither

There was plenty of excitement on the Portuguese coastline a couple of years back during early November. And I'm not referring to the amazing surf; nor to the turn of the roulette wheel. I'm talking about the constant buzz that was the World Bridge Championships.

Until recently, the latter stages of the Bermuda Bowl (Open) and Venice Cup (Ladies) would be held in an atmosphere of austere silence; for most of the players – eliminated – would have headed home.

Things have changed. These days the second week sees a fresh event take place, the Transnational Teams. Open to those gone from the main events, plus to anyone else (and as the name suggests, you do not need to play with partners and/or teammates from the same country), a fresh energy arrives, and ensures that the fortnight ends with a bang.

It was on this deal – from the Portuguese Transnationals – that the biggest penalty of the fourteen days occurred. West led the ten of spades against Five Diamonds doubled, East winning the jack and returning a heart.

Declarer won the ace of hearts, and could have secured down three by knocking out the ace of clubs, cashing one top trump, then running clubs and cross-ruffing. This would hardly have represented a victory – with Four Spades almost certain to fail on the likely singleton heart opening lead to the ace and a heart ruff. But it would not have been a calamity.

Winning the ace of hearts and playing ace and a second trump at Tricks Three and Four *was* a calamity. A huge one. For East was able to draw all the trumps, put his partner in with a second heart, receive a spade through the king to score both his spades, then put West back on play with a third heart to cash his

**Teams**

|  | ♠ K 4 2 |  |
|---|---|---|
|  | ♥ 8 |  |
|  | ♦ J 7 4 2 |  |
|  | ♣ J 9 8 6 4 |  |

| ♠ 10 9 8 6 5 3 |  | ♠ A Q J |
|---|---|---|
| ♥ K Q 9 5 | N | ♥ 10 6 4 2 |
| ♦ 8 | W    E | ♦ K Q 10 9 |
| ♣ A 10 | S | ♣ 3 2 |

|  | ♠ 7 |  |
|---|---|---|
|  | ♥ A J 7 3 |  |
|  | ♦ A 6 5 3 |  |
|  | ♣ K Q 7 5 |  |

| S | W | N | E |
|---|---|---|---|
| 1♦ | 1♠ | 3♦ (1) | 4♠ |
| 5♦ (2) | PASS | PASS | DOUBLE |
| END |  |  |  |

(1) Preemptive – in the modern style.
(2) Very poorly judged. South's hand is much better suited to defence than play (how much better to have ♦Axxx than ♦KQJx for defence).

**Contract: 5♦ doubled   Opening lead: ♠10**

long spades. Declarer won no more tricks and was limited to his two red aces. Down nine – 2300 points to East-West!

# Great Uncle John

You do not need to play Bridge for money to appreciate its joys fully – unlike Poker and Backgammon. However a small stake can add a certain froissant to proceedings. My Great Uncle John always played for a penny a hundred and kept a record all his life. I believe he died £11.21 in profit. This may not sound much, but it represents well over 100 more rubbers won than rubbers lost.

Great Uncle John's profits would have been severely dented if the same fate befell him as befell one James Walker, sitting West on this deal (try to cover up the other three hands before reading on). The critical card, as so often, was the opening lead. West cogitated – what did his partner's double of the Three Notrump contract mean?

Have you discussed what such a double would mean with your favourite partner? Does it mean 'Lead your bid suit'? Or does it mean 'Please try to find my suit'? In many ways the more logical interpretation is the latter – with the double actually steering partner away from the lead he was about to make (the same principle as the Lightner Slam Double).

West was unsure, but in the end he reasoned as follows: if my partner wants me to lead a heart (and I lead one), then I am 100% sure to be right; but if he doesn't (and I try another lead) then I am blindly guessing between the three other suits. Thus West finally placed the eight of hearts on the table – perhaps his partner held the king?

No good! Declarer won dummy's jack of hearts, then ran the six diamond winners and followed with the four spade winners. Eleven tricks were scored in the redoubled game – no less than 2000 points (including 700 for the rubber) to North-South.

Had West guessed to lead the queen of clubs, and then followed with a second club

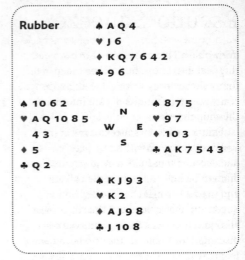

**Rubber**

|  | ♠ A Q 4 |  |
|  | ♥ J 6 |  |
|  | ♦ K Q 7 6 4 2 |  |
|  | ♣ 9 6 |  |

| ♠ 10 6 2 | | ♠ 8 7 5 |
| ♥ A Q 10 8 5 | | ♥ 9 7 |
| ♦ 4 3 | | ♦ 10 3 |
| ♦ 5 | | ♣ A K 7 5 4 3 |
| ♣ Q 2 | | |

|  | ♠ K J 9 3 |  |
|  | ♥ K 2 |  |
|  | ♦ A J 9 8 |  |
|  | ♣ J 10 8 |  |

| S | W | N | E |
|---|---|---|---|
| 1 NT | 2 ♥ | 3NT | DOUBLE |
| PASS | PASS | REDOUBLE | END |

**Contract: 3NT redoubled**

**Opening lead: ♥8**

when it held the trick, the defence would have taken all thirteen tricks. East would have run his six club winners and then switched to a heart through declarer's king. West would have won the last seven tricks with his hearts. Three Notrumps redoubled down nine (!) would score a massive 5200 points to East-West.

West choice of opening lead had swung 7200 points! Such a deficit – 72 pence at a penny a hundred – might take Great Uncle John six months hard grind at the table to recoup.

# Submarine Pseudo-Squeeze

We would all have hated to have been East on this deal. But I hope he will have seen the funny side before too long – what happened really was quite amusing. I am informed that the coup that declarer pulled off is called a 'submarine pseudo-squeeze'.

West kicked off with the jack of spades, and declarer won the king and ran his eight diamond winners. He discarded all four clubs and two hearts from hand, leaving ace-queen-three of spades and the king of hearts. His main hope was that a spade would be discarded to enable his three to become a length winner.

But West correctly came down to ten-nine-seven of spades and one other card. East was in no real difficulty, and discarded two spades, two hearts and three clubs.

The crunch moment was nearing. Declarer crossed to his queen of spades, and cashed his ace. With two cards remaining East held both his aces. He was fairly relaxed – presuming that declarer would be leading a club or a heart. But declarer, a wily fellow, did not. He led his losing spade. West won the ten, and East...

Poor East had to try to work out what West's last card was. Eventually he guessed to discard the ace of clubs and keep the ace of hearts.

West tabled his last card – the four of clubs. Disaster – dummy's ten took the last trick. East had made neither of his aces! Doubled slam made.

Dealer: North    Vulnerability: East-West

Rubber

|  | ♠ 4 2 |
|  | ♥ 5 |
|  | ♦ K Q J 10 7 4 3 2 |
|  | ♣ 10 7 |

| ♠ J 10 9 7 |   | ♠ 8 6 5 |
| ♥ 10 8 7 6 2 | N | ♥ A J 9 4 |
| ♦ 9 8 | W    E | ♦ 6 |
| ♣ 4 3 | S | ♣ A 9 8 5 2 |

|  | ♠ A K Q 3 |
|  | ♥ K Q 3 |
|  | ♦ A 5 |
|  | ♣ K Q J 6 |

| S | W | N | E |
|---|---|---|---|
|  |  | 5♦ (1) | PASS |
| 6NT (2) | PASS | PASS | DOUBLE (3) |
| END |  |  |  |

(1) Intended to block the opposition, in fact blocking partner...

(2) Unable to ask for aces (the bidding being above 4NT), South takes the plunge. In truth this bid is not sound – for why should partner hold an ace?

(3) Surely both aces must score...

**Contract: 6NT doubled    Opening lead: ♠J**

# Winning Tenuously

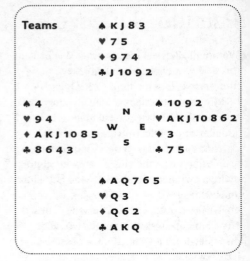

If you could always make the most effective opening lead, you would quickly move through the ranks, become a county champion, then an international star, and shortly after a world champion. It is that important.

On this deal, from the China Cup, you are West. Cover up the other three hands, look at the auction, and decide on your opening lead to Three Notrumps (doubled by partner). The lead of one suit will give you an unbelievable 2600 points. The lead of another will see the contract make. What is your choice?

West reasoned as follows. 'I could cash a top diamond, but if partner has a singleton and South has queen and two small cards, it is important that I do not rid partner of his one card. Instead I need to put partner on lead to play his singleton.' So far so good. He continued, 'Partner's double is probably based on a solid or semi-solid suit, and from the fact that the opponents have not sought to play in a major suit and from the fact that I hold four clubs, his suit is likely to be spades or hearts. If it is a completely solid suit, I am guessing blindly between the two. If it is a semi-solid suit, then holding a singleton may not be enough to enable him to run his winners. But if I hold a doubleton...'

It was all very tenuous reasoning, but such is the stuff of winners. At Trick One West placed the nine of hearts on the table. East won the king, then cashed the ace, felling South's queen. East elatedly continued with his five remaining heart winners, and West discarded his five losing black cards. After finishing his hearts, East correctly led his singleton diamond and West won his ten, cashed the ace-king (felling declarer's queen) and then tabled his last three cards, all diamond winners.

| S | W | N | E |
|---|---|---|---|
|  | 3♦ (1) | PASS | PASS |
| 3NT (2) | PASS | PASS | DOUBLE |
| END |  |  |  |

(1) Only a six-card suit, but otherwise the hand is perfect for a three-level opener.
(2) A better bid than a take-out double (flawed without hearts), or a Three Spade overcall (too many points and not 'spadey' enough). Theoretically better, I mean. But not in practice, as you will see...

**Contract: 3NT doubled   Opening lead: ♥9**

Declarer had not won a single trick. Nine down(!) represented an incredible 2600 points to North-South. But don't be too critical of their bidding. It is tough to bid over preempts and if West had led a black suit, declarer would have actually made his contract. Wow!

# Left-handed Box

Look at just West's hand and the auction – from the 2004 England vs Wales Home International match in Crawley, West Sussex.

*Question*: What is going on?

*Hint*: At the end of the auction, the Welsh South requests a left-handed bidding box.

The English West chose to lead the ace of spades against Six Notrumps doubled – perhaps a look at dummy would shed light on the surprising state of affairs. He continued with a low spade and declarer beat East's jack with the queen.

Declarer cashed the ace of diamonds, West discarding a club, and followed with the ace of hearts, a club to dummy's ace, and the king of hearts discarding a spade. He then took the marked diamond finesse (leading to the jack), scoring the remaining tricks with his five diamonds and king of spades. Twelve tricks and doubled slam made. Wales +1660.

Have you realised what happened? South pulled the wrong card (One Heart) out of his bidding box and did not notice his inadvertency until too late. Totally fixed over his partner's raise to Four Hearts (bidding Five Diamonds now would sound like a slam try in hearts, not an attempt to play), he took the practical escape route of jumping to Six Notrumps.

I presume that West smelt a rat (there is surely no hand that could open One Heart and then, over a game raise in the suit, leap to slam in notrumps). But suspecting that South meant to open One Diamond rather than One Heart did not solve his opening lead problem.

Cashing the ace of spades seems reasonable, but look what happens on an opening club lead (or a club switch at Trick Two – the king for choice – after cashing the ace of spades). Declarer wins dummy's ace and leads to the ace of diamonds. With no re-entry to dummy to take the marked finesse

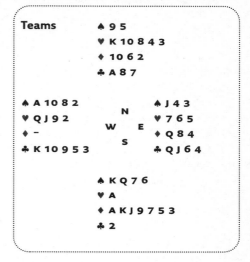

Teams

♠ 9 5
♥ K 10 8 4 3
♦ 10 6 2
♣ A 8 7

♠ A 10 8 2          ♠ J 4 3
♥ Q J 9 2           ♥ 7 6 5
♦ –                 ♦ Q 8 4
♣ K 10 9 5 3        ♣ Q J 6 4

♠ K Q 7 6
♥ A
♦ A K J 9 7 5 3
♣ 2

| S | W | N | E |
|---|---|---|---|
| 1♥ (?!) | PASS | 4♥ | PASS |
| 6NT (?!) | DOUBLE | END | |

This really was the auction. For why, see text. At the other table the auction went more normally: 1♦-Double-1♥-2♣-2♠-4♣-4♦-Pass-5♦-End. Making Six.

**Contract: 6NT doubled(!) Opening lead: ♠A**

in the suit, he has to give up the queen and watch four clubs being cashed. Five down – England +1400.

# CHAPTER 16

# Bridge around Britain

Figures vary hugely – between half a million and a staggering two-and-a-half million – as to the number of Bridge players in Britain. More hotel rooms are taken by Bridge players than any other single group, and Bridge vies neck-and-neck with fishing as the most popular recreational pursuit in the country. With people living longer and longer, and research showing that Bridge-playing keeps the brain active and slows down Alzheimer's more than just about any other activity, the game can look forward to a rosy future.

This chapter sees us tour the country: beginning in North West London's St John's Wood with a record-breaking 72-hour Bridge marathon. After a foray into Charity and Trials Bridge, we move up-country to Staffordshire and on to Cumbria. We then return to the scene of Britain's two strongest tournaments, Stratford upon Avon and Brighton. We finish in London, perhaps appropriately, at the House of Commons.

However never forget: the most important Bridge games are the ones played in your village hall, and in your living room.

# Record Breaker

Dealer: North          Vulnerability: Both*

What is the longest game of Bridge in which you have ever participated? I once played for 28 straight hours (predictably whilst a university student). But this pales into insignificance compared with the Guinness World Record breaking 72-hour game that took place recently at St. John's Wood Bridge Club.

The eight players, including internationals Gareth Birdsall and David Gold (incidentally the two biggest winners) played a total of 253 chicagos (over 1000 deals), averaging fourteen deals per hour (a fast rate for a short game, let alone for 72 continuous hours).

Lest you think that the standards slipped as the hours passed, here is one of the players, Hampshire's Gad Chadha, to demonstrate his card-playing skills in a thin Six Notrump slam.

Receiving a passive – but favourable – heart lead, declarer played low from dummy and beat East's jack with the ace. He returned a second heart to dummy's ten and East's king and a third heart was led back to dummy's queen.

Declarer crossed to his ace of spades (catering to a singleton queen), returned to dummy's ace of clubs, then successfully finessed the jack of spades. He cashed the king of spades (hoping for an even split) but West discarded (a diamond). The thirteenth heart saw both West and dummy throw diamonds, and East discard a club. But what could East discard when declarer followed by cashing dummy's king-queen of clubs?

Unable to let go a spade (or dummy's last spade would be promoted), East threw a diamond. But a diamond to the ace-king removed all the remaining cards in the suit and declarer scored the last trick – his twelfth – with the lowly four of diamonds.

Slam made.

**Rubber**

|  | North |  |
|---|---|---|
|  | ♠ 7 5 4 3 |  |
|  | ♥ Q 10 3 |  |
|  | ♦ 5 3 |  |
|  | ♣ A K Q 2 |  |

| West | | East |
|---|---|---|
| ♠ 9 8 | N | ♠ Q 10 6 2 |
| ♥ 7 6 5 | W   E | ♥ K J 8 |
| ♦ Q J 8 7 | S | ♦ 10 9 6 |
| ♣ J 8 7 5 | | ♣ 10 9 6 |

|  | South |  |
|---|---|---|
|  | ♠ A K J |  |
|  | ♥ A 9 4 2 |  |
|  | ♦ A K 4 2 |  |
|  | ♣ 4 3 |  |

| S | W | N | E |
|---|---|---|---|
|  |  | 1♣ (1) | PASS |
| 6NT (2) | END | | |

(1) Trying to pinch the 20 points for the vulnerable game, at the same time indicating a lead for partner should the deal belong to the opposition.

(2) Having a part-score when slamming often creates confusion. Unsure of which bids would be forcing (there is much to be said for playing all bids that are forcing without the part-score – e.g. a simple change of suit – remain forcing with the part-score), South takes the direct approach.

**Contract: 6NT**          **Opening lead: ♥7**

*North-South have 90 part-score.

# Vow of Silence

**Dealer: South**      **Vulnerability: Both**

Hampshire's David Bird has taken over Victor Mollo's handle as the best Bridge writer of wit. You will chuckle endlessly as you read (amongst others) his accounts of St Titus' Monastery. Take Brother Anthony, who has taken a vow of silence, and not uttered a word (or a bid) for 40 years. Finally, the Brother holds ♣KQJx and two aces and cannot resist doubling Five Clubs – only to find (surprise, surprise) that he can't beat it.

This deal comes from the Cancer Research UK's annual Bridge Tournament, with Bird's commentary. Six Hearts is an odds-on bet, appearing at first glance to depend on a 3-2 spade split (cashing the ace-king and giving up the third round, so promoting your fourth card). Can you do better?

Reflect that West would have led a top club if holding ace-king. With East marked with at least one of those honours, you can make your slam by using dummy's clubs (via ruffing finesses).

As Bird reports, win the diamond, lead the seven of trumps to dummy's eight (preserving the two) and noting the two-one split, then play dummy's queen of clubs. If East rises with the ace, you ruff, lead the nine of trumps to the ten, and pass the jack of clubs (discarding a spade). West wins the king but you can win his (say) diamond return, lead the two of trumps to the three, and discard your other spade loser on the promoted ten of clubs.

If East plays low on the queen of clubs, discard a spade. West wins the king and returns a diamond, so win, lead the nine of trumps to the ten and follow with the jack of clubs. East's ace is ruffed out (with a high trump), the two of trumps is led to the three, and the other small spade thrown on the ten of clubs. Twelve tricks and slam made.

Did you spot the ruffing club finesse?

**Pairs**

|                | ♠ 9 7 5 4        |                |
|                | ♥ 10 8 3         |                |
|                | ♦ 4 3            |                |
|                | ♣ Q J 10 3       |                |

```
          ♠ 9 7 5 4
          ♥ 10 8 3
          ♦ 4 3
          ♣ Q J 10 3

♠ Q 10 8 2         N          ♠ J
♥ 5 4                          ♥ 6
♦ Q J 10 2     W       E      ♦ 9 8 7 6 5
♣ K 9 6            S          ♣ A 8 7 5 4 2

          ♠ A K 6 3
          ♥ A K Q J 9 7 2
          ♦ A K
          ♣ -
```

| S | W | N | E |
|---|---|---|---|
| 2♣ (1) | PASS | 2♦ (2) | PASS |
| 2♥ | PASS | 3♥ | PASS |
| 6♥ (3) | END | | |

(1) 23+ points or any game-force.
(2) Zero to seven points – the conventional negative.
(3) Hard to find out whether partner's spades will prevent a loser, South takes the practical route.

**Contract: 6♥**      **Opening lead: ♦Q**

# Stage Two

The format varies from year to year, but as of a year or so ago... in order to win the World Bridge Championships for England you needed to form a team of four to six players. And then...

Stage One. Finish in the top three teams in the Pre-Trials (over two weekends) where you will be joined by five exempted teams.

Stage Two. Finish in the top four (out of eight) in the main Trials (over two weekends).

Stage Three. Win the Semifinal (128 deals).

Stage Four. Win the Final (160 deals).

Stage Five. Finish in the top five teams in the European Championships (two gruelling weeks).

Stage Six. Finally, win the World Championships (two more hard weeks).

And during that year-or-so-ago campaign... Fancied though the Forrester (our captain) squad of six players (including your author) was beforehand, we made very heavy weather of things, only squeaking through in fourth place. This deal assisted our cause.

Correctly expecting to take no spade tricks against Five Hearts doubled, West led a club. Can you see how declarer can take advantage?

East is marked with the king of diamonds for his One Notrump overcall (dooming the finesse), so the question is how to avoid losing to that card in addition to the ace-king of trumps. Endplay technique is required. This involves stripping East of his safe exits in the black suits before putting him on lead with his top trumps. A three-three club split is required and correct order of play is as follows:

Win the club lead with the ace, trump your spade, cash the king-queen of clubs (key play – stripping East of his clubs), and only then lead a trump. East wins his king, cashes the ace, but is then stuck.

**Dealer: North    Vulnerability: North-South**

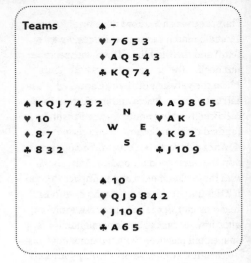

**Contract: 5♥ doubled    Opening lead: ♣3**

| S | W | N | E |
|---|---|---|---|
| | | 1♦ | 1NT |
| 2♥ | 4♠ | 5♥ | DOUBLE |
| END | | | |

If East leads a spade, declarer discards a diamond from his hand, trumps in dummy, and then discards a second diamond on the thirteenth club. If East leads a diamond, it is round to dummy's ace-queen, declarer's third diamond going on the thirteenth club. Contract made.

750 much needed (and rather fortunate) points to North-South. On to Stage Three!

# Neck and Neck

The scene was a Staffordshire Bridge Club. A needle match between the President's Team and the Captain's Team was neck and neck.

On the very last deal, the Captain's Team had bid to Two Hearts and made nine tricks. Bob Beech, sitting South for the President's Team, did rather better.

After a delicate auction to Four Spades, he won the queen of diamonds opening lead with the ace, and led a low trump from hand at Trick Two (the correct play in case West held a singleton ace). East beat dummy's king with the ace, cashed the king of diamonds, then exited passively with a trump.

Declarer won the jack of trumps, cashed the queen, then set about hearts. Deducing that West would be unlikely to overcall Two Diamonds, vulnerable, with three hearts headed by the jack, he cashed the ace of hearts, crossed to the queen, finessed the ten of hearts (West discarding a diamond), and cashed the king, discarding a club from dummy (as West discarded another diamond). Needing to avoid more than one club loser, and placing West with the strength for his bid, declarer now found an ingenious play.

At Trick Ten he led the king of clubs (key play). West won the ace (ducking would have been no use as declarer would merely lead towards dummy's queen). After winning his ace, West was completely endplayed. If he led a diamond, declarer would trump in one hand and discard his club loser from the other hand. West's actual decision to return the nine of clubs worked no better. Declarer played low from dummy and won the lead with his ten. Game, Set and Match for the President's Team!

East left the table kicking himself. If he had returned a club after cashing the king of diamonds, no endplay would have operated and the Captain's Team would have emerged the victors.

**Dealer: South**  **Vulnerability: Both**

**Teams**

|  | ♠ K 8 7 5 |  |
|---|---|---|
|  | ♥ Q 9 3 |  |
|  | ♦ 5 4 |  |
|  | ♣ Q 6 5 2 |  |

| ♠ 10 4 | | ♠ A 9 2 |
| ♥ 8 6 | N | ♥ J 7 5 2 |
| ♦ Q J 10 9 8 6 | W   E | ♦ K 7 2 |
| ♣ A J 9 | S | ♣ 7 4 3 |

|  | ♠ Q J 6 3 |  |
|---|---|---|
|  | ♥ A K 10 4 |  |
|  | ♦ A 3 |  |
|  | ♣ K 10 8 |  |

| S | W | N | E |
|---|---|---|---|
| 1♥ | 2♦ | 2♥ (1) | PASS |
| 2♠ (2) | PASS | 3♠ | PASS |
| 4♠ | END | | |

(1) A negative double – essentially for take-out with four spades – would be nice (if available).

(2) Key bid. South is worth one move towards game, and why not try Two Spades in case partner has four spades and three hearts?

**Contract: 4♠**  **Opening lead: ♦Q**

# Spring Ruffian

'Bridge for All', the brainchild of lady international Sandra Landy, is an attempt by the English Bridge Union to centralise Bridge teaching in this country. The scheme has its detractors, mainly on grounds of cost, or lack of flexibility. But there is little doubt that, by giving structure to the less experienced teachers, the scheme has improved teaching standards overall. As such, it should be lauded.

One *Spring Ruffian* (the Bridge for All magazine) contained an interesting deal, sent in by Cumbrian teacher Philip Wraight, in which one of his second year students managed to overcome a set-up defensive Trump Promotion.

West led his singleton spade to East's queen and East continued with the ace. Declarer correctly ruffed with the ten and the point of the deal was for West to discard – following the sound motto, 'Do not overruff with a trump that will win a trick anyway – and you might make two later.' West duly discarded (a diamond – a heart works no better) and it now appears as though declarer must lose two trumps – to the nine as well as the queen. Not so.

Declarer cashed the ace of trumps to reveal the bad news (East discarding) and then correctly abandoned trumps. He crossed to the queen of diamonds, returned to the queen of hearts, cashed the ace-king of diamonds (both opponents following and discarding spades from the dummy), then crossed to the ace-king of hearts.

At Trick Ten he led dummy's fourth heart and ruffed low, and then led a diamond. Down to just his three remaining trumps, West had no way to take more than one trick. He ruffed with the nine, but had to lead away from his queen-three around to declarer's king-jack. Eleven tricks and game made.

Wow! A star in the making.

**Rubber**

|  | ♠ J 10 9 8 |  |
|  | ♥ A K 7 2 |  |
|  | ♦ Q |  |
|  | ♣ 7 6 5 4 |  |

| ♠ 5 | **N** | ♠ A K Q 7 4 3 2 |
| ♥ 9 5 4 3 | **W**   **E** | ♥ J 10 8 |
| ♦ 9 7 6 5 | **S** | ♦ 8 4 2 |
| ♣ Q 9 3 2 |  | ♣ – |

|  | ♠ 6 |  |
|  | ♥ Q 6 |  |
|  | ♦ A K J 10 3 |  |
|  | ♣ A K J 10 8 |  |

| S | W | N | E |
|---|---|---|---|
| 1♦ | PASS | 1♥ | 1♠ (1) |
| 2♣ (2) | PASS | 3♣ | 3♠ |
| 5♣ (3) | END | | |

(1) Preempting is possible, but East looks at his three losers in each red suit and considers the unfavourable vulnerability.

(2) Close to a jump to 3♣ – a game force...

(3) ...but catches up once he hears support.

**Contract: 5♣**      **Opening lead: ♠5**

# Spring Fours

The Spring Foursomes has become England's premier open Bridge event. Perhaps this is because of its appealing double elimination knock-out format (you get two lives); perhaps it is because of its attractive location and timing: Stratford-upon-Avon during the first May Bank Holiday weekend; or perhaps it is because of the sponsorship of the late Boris Schapiro and his wife Helen, enabling better prize-money and a more professionally run event.

This deal from a recent Spring Fours sees the great Zia Mahmood defeat the undefeatable – the hallmark of a great.

Zia, East, risked a Lightner slam double of Six Spades (risky because they might run to Six Notrumps, or redouble when the ruff is the only defensive trick). West, London's Phil King, duly found the diamond opening lead (doing well to avoid the ace of hearts to 'have a look'). East ruffed, but not with the six and rather with the nine (key play). This was a cost-nothing play to create the illusion that he held king-nine doubleton trump.

At Trick Two East switched to a heart, declarer ruffing. Declarer then led the jack of trumps and West played low (note – not thoughtlessly covering an honour with an honour). Perhaps he should not have fallen for Zia's ruse, but declarer convinced himself that East now held the bare king and rose with dummy's ace. Down one.

Meanwhile at the other table East did not find the Lightner double. West led the ace of hearts (hoping to score the king of trumps in addition). Declarer ruffed, led the jack of trumps covered by the king and ace, and was soon claiming all thirteen tricks.

**Dealer: North**  **Vulnerability: Both**

Teams

|  | ♠ A Q 4 3 |  |
|  | ♥ K 9 6 5 |  |
|  | ♦ A K J 6 |  |
|  | ♣ 10 |  |

| ♠ K 6 | N | ♠ 9 5 |
| ♥ A 8 7 2 | W E | ♥ Q J 10 4 3 |
| ♦ 10 8 4 2 | S | ♦ – |
| ♣ K 7 4 | | ♣ 9 8 6 5 3 2 |

|  | ♠ J 10 8 7 2 |  |
|  | ♥ – |  |
|  | ♦ Q 9 7 5 3 |  |
|  | ♣ A Q J |  |

| S | W | N | E |
|---|---|---|---|
|  |  | 1♦ (1) | PASS |
| 1♠ | PASS | 4♣ (2) | PASS |
| 6♠ (3) | PASS | PASS | DOUBLE (4) |
| END | | | |

(1) Playing Five-card Majors.
(2) Splinter bid, showing a club shortage and a strong raise in spades.
(3) With no club or heart losers and a double fit, South can hardly do less.
(4) A Lightner slam double, asking partner for an unusual opening lead. Such a double is usually based on a void.

**Contract: 6♠ doubled**   **Opening lead: ♦8**

# Dreaded 'B'

Entries for the annual Brighton Teams (and some other events) are getting fewer. Is this a signal for Bridge to be introduced into the National Curriculum? I'm sure we Bridge-lovers could think of many good reasons for doing so. Here are five for starters:

Bridge teaches/enhances/creates (i) logic, (ii) cooperation, (iii) competition, (iv) concentration and (v) social skills. Plus it keeps youngsters off the street/Game Boy.

Back to Brighton. After a day-and-a-half of Swiss (playing matches against other teams with a similar concurrent score), the top eight teams play the 'A' Final. Teams nine to sixteen play the 'B' Final. And the rest continue the Swiss. Your author's team always seem to make the dreaded 'B' Final.

I recall that the adverse swing on this deal cost us the 'B' victory one year. It was a reasonable grand slam – in all but one respect. It failed. Declarer won West's singleton jack of clubs lead in hand, crossed to the ace of trumps (in case East held all four), then led a second trump. Had trumps split 2-2, he would have a trump left in dummy to ruff his fourth club. Not so – East discarded.

Leaving West's last trump outstanding, declarer turned to diamonds. He cashed the king, crossed to the ace, cashed the ace of hearts discarding a diamond, then ruffed a third diamond. Had both opponents followed, he would have drawn the last trump, crossed to the king of clubs, and discarded his fourth club on dummy's fourth diamond. But East discarded on the third diamond.

Declarer was down to his last option – clubs. He needed 3-3 clubs or, less likely (especially given that West held four diamonds), West (the opponent with the last trump) to have the club length; in that

scenario, declarer would be able to ruff his fourth club in dummy with West helplessly following suit.

However when declarer led a second club towards the king, West ruffed. Down one – shucks!

## Teams

**Dealer: South**  **Vulnerability: Both**

|  | ♠ A 9 7 |  |
|  | ♥ A 7 3 |  |
|  | ♦ A 6 5 4 |  |
|  | ♣ K 8 5 |  |

| ♠ 10 4 3 | | ♠ J |
| ♥ J 10 8 6 5 | N | ♥ K Q 9 4 2 |
| ♦ Q J 8 7 | W    E | ♦ 10 9 |
| ♣ J | S | ♣ 10 9 7 6 2 |

|  | ♠ K Q 8 6 5 2 |  |
|  | ♥ - |  |
|  | ♦ K 3 2 |  |
|  | ♣ A Q 4 3 |  |

| S | W | N | E |
|---|---|---|---|
| 1♠ | PASS | 2♦ (1) | PASS |
| 2♠ | PASS | 3♠ | PASS |
| 4♣ (2) | PASS | 4♦ (2) | PASS |
| 4♥ (2) | PASS | 5♣ (3) | PASS |
| 5♦ (3) | PASS | 5♥ (3) | PASS |
| 7♠ (4) | END | | |

(1) Playing 'Two-over-One', where a Two-Level response is forcing to game.
(2) First-round controls (i.e. ace or void).
(3) The suit having previously been cue-bid, first or second-round controls (i.e. king or singleton).
(4) 'I've heard enough.' South has no obvious losers (partner surely has ♠A for all his bidding).

**Contract: 7♠**  **Opening lead: ♣J**

# Late Finance Bill

There was once a late vote on a Finance Bill in the House of Commons one night. The question for the MPs was how to fill in the empty couple of hours?

It wasn't long before two packs of cards were being hunted down. A Bridge game was soon underway.

The early running was made by Sir Ray Whitney (West) and John Maples (East). And then this hand arrived...

Michael Mates, South, opened a bold (but reasonable) preemptive Three Hearts; West overcalled Four Diamonds – perhaps a take-out double was indicated but he was doubtless keen to make a Rubber call (he had a 90 part-score); North, Sir Archie Hamilton, without so much as a hesitation, jumped to Six Hearts. After two passes (South's being distinctly nervous – especially with three-quarters of his points now almost certain to be wasted), West metaphorically stood on his chair and doubled. But the bidding was not over. With the same speed as his Six Heart bid, North redoubled!

West chose to lead the ace of clubs (which looks best, holding the king and queen too). Mates, declarer, trumped the lead. He trumped a spade, trumped a second club, trumped a spade, then trumped a third club. Pleased to see the clubs split 3-3, he was now in a position to cross to the ace of trumps (West discarding) and lead a winning club.

East trumped with the king, but declarer hurriedly discarded the other red king. He trumped East's diamond lead, trumped a spade, and discarded his remaining spades on dummy's winning clubs. Redoubled slam made with just twelve points between the two hands!

Poor West! Had he chosen to lead the ace of diamonds, the contract would have been defeated trivially (East's king of trumps

certain to score). The ace of spades lead would also work – declarer would be an entry short to establish dummy's clubs. Try it.

*Postscript*: No more late bills means rather less Bridge is currently played in the Commons. Shame.

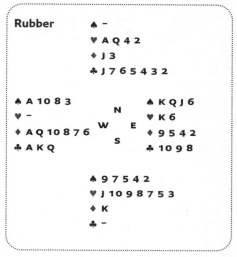

**Dealer: South    Vulnerability: East-West***

Rubber

|  | North |
|---|---|
| ♠ | – |
| ♥ | A Q 4 2 |
| ♦ | J 3 |
| ♣ | J 7 6 5 4 3 2 |

| West | | East |
|---|---|---|
| ♠ A 10 8 3 | | ♠ K Q J 6 |
| ♥ – | | ♥ K 6 |
| ♦ A Q 10 8 7 6 | | ♦ 9 5 4 2 |
| ♣ A K Q | | ♣ 10 9 8 |

|  | South |
|---|---|
| ♠ | 9 7 5 4 2 |
| ♥ | J 10 9 8 7 5 3 |
| ♦ | K |
| ♣ | – |

| S | W | N | E |
|---|---|---|---|
| 3♥ | 4♦ (1) | 6♥ | PASS |
| PASS | DOUBLE | REDOUBLE | END |

(1) Double perhaps better. Not that it would have ended any more happily, indeed doubtless the same.

**Contract: 6♥ redoubled   Opening lead: ♣A**

* vulnerable and 90.

# CHAPTER 17

# Bridge around the World

The only true common language of human beings, apart from music, is Bridge. Think about it. Sitting opposite a Papua New Guinean and bidding to a delicate slam is really something, I imagine.

I have good friends through Bridge all around the world. Can I hold a good conversation with many of them? Not really – the language barrier is too great. Can we share special moments through our knowledge of the intricacies of Bridge? Sure.

Bridge represents a meeting of cultures, a meeting of minds. There is no sexism, no racism, no religious fanaticism in Bridge. The very concepts are outside Bridge players' frame of reference.

The World Bridge Federation, under the dynamic leadership of Corsican Jose Damiani is spearheading a 'Bridge for Peace' campaign. It is fitting, therefore, that our first deal of the chapter is from a Bridge match between Israel and Palestine, their first ever sporting encounter of any kind.

# First-ever Meeting

**Dealer: North**    **Vulnerability: East-West**

**Teams**

```
                 ♠ K 9 3
                 ♥ A 8 5
                 ♦ 4 2
                 ♣ K Q 8 5 4

 ♠ 8 7 6 5 4          N          ♠ 10
 ♥ -                              ♥ 7 6 2
 ♦ K 8 6 5 3     W       E        ♦ A Q J 10 9 7
 ♣ A 10 7            S            ♣ 8 6 2

                 ♠ A Q J 2
                 ♥ K Q J 10 9 4 3
                 ♦ -
                 ♣ J 3
```

Palestine and Israel have their disagreements away from the table, of course, but sit a Palestinian Bridge team down against an Israeli team and the only differences that matter are those of hand evaluation and card play skills.

It was during the 2000 Transnational Teams that a Palestinian Team and an Israeli Team drew one another as opponents. I am reliably informed that the two had never previously met in any sporting context.

The auction – on our featured deal from the match – was exactly the same at both tables. Even West's final pass was equally reluctant – doubtless he was wondering whether or not to bid Seven Diamonds.

The play to South's Six Heart contract was not too tough. Both Wests led a diamond. Declarer ruffed, drew trumps in three rounds, cashed the four top spades, then forced out the ace of clubs. Twelve tricks and +980 to North-South at both tables. No swing to either team.

Though it would have taken a bold West to have sacrificed in Seven Diamonds, given the adverse vulnerability, it is interesting to speculate whether the bid would have been a point winner on the probable opening lead of the king of hearts.

Declarer, East, ruffs the heart in dummy and at Trick Two leads a spade (key play). South wins declarer's ten with the jack and switches to the jack of clubs (wishing he had led it originally). Declarer wins dummy's ace, ruffs a spade, ruffs a heart, ruffs a spade, ruffs a heart, and ruffs a fourth spade. He cashes the ace of trumps, crosses to dummy's king (drawing North's last trump) then leads the established fifth spade discarding a club. He just loses a spade and a club. Down two and +500 to North-South.

| S | W | N | E |
|---|---|---|---|
|  |  | 1♣ (1) | 2♦ (2) |
| 2♥ | 5♦ | PASS | PASS |
| 6♥ | END |  |  |

(1) Playing Strong Notrump.
(2) Weak Jump Overcall.

**Contract: 6♥**        **Opening lead: ♦5**

You will only rarely see an example of a profitable sacrifice of Seven over Six when you are vulnerable and your opponents are not.

# Jose Damiani

There is little doubt who is the most important person in the Bridge World today. It is the President of the World Bridge Federation, Frenchman (originally from Corsica) Jose Damiani.

Damiani is the great ambassador for Bridge, the Ely Culbertson of the modern era. Here is a recent – typical – speech of his from New York:

'There are not many sports that can help youngsters to improve their memory, concentration and reasoning skills, and at the same time help older people to avoid or reduce the effects of Alzheimer's or Parkinson's.'

How true.

Damiani was in New York to promote the first World Junior Individual Event. He is clearly (and rightfully) concerned about the lack of influx of young people to the game:

'In the old days, our Bridge population was renewed by families where the children learned to play Bridge with their parents. That is no longer the case, for reasons such as the advent of TV and video games, as well as the changing lifestyles of young people. Our Bridge community is getting older and older, and we should be aware of this danger. We want our children and our grandchildren to enjoy Bridge as we do. Teaching Bridge in schools is therefore essential for the long term.'

Damiani is a fine Bridge player himself, having recently won the Bronze Medal in the Senior Series (over 55s) at the European Championships. This deal from the event sees Damiani (East) and partner Albert Faigenbaum (West) defeating Five Spades, where many North-Souths were bidding and making Six.

West found the ten of diamonds lead. East ruffed and, needing two more tricks, now

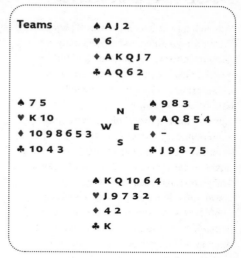

**Dealer: North   Vulnerability: North-South**

Teams

|   | ♠ A J 2 |
|---|---|
|   | ♥ 6 |
|   | ♦ A K Q J 7 |
|   | ♣ A Q 6 2 |

| ♠ 7 5 | | ♠ 9 8 3 |
|---|---|---|
| ♥ K 10 | N | ♥ A Q 8 5 4 |
| ♦ 10 9 8 6 5 3 | W   E | ♦ – |
| ♣ 10 4 3 | S | ♣ J 9 8 7 5 |

|   | ♠ K Q 10 6 4 |
|---|---|
|   | ♥ J 9 7 3 2 |
|   | ♦ 4 2 |
|   | ♣ K |

| S | W | N | E |
|---|---|---|---|
|   |   | 1♦ | 1♥ |
| 1♠ | PASS | 3♣ | PASS |
| 3NT | PASS | 4♠ (1) | PASS |
| 5♠ (2) | PASS | PASS (3) | PASS |

(1) Showing a huge hand with delayed (i.e. three-card) spade support and heart shortage.
(2) I must say that I would have Blackwooded into 6♠ with South's fine hand...
(3) ...Or raised to 6♠ with North's.

**Contract: 5♠          Opening lead: ♦10**

made the key move of returning a low heart away from his ace. His courage was rewarded when West won the king and gave him a second diamond ruff. Down one.

# Stuff of Dreams

**Dealer: South**　　　**Vulnerability: Both**

Playing against two of the finest players in the world, you listen carefully to the auction, draw the correct deductions, and bid to slam with just fifteen high-card points between your partnership. You then have the confidence to redouble when doubled. The contract duly makes and you write down +2070 on your scorecard.

It all sounds the stuff of dreams, but it was not. The deal occurred at the US Nationals. The victorious North-South were a comparatively unknown Los Angeles pair, Clark Millikan (South) and Stephen Castellino (North). Their illustrious opponents were Norway's Boye Brogeland (West) and England's Tony Forrester (East).

Look at North's actions in the auction. Initially settling for game, he re-evaluates once he hears East bid Four Spades. He reasons that East must have four spades for the bid, and West three spades for his take-out double. That leaves partner with no spades at all. He confidently raises his partner's Five Hearts to Six and then redoubles.

Should East-West have smelt a rat and run to Six Spades (or – better – Seven Clubs)? In practice it was virtually impossible for East-West to believe that they would only take one trick in defence with all their high-cards, and they both duly passed.

West led his singleton trump against the redoubled slam. Declarer won in dummy, ruffed a spade, then led the king of diamonds, but ruffed it when West played low. He ruffed a second spade, ruffed a diamond, ruffed a third spade, ruffed a third diamond, ruffed a fourth spade (with his last trump), ruffed a fourth diamond, cashed the two established spade winners in dummy, and merely conceded a club at the end.

**Teams**

```
              ♠ 10 7 6 5 4 3
              ♥ K Q J 5 4 3
              ♦ –
              ♣ 10
♠ A Q J               ♠ K 9 8 2
♥ 8             N     ♥ 2
♦ J 8 6 5    W   E    ♦ A 10 7 4
♣ A Q 9 6 5     S     ♣ K J 8 3
              ♠ –
              ♥ A 10 9 7 6
              ♦ K Q 9 3 2
              ♣ 7 4 2
```

| S | W | N | E |
|---|---|---|---|
| 1♥ (1) | DOUBLE | 4♥ | 4♠ |
| 5♥ | PASS | 6♥ (2) | DOUBLE |
| PASS | PASS | REDOUBLE | END |

(1) With a fine shape, two decent five-card suits and an easy rebid (diamonds), it is reasonable for South to open 1♥.

(2) Surely East-West must have seven spades to justify their bidding to Four Spades. With partner therefore holding a void – and presumably the ace of hearts – there can be but one loser in a heart contract.

**Contract: 6♥ redoubled　Opening lead: ♥8**

# Against 99 per cent of Wests

What is your first thought when you pick up a running suit? Mine is 'Notrumps!' A running suit (solid from the ace down to the jack/ten) is worth the same number of tricks in Notrumps as it is as trumps, and fewer tricks are needed to score game.

So reasoned South, on our featured deal. And against 99 per cent of defenders he would have been right. But not against Californian Kyle Larsen, sitting West. Cover up South and East's hand and you will fully appreciate the subtle magic of his defence to the Three Notrump contract.

West led the ace of diamonds, and received a discouraging signal of the two from partner. At Trick Two he cashed the ace of hearts. What should he do next?

It seems reasonable for West to cash the king of diamonds and lead the jack, to drive out the queen and set up his suit, with re-entries in both hearts and clubs. But declarer would now have nine easy tricks via seven spades, the promoted queen of diamonds, and the ace of clubs.

A switch at Trick Three to a club would be similarly disastrous, presenting declarer with the queen of clubs as his ninth trick. How about switching passively to a spade? This is better, but declarer runs off the seven winners in the suit. West needs to keep a guard for his king of clubs. But declarer exits with a diamond to West and waits for the inevitable club lead around to his ace-queen at Trick Twelve.

Rather than be squeezed himself, West preferred to squeeze declarer. And this he did by the simple but lovely manoeuvre of cashing the king of hearts at trick three (key play). He did not mind setting up dummy's long suit – there were no entries.

**Teams**

|  |  |  |
|---|---|---|
| ♠ 8 2 |  |  |
| ♥ Q J 8 5 3 2 |  |  |
| ♦ 5 3 |  |  |
| ♣ J 10 9 |  |  |

| ♠ 10 3 | N | ♠ 6 5 |
|---|---|---|
| ♥ A K 9 | W       E | ♥ 7 6 4 |
| ♦ A K J 10 4 | S | ♦ 8 7 2 |
| ♣ K 6 2 |  | ♣ 8 7 5 4 3 |

|  |
|---|
| ♠ A K Q J 9 7 4 |
| ♥ 10 |
| ♦ Q 9 6 |
| ♣ A Q |

| S | W | N | E |
|---|---|---|---|
|  | 1 ♦ | PASS | PASS |
| DOUBLE | PASS | 1 ♥ | PASS |
| 3NT (1) | END |  |  |

(1) Running suit plus slow diamond stopper.

**Contract: 3NT**          **Opening lead: ♦A**

What could declarer discard? A diamond (unguarding his queen) was clearly fatal, as was the queen of clubs (enabling West to exit with a low club to the ace, and wait for two tricks at the end). So away went a winning spade.

But with declarer now holding one fewer winner, West could cash the king of diamonds, exit with the jack, and wait for his king of clubs at Trick Thirteen. Down one.

# Tarzan

Team Orange, the Dutch national team which gets together every Friday to train (their companies pay for their leave), have just won the European Open Teams in Tenerife. One of their three pairs, Simon de Wijs and Bauke Muller, call their bidding system Tarzan. Can you work out why (answer at the end)?

Seven Spades was not a good grand slam. However an opening heart lead from West would render precisely twelve tricks in a spade contract an unlikely number (either eleven or thirteen rate to be available depending on the diamond finesse – a so-called 'Five or Seven hand'); so perhaps the Dutch were justified in bidding Seven, once they reached the Six-level.

Declarer won the spade lead in hand and, with just eleven top tricks, shut his eyes and finessed the queen of diamonds at Trick Two. Success! He ruffed a low diamond, crossed to the jack of trumps (drawing the trumps), ruffed another low diamond (both following to reveal the four-three split), then crossed to the king of clubs and discarded his club and heart losers on the ace and promoted five of diamonds. Thirteen tricks and grand slam made.

Note that if an opponent shows out on the third diamond, declarer has a fallback position. He cashes the ace of clubs, crosses to the king, discards his third club on dummy's ace of diamonds, then ruffs a club. If the clubs split 3-3, he is able to cross to the ace of hearts and discard his losing heart on the promoted thirteenth club.

Why Tarzan? Answer: Wijs-Muller... Johnny Weissmuller... Tarzan.

**Dealer: South    Vulnerability: Neither**

**Teams**

|  | ♠ J 6 |  |
|---|---|---|
|  | ♥ A 10 |  |
|  | ♦ A Q 5 3 2 |  |
|  | ♣ K 6 3 2 |  |

| ♠ 7 3 | | ♠ 9 4 |
| ♥ K 9 7 4 | N | ♥ Q J 6 5 3 |
| ♦ K 10 9 8 | W E | ♦ J 6 4 |
| ♣ 9 7 5 | S | ♣ Q J 4 |

|  | ♠ A K Q 10 8 5 2 |  |
|---|---|---|
|  | ♥ 8 2 |  |
|  | ♦ 7 |  |
|  | ♣ A 10 8 |  |

| S | W | N | E |
|---|---|---|---|
| 1♠ (1) | PASS | 2♦ | PASS |
| 3♠ | PASS | 4♣ (2) | PASS |
| 4♦ (2) | PASS | 4♥ (2) | PASS |
| 4NT (3) | PASS | 5♥ (4) | PASS |
| 5NT (5) | PASS | 7♠ (6) | END |

(1) The days of the eight-playing-tricks Strong Two are long gone at top level (perhaps sadly).
(2) First or second-round control-showing bids agreeing spades.
(3) Roman Key Card Blackwood.
(4) Two of the 'five aces' (incl ♠K); no ♠Q.
(5) Nominally asking for kings, but crucially confirming all the key cards – a necessary courtesy as partner is unlimited – and inviting the grand.
(6) A pretty bold, Tarzan-like punt.

**Contract: 7♠        Opening lead: ♠3**

# All England

The European Champions Cup is contested by national champion Bridge Clubs from the top ten European Countries of the previous European Championships.

The three-time winning Italian team masquerades as the Tennis Club Parioli, although the girths of the six players suggest that they rarely venture on to the tennis court (their lead pair, Alfredo Versace and Lorenzo Lauria, assured me that they did once knock up together ... several years ago... for about ten minutes).

Your author once qualified as the All England Bridge Club. Living up to our 'All England' billing, we did about as well as British tennis players have done in recent years in the Winbledon Tennis Final (i.e. not reach it).

The crucial deal of the match against the Russians that year is a good illustration of an important principle concerning the choice of two trump suits: you should select the one with the closer equality of trump length, leaving the side suit with the greater disparity (thus more potential for discards).

The All England Club tried Seven Clubs, which had to fail. Declarer can draw trumps and run diamonds, but still has a spade loser – down one.

Seven Diamonds, however, succeeds (see featured auction). Declarer wins the spade lead with dummy's ace, draws trumps in three rounds, then cashes six rounds of clubs, discarding dummy's three spades. He ruffs his queen of spades with dummy's remaining trump, and the grand slam is his.

**Dealer: North          Vulnerability: Neither**

Teams
```
                  ♠ A 9 8 2
                  ♥ Q 8
                  ♦ A Q 8 6
                  ♣ A 7 4

♠ 5                           ♠ K J 7 6 4 3
♥ K J 10 9 7       N          ♥ A 5 3
  6 4 2          W   E        ♦ 4
♦ 5 3 2            S          ♣ J 9 5
♣ 3

                  ♠ Q 10
                  ♥ –
                  ♦ K J 10 9 7
                  ♣ K Q 10 8 6 2
```

| S | W | N | E |
|---|---|---|---|
|  |  | 1♠ | PASS |
| 2♣ | PASS (1) | 2NT | PASS |
| 3♦ | PASS | 4♦ (2) | PASS |
| 5♥ (3) | PASS | 7♦ (2) | END |

(1) Only four points, but hugely timid not to try to disrupt. East-West can make ten tricks in Hearts.

(2) Choosing diamonds, a known four(+)-four fit rather than clubs (five(+)-three).

(3) Void-showing (all splinter jumps at the Five-level show voids), inviting a grand slam.

**Contract: 7♦          Opening lead: ♠5**

# Michael

I spent a charming weekend in Copenhagen a while ago, participating in the Hecht Cup. Though my partner in the main event was the illustrious Zia Mahmood, I had more success with my Pro-Am partner on the eve of the main event.

I only knew him as Michael and when he said he was just an occasional player, my expectations changed from desire to do well to desire to enjoy the evening. In fact I achieved both ends – he was a very capable card-player with a penchant for doing the right thing at the right time... as he showed on this deal, our penultimate of the chapter.

Michael, South, can hardly be blamed for taking out my double of Five Clubs (which would have gone one down – losing three aces). With seven hearts – and jump support in the suit from partner – it was reasonable to try to make the eleven-trick contract.

However Five Hearts looks certain to fail – with a seemingly unavoidable loser in spades and diamonds in addition to the ace of trumps. Armed with the knowledge that West had extreme length in clubs for his solo bidding to Five Clubs, Michael hatched a plan.

He won West's king of clubs opening lead with dummy's ace, and at Trick Two led a low spade (key play). This went to East's five, declarer's six, and West's ten. West then tried to cash the queen of clubs, an understandable play, but a fatal one.

Declarer trumped, crossed to the ace of spades, trumped a third spade (West following with the king), then cashed the ace of diamonds. When he followed by leading the king, West paused. It would do him no good to trump with his ace, so he discarded a club. However this was merely prolonging the agony, for declarer's next play was a trump.

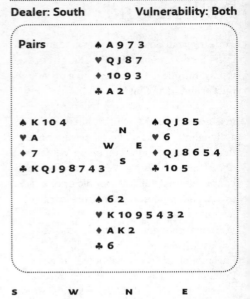

**Dealer: South**          **Vulnerability: Both**

**Pairs**          ♠ A 9 7 3
                   ♥ Q J 8 7
                   ♦ 10 9 3
                   ♣ A 2

♠ K 10 4                        ♠ Q J 8 5
♥ A                             ♥ 6
♦ 7                             ♦ Q J 8 6 5 4
♣ K Q J 9 8 7 4 3               ♣ 10 5

                   ♠ 6 2
                   ♥ K 10 9 5 4 3 2
                   ♦ A K 2
                   ♣ 6

| S | W | N | E |
|---|---|---|---|
| 1♥ | 2♣ | 3♥ | PASS |
| 4♥ | 5♣ | DOUBLE | PASS |
| 5♥ | END | | |

**Contract: 5♥**          **Opening lead: ♣K**

West won his singleton ace, but had only clubs remaining. Declarer trumped the club return in dummy and and discarded his diamond loser from hand. Game made.

Though any other play but a club at Trick Three by West would have left declarer an entry short for his black suit elimination, this does not detract from declarer's elegant line. Perhaps the simplest defence for West to avoid the throw-in is for him to cash his singleton ace of trumps before exiting.

# Gallic Grunting

You are an unknown foreigner playing in the Biarritz Bridge Festival. You are playing against one of the most famous and popular French players of all time, the 'enfant terrible' Paul Chemla (now in his late fifties). He has a huge entourage of spectators ('kibitzers') rooting for him and he has just doubled you in a friskily bid game contract.

You would be forgiven for not giving your best performance, psyched out by the situation. Not so Marshall Lewis, sitting South.

West led the jack of of hearts against Four Spades and East, Chemla, won the ace and returned a second heart. Declarer ruffed and played a diamond to the jack. When the finesse succeeded, declarer breathed more easily. But East's double of the final contract was ominous, suggesting a bad trump split.

Declarer's next move was to lead a trump from dummy, correctly withholding his ace when East split his honours, playing the jack. East led a third heart, in an effort to reduce the opposing trumps (nothing would have worked better), and declarer correctly discarded a diamond from his hand and ruffed in dummy. He led another trump, dummy's last, to East's queen and his ace, and West discarded. Undeterred, he played his last diamond to dummy's queen, both opponents following low, cashed the ace of clubs, and then led the ace of diamonds.

East had no reply. If he ruffed with the king, declarer would be able to ruff his heart return, draw his nine of trumps with the ten, and then play club winners; if he ruffed with the nine, declarer would overruff with the ten and play minor suit winners, again restricting East to his king of trumps.

In fact East chose to discard a club on the ace of diamonds. But declarer simply discarded a club from his hand and led a fourth diamond. Both East and declarer discarded clubs a second time – and then again when dummy's fifth diamond was led.

At Trick Twelve a club was led from dummy. East held his king-nine of trumps sitting under declarer's ten-five. He ruffed the club with the nine but declarer overruffed with the ten. The doubled contract had made.

There followed some Gallic grunting from unappreciative kibitzers. They had not come to watch their hero lose!

---

**Dealer: South**  **Vulnerability: Both**

Teams

|  | ♠ 8 7 6 |  |
|  | ♥ Q 8 |  |
|  | ♦ A Q J 4 3 |  |
|  | ♣ A K 4 |  |

| ♠ 3 | | ♠ K Q J 9 |
| ♥ K J 10 4 3 2 | N | ♥ A 9 6 5 |
| ♦ K 6 2 | W E | ♦ 10 8 |
| ♣ 7 3 2 | S | ♣ 8 6 5 |

|  | ♠ A 10 5 4 2 |  |
|  | ♥ 7 |  |
|  | ♦ 9 7 5 |  |
|  | ♣ Q J 10 9 |  |

| S | W | N | E |
|---|---|---|---|
| PASS | 2♥ (1) | 3♦ | 3♥ |
| 3♠ | PASS | 4♠ | DOUBLE |
| END | | | |

(1) Weak Two, five to ten points and a six-card suit.

**Contract: 4♠ doubled**   **Opening lead: ♥J**

# CHAPTER 18

# Stars of the Future

Bridge players rarely reach their peak until their mid-thirties because, unlike ball games, and indeed chess, so much of Bridge is based on experience, on understanding human nature, and the maturity of being able to cooperate with partner and coping with their foibles. However there is no doubt that the earlier you begin, the better you can be. Tiger Woods (golf, need I say?) and the Williams sisters (tennis) will testify to that, with the tool of their trade in their little hands by the age of two.

I remember playing in the World Pairs final a few years ago against a gangly boy who looked young enough to be still at school. He played a hand brilliantly, endplaying me for a 'top'. Indeed he was still at school – and just fifteen years old. Argentina's Agustin Madala discovered his ability at the game early. Let us hope that other such Bridge talents are discovered young.

Things are moving in the right direction in this country, with Bridge or MiniBridge (essentially Bridge without bidding) slowly being introduced into schools. However this tends only to occur when there is a keen Bridge-playing teacher, and dies out when that teacher leaves/retires.

Perhaps Britain should follow the same direction as such countries as Poland, Italy, Holland and Indonesia. In these – and other such forward-thinking countries – Bridge forms part of their standard national curriculum (or the equivalent). It is no surprise that those counties are beginning to ease ahead of the others in international championships.

# Junior Camps

Junior Bridge (under 25) is flourishing. Junior Bridge Camps abound, the World Junior and Schools Championships have recently taken place in Torquay, and the overall standard of play is getting better and better.

With no fear of failure, Juniors seem to make more spectacular plays than their more seasoned counterparts. Naturally one or two of these shots result in egg on the face, but some – like this deal – are so brilliant that they are worthy of a newspaper or book. The hero was Israel's Ophir Reshef, sitting South, and the venue was the Frostburg (Maryland, USA) Junior Camp.

If West leads a club against the Three Notrump contract – setting up three defensive tricks in the suit to go with the two red aces – declarer would have to fail. A heart lead to East's ace and a club switch would similarly defeat the contract. But when West chose to lead his singleton heart and East won his ace, declarer dropped the queen!

This was a brilliant stroke. If declarer had followed low, East would surely have realised that there was no future in hearts (declarer marked with the king-queen as West would lead the honour from an honour doubleton holding). East would doubtless have switched to the queen of clubs, and continued the suit – fatally for declarer – when he won the ace of diamonds.

However the young declarer dropping the queen of hearts made it look to East as though he held king-queen doubleton, and West six-three doubleton. To give East credit, he did sniff the air suspiciously for a few minutes. But he finally took the bait and led a low heart. If this had drawn declarer's king, then he had three established winners in the suit to be cashed when he won the ace of diamonds.

It was not to be – declarer's ruse had

worked. He played low from hand (East-West were playing Five-card Majors, so West's heart was known to be singleton) and won cheaply in dummy. He knocked out the ace of diamonds, and was soon chalking up ten tricks (three spades, two hearts, four diamonds and a club).

**Dealer: East    Vulnerability: North-South**

**Pairs**

|  | North |  |
|---|---|---|
|  | ♠ A Q | |
|  | ♥ 9 7 5 4 | |
|  | ♦ K Q J 8 7 | |
|  | ♣ A 6 | |

West
♠ J 6 4 3 2
♥ 6
♦ 9 4 2
♣ K 10 7 2

East
♠ 9 7 5
♥ A J 10 8 2
♦ A
♣ Q J 9 8

South
♠ K 10 8
♥ K Q 3
♦ 10 6 5 3
♣ 5 4 3

| S | W | N | E |
|---|---|---|---|
|  |  |  | 1♥ (1) |
| PASS | 1♠ (2) | 2♦ | PASS |
| 3♦ | PASS | 3♥ (3) | PASS |
| 3NT | END | | |

(1) Playing Five-card Majors.
(2) Responding super-light has become the modern trend. The logic is sound: if partner has a good opener (with a fit) then game might be on; if he does not, then the opponents may well have a contract. Bidding will probably make life more awkward for them.
(3) Asking for a heart stopper for Notrumps.

**Contract: 3NT          Opening lead: ♥6**

# Nature, Nurture

A surprisingly large number of the offspring of expert Bridge players around the world are highly proficient players in their own right. Is this because of nature – a passing on of the requisite Bridge-oriented genes? Or is it due to nurture – being exposed to Bridge at a very young age? Doubtless it's a bit of both.

Take Martin Schaltz from Denmark, son of two international champions Dorthe and Peter. He is a mainstay of the Danish Junior (under 25) Team and has recently won the Silver Medal in the Danish Open Team Championship. All this before even turning eighteen.

Don't worry if you cannot follow the somewhat involved auction on this deal from the final of that Danish Team Championship; extrapolating the key details, West has shown four spades and six hearts. Can you do as well as Martin, sitting South, and chalk up your Six Club slam? West leads out two top hearts.

After ruffing the second heart, declarer cashed the jack of trumps and led a low trump to dummy's ten. With West following both times, his likely shape (based on his jump in spades and subsequent Five Heart bid) appeared to be 4♠6♥1♦2♣. East was therefore four times more likely than his partner to hold the jack of diamonds.

At Trick Five declarer found the winning play. He led a diamond and finessed his nine (key play). When West followed low, he could cash the ace of spades, ruff a spade with dummy's king, ruff a heart, draw East's last trump, cash the queen of diamonds, then lead his third diamond over to dummy's three remaining winners in the suit. Twelve tricks and slam made.

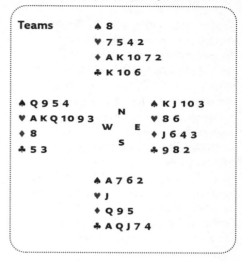

**Dealer: West    Vulnerability: North-South**

Teams

```
               ♠ 8
               ♥ 7 5 4 2
               ♦ A K 10 7 2
               ♣ K 10 6

♠ Q 9 5 4              ♠ K J 10 3
♥ A K Q 10 9 3    N    ♥ 8 6
♦ 8          W       E  ♦ J 6 4 3
♣ 5 3              S    ♣ 9 8 2

               ♠ A 7 6 2
               ♥ J
               ♦ Q 9 5
               ♣ A Q J 7 4
```

| S | W | N | E |
|---|---|---|---|
| | 1♥ | PASS (1) | 1♠ (2) |
| 2♣ | 3♠ (3) | DOUBLE (4) | PASS |
| 4♥ (5) | PASS | 4♠ (5) | DOUBLE |
| REDOUBLE (6) | 5♥ | 6♣ | END |

(1) Too dangerous to overcall 2♦ at the adverse vulnerability.
(2) Shaded but routine in the modern game.
(3) Close to a semi-preemptive 4♠.
(4) Take-out – showing club support and a side diamond suit.
(5) Control-showing bids, looking for slam.
(6) Showing ♠A and further slam-interest.

**Contract: 6♣**          **Opening lead: ♥A**

# Rule of 20

Thirteen points used to be the minimum requirement for an opening bid. But standards have been slipping steadily and these days many use the Rule of 20 (recommended): 'Open the bidding (at the one-level) when your high-card points added to the number of cards in your two longest suits get to at least 20.'

Indeed the world's leading pair over the past couple of decades – USA's Meckstroth-Rodwell – go even further. They think nothing of opening balanced elevens and distributional nines and tens – effectively a Rule of about eighteen. But they do extract the maximum in the card-play. My advice is to stick to the Rule of 20.

On this deal North opened a hand with just nine points – but one that satisfied the Rule of 20. His partner was one of the most promising juniors in the country, Manchester's Michael Byrne. With his full-looking seventeen points, South must have been thinking 'slam'. In the event it took fine technique for him to make game.

West led the four of hearts against the Three Notrump contract. Declarer beat East's ten with the queen and led the ten of diamonds, West playing low. It was crunch time – should he run the ten or rise with dummy's king?

Though the best odds in isolation of avoiding a second diamond loser (in other words preventing the queen from scoring) are to run the ten, declarer looked deeper. If East won the lead (with the queen or ace), a heart return through his king to West's ace (East would have played the ace at Trick One if he held it) would doom the contract for sure.

Declarer needed West to hold the ace of diamonds to have a chance. He correctly rose with dummy's king and was rewarded when the queen fell from East. It was now a simple

matter to lead a second diamond to West's ace. When West failed to cash the ace of hearts, declarer wound up scoring all the remainder. Twelve tricks and game made.

**Dealer: North**     **Vulnerability: Neither**

| Teams | ♠ A J 8 2 |
| | ♥ 7 |
| | ♦ K J 9 7 5 3 2 |
| | ♣ 4 |

| ♠ 9 4 | | ♠ Q 7 5 3 |
| ♥ A J 9 4 2 | **N** | ♥ 10 6 5 3 |
| ♦ A 4 | **W    E** | ♦ Q |
| ♣ 8 7 3 2 | **S** | ♣ J 10 9 6 |

| | ♠ K 10 6 |
| | ♥ K Q 8 |
| | ♦ 10 8 6 |
| | ♣ A K Q 5 |

| S | W | N | E |
|------|------|------|------|
| | | 1 ♦ | PASS |
| 2 ♣ | PASS | 2 ♦ | PASS |
| 2 ♥ (1) | PASS | 3 ♦ | PASS |
| 3NT | END | | |

(1) Fabricates a bid in order to force partner to reveal more. An encouraging squeak and South might have gone slamming.

**Contract: 3NT**     **Opening lead: ♥4**

# Universities Championship

This deal comes from the Universities Championship Final and sees the Cambridge Captain, Stuart Haring, use Elimination and Throw-in technique to make a tricky Five Diamond contract.

West led the king of spades and declarer won dummy's ace. Staring at a second-round heart loser and a third-round club loser, it appears that the game requires there to be no trump loser. But Haring saw other possibilities and at Trick Two led a heart to his ten.

West won his king of hearts and switched to the two of clubs (best), declarer playing low from dummy and beating East's queen with the king. He next cashed the ace of trumps (all following small), the other red ace (with the same result), and led a second trump to dummy's king. West discarded a spade on this second trump (not so surprising given his preempt) thus revealing a trump loser, but declarer was undaunted.

At Trick Seven, declarer led dummy's jack of hearts for a ruffing finesse, discarding a club from hand when East followed low. He ruffed a fourth heart, bringing down East's queen, then crossed to dummy's ace of clubs to lead the established fifth heart. It would have done East no good to ruff with his master trump, so he discarded a spade (declarer throwing a club). But this only postponed the agony for him.

Both dummy and declarer's last three cards were two trumps and a losing club, East holding two spades and the master trump. A trump was led to East who had to lead a spade, allowing declarer to ruff in one hand and discard the club loser from the other. Eleven tricks and game made.

**Dealer: South**     **Vulnerability: Neither**

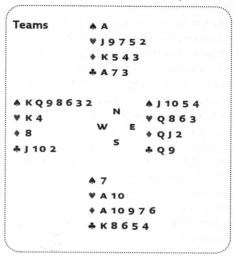

Teams

|  | North |  |
|---|---|---|
|  | ♠ A | |
|  | ♥ J 9 7 5 2 | |
|  | ♦ K 5 4 3 | |
|  | ♣ A 7 3 | |

| West | | East |
|---|---|---|
| ♠ K Q 9 8 6 3 2 | | ♠ J 10 5 4 |
| ♥ K 4 | | ♥ Q 8 6 3 |
| ♦ 8 | | ♦ Q J 2 |
| ♣ J 10 2 | | ♣ Q 9 |

|  | South | |
|---|---|---|
|  | ♠ 7 | |
|  | ♥ A 10 | |
|  | ♦ A 10 9 7 6 | |
|  | ♣ K 8 6 5 4 | |

| S | W | N | E |
|---|---|---|---|
| 1♦ | 3♠ | DOUBLE (1) | 4♠ (2) |
| 5♣ | PASS | 5♦ | END |

(1) Negative – promising (in this auction) hearts plus the values to compete at the four-level (around 10+ points).
(2) Raising partner's barrage one further level.

**Contract: 5♦**     **Opening lead: ♠K**

# Junior Camrose

24-year-old Jake Dunn (he may be a year or so older as you read this) has represented Wales in a record twelve Junior Camrose ('JC') Trophies (the annual Home Countries competition for under-25s). With England having a big demographic edge, the battle between Wales, Scotland and Ireland is normally for second place.

Here is Jake (sitting South) in action on a fascinating JC slam deal. Receiving the ten of diamonds lead, he would have had twelve easy tricks had East unthinkingly risen with the ace (presenting him with two tricks in the suit). Instead East correctly ducked and declarer was a trick short.

Declarer looked at the club suit. Looking at the suit in isolation, there were two ways to make an extra trick without losing one. He could cash the ace-king and hope for the queen to drop doubleton; or he could run the jack and, if covered by the queen, win the king and return to hand to run the nine, succeeding when West has both the missing queen and ten (or fails to cover the jack with, say, Qxxx).

Neither approach was particularly appealing in percentage terms, so Jake went a third route. Can you see how he landed his slam in spite of East holding the guarded queen of clubs (rendering both the above methods a failure)?

After winning Trick One with the queen of diamonds, declarer crossed to the king of clubs (no queen), ran dummy's spades (discarding three diamonds), then cashed the three top hearts finishing in hand. His last three cards were ♦K and ♣J9, dummy holding ♣A82.

What could East retain? If he kept ♦AJ and ♣Q, declarer could drop his queen of clubs. At the table East chose to reduce to ♦A and ♣Q10. But declarer exited with the

**Dealer: South**    **Vulnerability: Both**

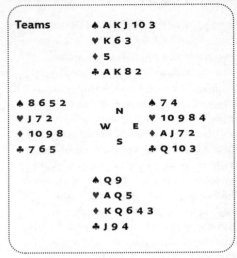

**Teams**

|  | ♠ A K J 10 3 |  |
| --- | --- | --- |
|  | ♥ K 6 3 |  |
|  | ♦ 5 |  |
|  | ♣ A K 8 2 |  |
| ♠ 8 6 5 2 |  | ♠ 7 4 |
| ♥ J 7 2 | N | ♥ 10 9 8 4 |
| ♦ 10 9 8 | W    E | ♦ A J 7 2 |
| ♣ 7 6 5 | S | ♣ Q 10 3 |
|  | ♠ Q 9 |  |
|  | ♥ A Q 5 |  |
|  | ♦ K Q 6 4 3 |  |
|  | ♣ J 9 4 |  |

| S | W | N | E |
| --- | --- | --- | --- |
| 1 NT | PASS | 2♥ (1) | PASS |
| 2♠ | PASS | 3♣ | PASS |
| 3NT | PASS | 4♥ (2) | PASS |
| 6NT (3) | END |  |  |

(1) Transfer bid – showing five spades.
(2) 'Patterning out' – i.e. implying his exact shape (and slammy values).
(3) With a maximum point-count but no fit.

**Contract: 6NT**    **Opening lead:** ♦10

king of diamonds to his ace and East had to lead away from the queen of clubs at Trick Twelve, enabling declarer to score his jack as well as dummy's ace. Twelve tricks, slam made, and a perfectly executed Strip Squeeze.

# Diabolical

Eighteen-year-old Englishman Oliver Burgess (sitting West) will fondly remember this deal from a recent Junior European Championships. First, team-mate David Gold, South at another table, demonstrated that Seven Spades makes on a normal lead.

Receiving the jack of diamonds lead, David won dummy's queen and drew trumps in three rounds. He then tried a second top diamond, hoping for a three-two split. It was not to be – East discarding – so he cashed the third top diamond, ruffed a low diamond, then led the king of clubs (the four-one diamond split meant he now needed a trick in the suit). West played low, but declarer discarded a heart from dummy, and took the rest with the ace-king of hearts in hand and a trump and two established diamonds in dummy. Thirteen tricks and grand slam made.

Meanwhile Oliver's opening lead was a diabolical jack of clubs! He knew – from North's Six Club bid – that his ace of clubs would be ruffed. Watch what happened.

Not suspecting that West would underlead an ace against a Grand Slam, the Polish declarer ruffed in dummy. The four-one diamond split now rendered the contract unmakeable, though he gave it his best shot, cashing the king of trumps, crossing to the ace, and then trying two top diamonds. East ruffed and the grand ended up down two.

Would declarer have succeeded on the more mundane ace of clubs lead? Yes – just. Ruff the lead, cash the king-queen of trumps, cross to the king of hearts, ruff a club, cross to the ace of hearts, cash the ace of trumps (drawing the last trump), then cash the king-queen of clubs and ace-king-queen of diamonds. Thirteen tricks. Only a lower club lead beats the grand slam!

**Dealer: North   Vulnerability: East-West**

Teams

North
- ♠ K Q 10 4
- ♥ 10 9 7
- ♦ A K Q 7 3 2
- ♣ –

West
- ♠ J 6
- ♥ 6 3
- ♦ J 10 9 5
- ♣ A J 10 6 3

East
- ♠ 9 8 7
- ♥ Q J 8 5 2
- ♦ 8
- ♣ 9 8 7 4

South
- ♠ A 5 3 2
- ♥ A K 4
- ♦ 6 4
- ♣ K Q 5 2

| S | W | N | E |
|---|---|---|---|
| | | 1 ♦ | PASS |
| 1 ♠ | PASS | 4 ♦ (1) | PASS |
| 4NT (2) | PASS | 6 ♣ (3) | PASS |
| 6 ♥ (4) | PASS | 7 ♠ | END |

(1) A raise to 4♠ with good diamonds.
(2) Roman Key Card Blackwood – spades agreed.
(3) In the partnership methods this showed two of the 'five aces' (including ♠K) plus a club void.
(4) Asking for ♠Q for a grand slam.

**Contract: 7♠**          **Opening lead: ♣J**

# Universal Language

There is no doubt that Bridge at a social level is enjoying a huge revival, especially in Europe. To encourage the revival at international level, biennial Junior (under 25) Bridge Camps have been started. In a recent such camp, Poland played host, and the camp was attended by over 250 young players worldwide.

Proving yet again that Bridge is a universal language, the participants partnered those of different nationalities. This ensured a natural, direct style of bidding that must be best for the future accessibility of the game.

The auction on this final deal – from the camp – was certainly direct. It left West to find a blind opening lead.

Should West try the ace of clubs? Or did North's failure to use Blackwood suggest a void in the suit? Should he attack with a heart, risking squashing his queen? Should he opt for a diamond, possibly setting up a trick there? Or should he opt for a safe trump?

It was a nightmare of a decision, with only the attacking heart lead defeating the contract. Eventually the nine of trumps hit the table.

Declarer now gave us a lesson in finessing technique. Look at the diamond suit – how should he try to score three tricks in the suit? *Answer*: in order to promote the queen and jack, he must lead the suit twice from dummy (key).

He won the trump lead in hand, crossed to dummy's ace (drawing the last missing trump), then led a low diamond (key play). East would have made things easy for declarer by rising with the king (declarer would make his queen and jack, then discard the heart loser on dummy's ace). However East played low.

**Dealer: South**  **Vulnerability: East-West**

**Pairs**

|         | ♠ A 10 6 4 2 |         |
|---------|--------------|---------|
|         | ♥ A 10 6 5   |         |
|         | ♦ A 7 4 3    |         |
|         | ♣ –          |         |

| ♠ 9          |       | ♠ J 8        |
|--------------|-------|--------------|
| ♥ Q 9 8      |   N   | ♥ K 7 4 3    |
| ♦ 8 2        | W   E | ♦ K 10 9 6   |
| ♣ A J 10 6 5 3 2 |   S   | ♣ Q 9 7      |

|         | ♠ K Q 7 5 3 |         |
|---------|-------------|---------|
|         | ♥ J 2       |         |
|         | ♦ Q J 5     |         |
|         | ♣ K 8 4     |         |

| S | W | N | E |
|---|---|---|---|
| 1♠ (1) | PASS (2) | 6♠ (3) | END |

(1) Playing Five-Card Majors and Strong Notrump.
(2) Showing surprising restraint. I never bid that way when I was a Junior – even Vulnerable!
(3) That's more like the Junior Bridge I remember!

**Contract: 6♠**  **Opening lead: ♠9**

Declarer won the queen, ruffed a club, then led a second low diamond. East rose with the king this time, and led a second club. Declarer ruffed in dummy, crossed to the jack of diamonds, ruffed a third club (with dummy's last trump), cashed the ace of diamonds (discarding a heart), cashed the ace of hearts and claimed.

Slam made.

# CHAPTER 19

# A Personal Reflection

'Oh, not boring Bridge', I used to sigh when a game of family Bridge was suggested after supper. I owe my parents much, for they persisted, and when, aged about eleven, I pulled out a Bridge book from the mobile library (which had disappointingly run out of 'Jennings' books, and was just about to pull away), then started to read, I soon became hooked.

Teenage years were spent dealing out cards, sometimes with my two younger brothers (as you can imagine, that got the competitive juices flowing) and mother; sometimes on my own (a very instructive exercise). I remember my first ever Duplicate: arriving at my local Club (Abingdon) very nervously with brother James (naturally we were youngest by some years); feeling we'd done okay, although fading somewhat as we played on well past our normal bedtime; a sleepless night reliving every board; a second-rate performance in next morning's double-maths period; then arriving back next week to a mixture of hushed whisper and congratulation: we had won by a distance with 68%.

University life saw Bridge take more and more prominence, as my studies took commensurately less. All-night sessions were frequent: I remember making nearly £9 one night – at 5p per hundred; and another night (...and day... and night) playing 28 successive hours, then arriving back at my House of Residence, putting a pizza in the oven, and then promptly falling asleep. The ensuing fire was mercifully put out just in time by a fellow resident student.

My first ever major event, aged 22, took me to Miami and...

Let me illustrate some of the highs and lows of the next twenty years, with some of my most memorable deals, none of which have ever been featured in *The Times*. Forgive any lack of modesty, but it is rare that I feel it appropriate to write myself up.

# Young Tigers

Miami 1986: the World Open Championships. As a raw 22-year-old on my first real Bridge adventure, I remember negotiating an incredibly cheap room rate for my partner Glyn Liggins and teammates Claudio Di Lullo and Dave Leigh (where are they now?). I remember playing swimming pool volleyball between sessions, and in the middle of the night (angering the hitherto kind hotel manager). And I remember playing Bridge. Lots of it.

The opening Teams seemed to go on for ever (indeed it became known as 'The Endless Teams'), such that Glyn and I were pretty exhausted by the end (we finished a respectable 43rd). Pairs to follow, and a lack-lustre start saw us near the foot of the table for the first three sessions.

A good final session saw us catapult from 270th to 147th (out of 320), with 151 pairs qualifying for the semifinal. Glyn, still in bed thinking we had no chance to qualify (and, frankly, looking forward to a rest) was awoken, and we began our charge through the field during the four-session semifinals, being the only British Pair to make the 48-pair final.

I remember the late Jeremy Flint, then correspondent, refer to us in *The Times* as 'The Young Tigers', and being proud as punch. Our card-play may have been less experienced, but we Tigers survived on close doubles for down one. Plus there were a few youthful liberties, such as this deal, my favourite of the whole two weeks.

Not for the faint-hearted (or sane), my psychic Two overcall goaded North-South into Six Notrumps. Out came my surprise attack, the king of spades, and the Swedish declarer, placing me with ♥K10xxxx (I was vulnerable, after all), reasonably decided to play for all thirteen tricks. He therefore won

**Dealer: South      Vulnerability: Both**

Pairs

|  | ♠ 3 |  |
|---|---|---|
|  | ♥ A Q 9 8 |  |
|  | ♦ A Q J 10 4 3 2 |  |
|  | ♣ 4 |  |

| ♠ K Q 10 8 7 6 5 | | ♠ J 2 |
| ♥ 7 5 | N | ♥ K 10 6 3 2 |
| ♦ – | W    E | ♦ 9 8 7 |
| ♣ 8 6 5 3 | S | ♣ K J 9 |

|  | ♠ A 9 4 |  |
|---|---|---|
|  | ♥ J 4 |  |
|  | ♦ K 6 5 |  |
|  | ♣ A Q 10 7 2 |  |

| S | W (ROBSON) | N | E |
|---|---|---|---|
| 1NT (1) | 2♥! (2) | 6NT (3) | END |

(1) 14-16.
(2) No this is not a misprint. Your young author psyched Two Hearts, prepared to run to spades if doubled.
(3) Upgrading his hand in the light of the seemingly well-placed heart honours, and choosing the higher-scoring slam (Matchpoint scoring).

**Contract: 6NT      Opening lead: ♠K**

the ace of spades, then took the 'marked' heart finesse, running the jack.

You can imagine his horror (actually he was very sporting) when East, Glyn, won the king, and returned a second spade. Six more of those meant down six.

# World Junior

The late Eighties saw your author finish his Postgraduate Certificate in Education at Bristol University, abandon being a local supply teacher, and move to London to pursue Bridge full-time.

It did not start glamorously. I remember trying to make the accounts balance at 3am behind the Young Chelsea Bridge Club bar (they never did, and the genial owner Warwick Pitch, would always rectify them in two minutes the next morning). I remember all-night rubber sessions at the now defunct London School of Bridge (LSB) on the Kings Road, where I hosted, and, later, did my first real Bridge teaching. And I remember Junior Bridge.

I was regarded as something of a maverick: brilliant natural card-player, wild unreliable bidder. I was asked to play with the then number one Junior, John Pottage (who has since stopped playing). After an underachieving start, we peaked as I neared the age limit of 25 (thank you, Mummy, for giving birth to me two weeks late, on January 5th).

1989 was the beginning of a purple patch. John and I spearheaded a team win in the Common Market Championships, and then came the big one: the World Junior Team Championships in Nottingham (which we only qualified for by being the host nation).

Everything went perfectly, and even misplayed hands, such as this one, turned out okay. Declaring Four Hearts as South, I successfully finessed dummy's queen of spades at Trick One, then hurriedly discarded a diamond on the ace of spades (a should-have-been fatal error; start trumps instead, relying on the ace of diamonds to be onside, and I would have been home and dry).

At Trick Three I led a trump to the jack, winning, then followed with a club. West rose with the ace and led the king of spades, allowing East to dispose of a club as I ruffed. I led a club to dummy and followed with a

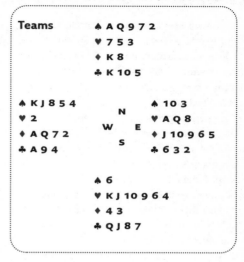

**Dealer: West    Vulnerability: North-South**

Teams

♠ A Q 9 7 2
♥ 7 5 3
♦ K 8
♣ K 10 5

♠ K J 8 5 4
♥ 2
♦ A Q 7 2
♣ A 9 4

♠ 10 3
♥ A Q 8
♦ J 10 9 6 5
♣ 6 3 2

♠ 6
♥ K J 10 9 6 4
♦ 4 3
♣ Q J 8 7

| S (ROBSON) | W | N | E |
|---|---|---|---|
| | 1♠ | PASS | 1NT |
| 3♥ (1) | PASS | 4♥ (2) | END |

(1) Weak Jump overcall.
(2) 'Andrew may be a little crazy, but he is vulnerable'.

**Contract: 4♥**            **Opening lead: ♠5**

second trump. East won the ace (West discarding an encouraging diamond), and my fate seemed set. East would (and did) lead a diamond to his partner's ace, and secure a club ruff. Down one

I had one chance. When West won the ace of diamonds, I called for dummy's king, as though I had not seen the ace. West fell for the bait, trying to cash the queen of diamonds. Breathing a sigh of relief, I could ruff, cash the king of trumps, felling East's queen, and claim my game.

Being a World Champion felt really good, but with a tinge of sadness. My age forced me to bow out of Junior Bridge. The challenge of the Open game awaited...

# Impostor

Tony Forrester was the undisputed No. 1 player in the country at the time, but his successful partnership with Raymond Brock was ending. I was determined to become Tony's partner, and, after some deliberation, he agreed.

A period followed that was the stuff of dreams. In the space of ten days in early January 1990, Tony and I won the two most prestigious invitational events in the Bridge World, the Cap Gemini in The Hague, and the Sunday Times/Macallan in London. Beating heroes such as Italy's Benito Garrozzo, and USA's Meckstroth-Rodwell, was almost too fantastic to be true.

In the space of two years, I had moved from relative unknown British Junior to world beating Open player. 'Who is this Robson?' I was the talk of the town. I remember feeling something of an impostor: how can I be winning all this, when I am barely out of shorts (or the Bridge equivalent)?

What were the secrets of the Forrester-Robson glory days? (a) Tony never made a mistake (although I did), (b) my 'flair' bids seemed to work more often than not, (c) we seemed to have the better of the luck.

Take this Cap Gemini deal, perhaps the most fortunate hand I have ever played. Bizarrely, my partner was the genial and talented Dutchman Kees Tammens, substituting for poor Tony who was in his sickbed that day.

Because the two hands, mine and dummy's, were mirrored, i.e. exactly the same shape, Six Notrumps was a filthy slam, with almost no hope of making. There was one tiny chance: I played for it.

Winning the spade lead, I cashed all my black suit winners, then played ace, king, and a third diamond. West won and, as I had to hope, held no black-suit cards to cash,

**Dealer: South    Vulnerability: Neither**

Teams
- ♠ A 7 6
- ♥ A 10 3
- ♦ A 8 4 3
- ♣ K Q 7

West:
- ♠ J 10 8
- ♥ Q J 5 2
- ♦ J 10 7
- ♣ 10 6 5

East:
- ♠ 9 5 4 2
- ♥ 9 7 6
- ♦ Q 6
- ♣ J 9 3 2

South:
- ♠ K Q 3
- ♥ K 8 4
- ♦ K 10 5 2
- ♣ A 8 4

| S (ROBSON) | W | N | E |
|---|---|---|---|
| 1 NT (1) | PASS | 6NT (2) | END |

(1) 15-17 with Kees (Tony and I played 14-16).
(2) A tad optimistic, with the barren 4333 shape.

**Contract: 6NT          Opening lead: ♠J**

therefore had to lead a heart. If he held ♥Q9xx/♥J9xx, he could defeat the slam by switching to his honour, and West, Dutch Champion Berry Westra, would certainly have known this textbook position.

When West switched to a low heart, I played for my only chance, rising with the ten and hoping that West held both honours. Phew! The ten won, and I could claim my slam. Lucky boy!

# Purest Test

Despite this fairy-tale start to my career in the Open game, I still felt that I really shouldn't be there, right at the top. I made mistakes, surely at a more basic level than other world experts.

The 1990 Par Contest, the first such event for many decades and perhaps the purest test of ability, somewhat changed my perception.

There are few more daunting prospects for a Bridge player, than sitting behind a computer terminal (remember this was before the computer/internet era), whilst playing some of the trickiest declarer-play problems imaginable. Make a wrong move, and you will hear a frightening, point-deducting, and morale-shattering bleep. Three bleeps per problem and you score no points.

I finished fifth (out of 20 or so invited world experts), a place above partner Tony Forrester, and was only beaten by 'single-dummy' specialists.

Here is Problem Five out of twelve, one of the four or five I solved completely correctly (i.e. bleep-free). East wins the trump lead with the ace, and returns a second trump, inconveniently preventing you from ruffing three spades in dummy.

Hearts appear 6-3 on the bidding. You must hope that East has the ace, which can be ruffed out on the third-round of the suit, and so promote the king. Dummy entries are very short, however.

The key play is to lead the two of diamonds at Trick Three. This puts West in a fork: unable to rise with the ace (and give you three diamond tricks), he must play low. You win dummy's jack, then ruff a heart, cash the ace of spades, ruff a second spade, ruff a second heart, ruff a third spade, and ruff a third heart (bringing down East's ace).

At Trick Nine you lead the king of

**Par**

|  | ♠ J |
|  | ♥ K 9 7 4 |
|  | ♦ Q J 5 4 |
|  | ♣ 7 6 5 4 |

| ♠ K Q 5 | | ♠ 10 9 7 6 |
| ♥ Q J 8 6 3 2 | N | ♥ A 10 5 |
| ♦ A 8 3 | W    E | ♦ 10 9 7 6 |
| ♣ 3 | S | ♣ A 2 |

|  | ♠ A 8 4 3 2 |
|  | ♥ – |
|  | ♦ K 2 |
|  | ♣ K Q J 10 9 8 |

| S | W | N | E |
|---|---|---|---|
| 1♣ | 1♥ | 2♣ | 2♥ |
| 2♠ | 4♥ | DOUBLE | PASS |
| 4♠ | PASS | 5♣ | END |

The auction, opening lead, and dummy are given. You have to make your contract.

**Contract: 5♣**          **Opening lead: ♣3**

diamonds, and again West is forked. If he wins the ace, he has to lead a red card, giving access to dummy's stranded king of hearts and queen of diamonds: away go declarer's two remaining spades and the game is made.

However West ducking the king of diamonds is no better, for now you switch tacks, giving up the fourth spade to East, ruffing the diamond return, and cashing the now-established fifth spade. Either way: eleven tricks and game made.

# Killarney

The good times continue in 1991, during which Tony Forrester and I spend almost half the year globetrotting. The year kicks off with high placings in the Cap Gemini (2nd), and *Sunday Times*/Macallan (4th), and reaches a peak in Killarney, Ireland, in the summer.

Tony and I spearhead a British Team victory – by a record margin – in the biennial European Team Championships, considered by many to be the toughest event in the World calendar. I have always regarded this as my greatest-ever achievement.

This Killarney deal sees your author declare a Six Diamond slam that depends on avoiding two club losers. The simple approach is to lead to dummy's queen, but there were options if the king of clubs was offside (i.e. with East). Where was that all-important king?

Winning the heart lead with the ace, I drew trumps, cashed spades, then eliminated hearts by crossing to the king and leading a third round. I noted that East, known to hold the queen of hearts from West's opening lead of the jack, refrained from playing it. This was surely an indication that he didn't want to be endplayed with the card, forced to lead away from his king of clubs.

Placing the crucial king with East, I ruffed the third heart and led a club to West's low card and dummy's nine (key play). East won the jack but was now endplayed to lead away from his king (around to dummy's queen), or lead a major (enabling me to ruff in one hand and discard a club from the other). Twelve tricks and game made.

Note that West could have given me an awkward guess by inserting the ten of clubs. Would I have covered with dummy's queen, playing his partner for the jack (the winning option); or ducked (playing West for the jack)?

In truth, I did nothing brilliant, and would

argue that our positive swing on the deal (slam failed in the other room) was at least as much due to the brilliance of team-mate John Armstrong (East). For when a third heart was led from the dummy (declarer playing identically to me), John rose with the queen, feigning indifference to being endplayed. Now placing the king of clubs with West, declarer ruffed and led a club to dummy's queen. East won the king and returned a club, ensuring that the defence came to a second trick in the suit. Down one.

**Dealer: South**          **Vulnerability: Both**

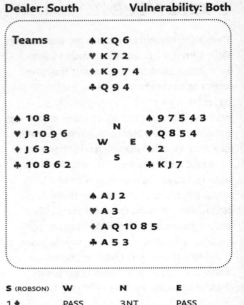

Teams

|   |   |
|---|---|
| ♠ K Q 6 | |
| ♥ K 7 2 | |
| ♦ K 9 7 4 | |
| ♣ Q 9 4 | |

| ♠ 10 8 | ♠ 9 7 5 4 3 |
| ♥ J 10 9 6 | ♥ Q 8 5 4 |
| ♦ J 6 3 | ♦ 2 |
| ♣ 10 8 6 2 | ♣ K J 7 |

| ♠ A J 2 |
| ♥ A 3 |
| ♦ A Q 10 8 5 |
| ♣ A 5 3 |

| S (ROBSON) | W | N | E |
|---|---|---|---|
| 1♦ | PASS | 3NT | PASS |
| 6♦ | END | | |

**Contract: 6♦**          **Opening lead: ♥J**

# Could've, Should've

Dealer: West       Vulnerability: Both

My Bridge was still far from error-free, but I always sought to learn from my mistakes. Sometimes I had the opportunity to teach others from these errors too.

I remember my 1991 Bols Bridge Tip (winning 2nd place): 'Play a pre-emptor who leads his suit for a singleton trump.' This was triggered  by a Cap Gemini deal I mucked up.

Why should a pre-emptor who leads his suit normally have a singleton trump? Simple really. A pre-emptor's most likely shape (by far) is 7321; he will surely lead his singleton against your trump contract... unless it's in trumps.

On the deal in question, I would have done better to pass Three Notrumps (or better, double) and lead the king of hearts. However West's ace of clubs lead gave me a chance in Four Hearts. I ruffed, and now crossed to the king of spades, discarded a diamond loser on the promoted king of clubs, then led a trump to the king. Essentially I was playing for both majors to split, with the queen of spades being doubleton (for the lack of a dummy entry to finesse). I ended up down two.

I should have reasoned that West's failure to lead a side-suit singleton meant he was likely to be 7321 with a singleton trump.

The indicated line is as follows:

Cross to the king of spades, discard a diamond on the king of clubs, then lead the jack of spades (the last time I can finesse). Assuming East plays low, I now lead a trump and, playing East for ♥A10xx (by far his most likely four-card holding), finesse the nine. I can now force out the ace of trumps, and claim my game, losing two diamonds and a trump.

If, at Trick Three, East covers the jack of spades with the queen, I win the ace and lead the king of trumps. Whether or not this is taken by the ace, I can cross to the promoted

**Teams**

|                |            |              |           |
|----------------|------------|--------------|-----------|
|                |            | ♠ K J 10 4   |           |
|                |            | ♥ 6 4        |           |
|                |            | ♦ J 8 4 3    |           |
|                |            | ♣ K 4 3      |           |
| ♠ 5 2          |            |              | ♠ Q 7 6   |
| ♥ 8            |            | N            | ♥ A 10 7 2 |
| ♦ K 6 5        | W          | E            | ♦ A Q 7   |
| ♣ A J 10 9 6   |            | S            | ♣ Q 8 7   |
| 5 2            |            |              |           |
|                |            | ♠ A 9 8 3    |           |
|                |            | ♥ K Q J 9 5 3 |          |
|                |            | ♦ 10 9 2     |           |
|                |            | ♣ –          |           |

| S (ROBSON) | W | N | E |
|---|---|---|---|
| | 3♣ | PASS | 3NT |
| 4♥ | END | | |

**Contract: 4♥          Opening lead: ♣A**

ten of spades and lead a second trump to the nine.

Either way – vulnerable game made. Could've, should've.

# Naturals vs Scientists

The year 1992 saw disappointing finishes in the January invitation events, after which there followed the famous Naturals vs Scientists match.

As a Natural, Tony Forrester and I were allowed no conventions, other than a notrump range (we chose our normal 14-16), a take-out double, and Blackwood. No Stayman, no Transfers, no Fourth Suit Forcing, no Unassuming Cue Bid (the latter two being the biggest losses).

£50,000 was the prize for the winning team, our sponsor being Portland Club member Demetri Marchessini, who championed the Natural cause. Sad to report, the Scientists took the loot (back to their native USA). However it was generally agreed that inferior cardplay was as much to blame (for our loss) as lack of bidding methods.

Take this missed opportunity by your author. In a shaky Four Spades, the defence began with two rounds of clubs. I ruffed, and realised that I would be fatally shortened if I drew trumps and then tried to knock out the red aces. Instead I led the jack of diamonds at Trick Two.

I was hoping to create the impression I held a doubleton diamond, and the ruse was successful. West ducked the jack, but, on winning a second diamond, failed to give his partner a ruff. Doubtless he thought that East's count signal – indicating an even number – was based on four cards rather than two. He led a third club.

I ruffed the club and led a heart. West played a deceptive jack (I would have finessed the ten), so I covered with the king, ducked by East. I now led a trump to the nine, the finesse successful, and cashed the ace of trumps.

On this trick, East, Eric Rodwell, made the fine play of dropping the queen, the card he was known to hold. Leaving the last trump outstanding, as I had to, I led a heart to the ten, which East again ducked, and a third

heart to East's ace. East continued his fine defence by leading a fourth club, on which I discarded a diamond from hand and ruffed in dummy.

In the two-card ending, dummy held the thirteenth heart and a top diamond; I held a top trump and a diamond. With the benefit of hindsight, it should have been clear to lead the last heart, playing East to have the last trump (and to have false-carded with the queen). East would ruff, whereupon I could overruff, cash the diamond, and (so I was later told) win the Brilliancy Prize for Best Played Hand.

Sadly I led the king of diamonds, and East pounced on the trick, ruffing. Down one. Truly defeat snatched from the jaws of victory.

---

**Dealer: West          Vulnerability: Neither**

**Teams**

|                  | ♠ J 10 5          |                  |
|                  | ♥ K 10 8 7        |                  |
|                  | ♦ K Q 8           |                  |
|                  | ♣ 7 5 3           |                  |

| ♠ 7 3            |         | ♠ Q 8 2          |
| ♥ J 9 2          | N       | ♥ A 4 3          |
| ♦ A 10 9 2       | W   E   | ♦ 5 3            |
| ♣ A 10 6 4       | S       | ♣ K Q J 9 2      |

|                  | ♠ A K 9 6 4       |                  |
|                  | ♥ Q 6 5           |                  |
|                  | ♦ J 7 6 4         |                  |
|                  | ♣ 8               |                  |

| S (ROBSON) | W | N | E |
|---|---|---|---|
|  | PASS | PASS | 2♣ (1) |
| 2♠ | 4♣ | 4♠ | |

(1) 11-15 with five or usually six clubs (precision-style).

**Contract: 4♠          Opening lead: ♣A**

# 'Nicely Played'

I played less Tournament Bridge during the mid-Nineties. I managed The Acol Bridge Club in 1993/4, then, after a brief pause, started my own club in September 1995 above a pub in Chelsea.

The Andrew Robson Bridge Club grew beyond my wildest dreams, necessitating a move to Parsons Green (in 1999) to our own dedicated premises. It now has some 2000 members (I am told this makes it the biggest Bridge Club in the world).

I also started writing on Bridge: for the *Oldie*, the *Spectator*, the *Express on Sunday*, and *Country Life* (for which I still write weekly). Less time for playing was a regret, but reaching out to thousands through writing and teaching is perhaps more worthwhile.

My partnership with Tony Forrester was nearing its natural conclusion (we stopped playing in 1997), but we did have a few more moments to savour. Take the international match against Indonesia in 1996.

Tony and I had a spectacular disaster to end spectacular disasters, going for 3400 in Three Spades redoubled (down six). (I passed Tony in an SOS 'get me out of here' redouble; our trump suit was 6542 facing 8; I recall he played it rather well to make three tricks.) This was the very next deal:

Declaring Five Clubs doubled after a revealing auction, the defence led two rounds of spades. East's likely trump holding was Kxx. I could pick up his trumps via a finesse, but would need both of dummy's trumps, and therefore could not afford to ruff a third heart.

Needing to make something of the diamonds, I ran the ten of the suit at Trick Two. East won the jack, and exited with a small heart. This gave me a less interesting way of getting home, able to play low from hand, beat West's jack with the ace, run dummy's ten, and then lead the jack of

**Dealer: West    Vulnerability: Neither**

Teams

```
                ♠ J 5 3
                ♥ K 10
                ♦ A Q 6 4 3 2
                ♣ J 3

  ♠ K 10 9 8 6          N        ♠ A Q 7 4
  ♥ J 8 6 4 2                    ♥ Q 7 3
  ♦ 7 5          W         E     ♦ K J 9
  ♣ 5                   S        ♣ K 9 2

                ♠ 2
                ♥ A 9 5
                ♦ 10 8
                ♣ A Q 10 8 7 6 4
```

| S (ROBSON) | W | N | E |
|---|---|---|---|
| | 2♣ (1) | 2♦ | 4♠ |
| 5♣ | PASS | PASS | DOUBLE |
| END | | | |

(1) Weak with both majors (5-4 or 5-5).

**Contract: 5♣ doubled   Opening lead: ♠10**

trumps. But I did not need to rely on East having a heart honour.

Instead of rising with the ace of hearts, I played a diamond to the ace, then led the jack of trumps. East played low (as he had to – cover and I could ruff a heart), but now I switched tacks, ruffing a diamond to set up the suit, crossing to the king of hearts, and leading a promoted long diamond.

If East ruffed, I could overruff, ruff a heart, and the king of trumps would fall under the ace. If East discarded, I could throw my losing heart, then lead the second trump and finesse against East's king. Eleven tricks, game made, and a generous, 'Nicely played,' from Tony (who was naturally still smarting from the -3400).

# Bleep-Free

I was somewhat injury-prone even before my horrific cliff-fall in 2001, and it was with a broken wrist (whilst playing cricket), and a card-holder, that I arrived at the 1998 World Championships in Lille. Not that I needed two hands (the human variety) for the second (and only) Par Contest to be held in the last 50 years.

Each of the 35 invited experts were seated at a computer terminal. In the same format as eight years before in Geneva, you saw dummy's cards, but not the opponents'. You sought to avoid the dreaded 'bleep'. For three bleeps per deal, and you score no points, and must move on to the next of the twelve diabolical declarer-play problems.

In Lille, there was a 36th competitor, GIB. GIB, one of the world's leading computer Bridge programs, was leading after three (of four) sessions, but evidently got 'tired', finishing twelfth.

I finished eighth, not bad, given the aching wrist. Whilst being a slightly lower position than Geneva, the overall standard was much better, and my absolute score was higher. Furthermore, I was really out of practice, having spent more time walking from Coast-to-Coast of England, and teaching and managing at my Bridge Club, than playing at the table so far that year.

My favourite deal, and one of the easier ones (!), which I managed bleep-free, was this horrendous Six Clubs. Is there any layout that permits success?

The answer is just one. With a certain trump loser, you must score four spade tricks, and discard a heart on the fourth. Lacking the entries to hand to ruff two diamonds, you must make something of the hearts, which you can only do if West has honour-honour doubleton. The desired position can only be reached if West's shape

**Dealer: South      Vulnerability: Neither**

| Par | ♠ A J 10 9 |
|---|---|
| | ♥ A 10 9 4 3 |
| | ♦ A |
| | ♣ 6 5 4 |

| ♠ 4 3 | | ♠ Q 8 7 6 |
|---|---|---|
| ♥ Q J | **N** | ♥ K 8 6 5 |
| ♦ J 10 9 7 5 | **W   E** | ♦ K Q |
| ♣ 3 2 | **S** | ♣ J 10 2 |
| ♣ Q 9 | | |

| | ♠ K 5 2 |
|---|---|
| | ♥ 7 2 |
| | ♦ 8 6 4 |
| | ♣ A K 8 7 3 |

**S     W     N       E**

Contract = 6♣ (Don't try to find a sensible sequence: there cannot be one, and the resulting slam is appalling!)

**Contract: 6♣         Opening lead: ♦J**

is precisely 2272 (as you will see), so, with East having more spades, you should play him for the queen.

The indicated line is to lead and run the jack of spades at Trick Two, then run the ten (East playing low – best). Cross to the ace-king of trumps, cash the king of spades, cross to the ace of hearts, discard a heart on the ace of spades, and ruff a low heart (both West's honours appearing).

At Trick Ten, ruff a diamond, then lead the ten of hearts for a ruffing finesse. East covers with the king (best), but you ruff, and exit with a trump. East wins, but his last card is a small heart, taken by dummy's nine, as you throw away your losing diamond. Twelve tricks and slam made.

But please stop in a part-score next time!

# Last Train

During 1998 and 1999, I played more Bridge Stateside than in Britain, and with some success. My team (with partner Rita Shugart, and team-mates Tony Forrester and talented Norwegian Geir Helgemo) won the prestigious Reisinger both years. This made Tony and me the first Englishmen to win an American 'Major'.

The ten-team final in Boston in 1999 saw one of the oh-so-rare days, where everything Rita and I did turned to gold. I recall holding ♠A75, ♥A10864, ♦K93, ♣64, and hearing the (unopposed) auction go: 1NT–2♣ (Stayman)–2♠–3NT. With both opponents having advertised a major suit, I led the four of clubs! This deceptive ruse worked like a charm, declarer misplaying the entire hand, thinking I held good clubs.

Funnily enough though, the deal I remember most from that USA-dominated period occurred during a training match. East, Michael Rosenberg, winner of the 1998 Par Contest and true card-play magician, said that he had never defended a hand where he had been so sure the contract would fail, yet it did not. Praise indeed. Here it is:

West, Zia Mahmood, found the normal (but not best) opening lead of the jack of diamonds, which ran to my queen. I led a trump to the queen, to discover the bad news-good news. The bad news was that trumps split 4-0; the good news was that it was East, finessable, with the four.

East beat the queen with the ace, and returned a second diamond. I could not ruff a diamond, or I would be unable to pick up East's remaining trumps via two finesses. So I rose with the ace, discarding a heart.

I crossed to a top heart, and played a trump to East's seven and my eight. I then crossed to the other top heart, and led a third heart, ruffing out East's queen.

I next crossed to the ace of clubs and led a

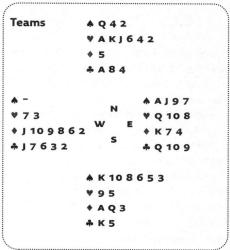

**Dealer: South    Vulnerability: Neither**

**Teams**

|  | ♠ Q 4 2 |  |
|  | ♥ A K J 6 4 2 |  |
|  | ♦ 5 |  |
|  | ♣ A 8 4 |  |

| ♠ - | | ♠ A J 9 7 |
| ♥ 7 3 | N | ♥ Q 10 8 |
| ♦ J 10 9 8 6 2 | W    E | ♦ K 7 4 |
| ♣ J 7 6 3 2 | S | ♣ Q 10 9 |

|  | ♠ K 10 8 6 5 3 |  |
|  | ♥ 9 5 |  |
|  | ♦ A Q 3 |  |
|  | ♣ K 5 |  |

| S (ROBSON) | W | N | E |
|---|---|---|---|
| 1♠ | PASS | 2♥ | PASS |
| 2♠ | PASS | 4♦ (1) | PASS |
| 4♥ (2) | PASS | 4NT (3) | PASS |
| 5♥ (4) | PASS | 6♠ | END |

(1) Splinter Bid, showing spade support, diamond shortage, and slam interest.
(2) 'Last Train' (to Clarkesville), a highly useful modern treatment, whereby the 'bid-in-the-middle' (i.e. the only bid between sign-off and slam-advance) says, 'I'm interested in slam, but cannot commit beyond game.' It says nothing about the suit actually bid.
(3) Roman Key Card Blackwood.
(4) Two of the 'five aces', where the king of trumps (here, spades) counts as an ace; but no queen of trumps.

**Contract: 6♠**          **Opening lead:** ♦J

winning heart. East, helpless, ruffed, but I could now overruff, ruff a diamond, lead another heart, ruffed and overruffed, and table my last trump and the king of clubs. Slam made – there was no defence.

# Count Declarer's Tricks

There has been one other major influence on my Bridge-playing life, who has received little mention to date: charismatic Pakistani-born Zia Mahmood.

Although Zia is qualified to play for the USA, and therefore only available for the occasional game, we did win the Cap Gemini in 2000 and 2001. I felt confident the second time, because I saw a car on the way to the airport with the number-plate CAP 2! Less than a month later, I almost lost my life in a hill-walking accident in the Lake District which I alluded to earlier.

Britain's most prestigious invitational event (since the demise of the *Sunday Times/Macallan*), the Lederer Memorial Trophy, has also been kind to Zia and me. As part of the 'All Stars' (team of four), we won in five successive years from 1998 to 2002.

This deal from the 1998 Lederer won me the Best Defended Hand of the Year, although in truth I thought it barely worth all the accolades it received. West, Zia, led the king of clubs against the Six Spade slam. Declarer won the ace, and led a diamond to the king. I was the ace, and it was crunch time.

The key was to count declarer's tricks. If I, say, woodenly returned a club, hoping to score my jack of trumps later, I would be disappointed. For declarer is known to have four side-suit winners (ace-king of hearts, queen of diamonds, and ace of clubs). He would simply cross-ruff all his eight trumps, to make twelve tricks and slam made.

The way to reduce declarer's tally of trump tricks was to switch to a trump. Yes, away from ♠Jxxx. Declarer could still have made the slam after my trump switch, because of the miraculous heart position. Reasonably, he played to set up the fifth

**Dealer: North**  **Vulnerability: Both**

Teams

|  | ♠ K 10 7 |  |
|---|---|---|
|  | ♥ K 9 6 5 2 |  |
|  | ♦ K Q 9 8 4 |  |
|  | ♣ - |  |

| ♠ 2 |  | ♠ J 8 5 3 |
|---|---|---|
| ♥ 7 4 3 | **N** | ♥ Q J |
| ♦ J 10 3 2 | **W      E** | ♦ A 7 6 |
| ♣ K Q 9 7 2 | **S** | ♣ 10 8 5 4 |

|  | ♠ A Q 9 6 4 |  |
|---|---|---|
|  | ♥ A 10 8 |  |
|  | ♦ 5 |  |
|  | ♣ A J 6 3 |  |

| S | W | N | E (ROBSON) |
|---|---|---|---|
|  |  | 1 ♥ | PASS |
| 1 ♠ | PASS | 2 ♦ | PASS |
| 3 ♣ (1) | PASS | 3 ♠ | PASS |
| 4NT (2) | PASS | 5 ♦ (3) | PASS |
| 6 ♠ | END |  |  |

(1) Fourth Suit Forcing. 'We're going to game – more information please.'
(2) Roman Key Card Blackwood, agreeing spades.
(3) One (or four) of 'five aces' (including the king of spades).

**Contract: 6♠**       **Opening lead: ♣K**

diamond, and ended up down two when trumps did not split.

It's worth remembering that defensive tip: counting declarer's tricks. I have found it most useful over the years.

# Le Manoir

It was a life-changing year for me in 2000. Much more important (even) than becoming *The Times* Bridge Correspondent (in June), I married Lorna in January, and was a Dad by the end of the year.

As any parent knows, life before children is very different to life after, and any comparison is futile and entirely inappropriate. You adore your wife and children (I have two lovely daughters, Hannah and Mimi), but of course child-rearing is by its very nature a selfless task.

Carefree gallivanting around the globe is replaced by fetching and carrying small people; weekend Bridge-playing is replaced by more writing and teaching during the week.

There might be less Bridge-playing, but there is far from none. I was thrilled to win Britain's premier knock-out event, the Gold Cup, in 2002 and again in 2003. The very day I won (for the first time) in 2002, my parents were hosting their 40th Wedding Anniversary celebration at Le Manoir au Quat' Saisons restaurant. I felt I had to win to justify (to myself) my non-attendance. In the event, I felt this huge force (from Oxfordshire) with me all day, and we won by a record 151 imps.

My partner on that occasion, and the year after, was co-teacher at my club, David Bakhshi, one of the English talents to emerge over the last decade. Here is a Gold Cup deal in partnership with David.

West led a reasonable (but unfortunate) club against my Four Spades. I won the ten, and at Trick two led a heart. West almost certainly held both red aces to justify his double, and he was likely to rise with the ace in case I held a singleton heart. He did.

West returned a passive second heart (best), and I won the king and ruffed a third heart low (safe – West would hardly double One Spade with just two hearts). What next?

I wanted to ruff my jack of clubs, but how

**Teams**

|  | ♠ A 6 4 |  |
|  | ♥ K 10 8 7 |  |
|  | ♦ 8 6 5 3 2 |  |
|  | ♣ 7 |  |

| ♠ 9 | | ♠ J 8 3 2 |
| ♥ A 3 2 | N | ♥ Q J 6 4 |
| ♦ A J 10 9 | W   E | ♦ Q 4 |
| ♣ Q 8 6 5 2 | S | ♣ 9 4 3 |

|  | ♠ K Q 10 7 5 |  |
|  | ♥ 9 5 |  |
|  | ♦ K 7 |  |
|  | ♣ A K J 10 |  |

| S (ROBSON) | W | N | E |
|---|---|---|---|
| 1♠ (1) | DOUBLE | 2♣ (2) | 2♥ |
| 4♠ | END | | |

(1) Playing Five-card Majors.
(2) A conventional bid, showing a decent three-card spade raise (8-10 points or compensating shape).

**Contract: 4♠**      **Opening lead: ♣5**

would I then play trumps? Would I cash the ace and finesse the ten (West rated to be short for his take-out double)? Or not? Unwilling to guess, I saw an improvement, involving drawing trumps and endplaying West in the minors.

I cashed the king of trumps, crossed to the ace (West did discard), finessed the ten, and cashed the queen. To what five cards could West reduce?

Helpless, at the table West came down to three clubs and two diamonds, but I played ace-king-jack of clubs to his queen, and waited for him to lead away from his ace of diamonds, enabling me to score my king. Ten tricks and game made.

# Rubber Bridge

Although, unlike Zia, Rubber Bridge is not my first love (I prefer the cut-and-thrust of Matchpointed Pairs), I learnt to play at the Rubber Table, so it is very dear to my heart. Family Rubber Bridge, student Rubber Bridge, hosting at London Rubber Clubs Green Street and the London School of Bridge (both now defunct), I must have played many tens of thousands of Rubber Bridge deals over the past 30 years.

These days, I have less time – or cause – to play much Rubber. However there is one group of players with whom I still love to play. Not because I hope to fleece them, you understand (although I do have a small edge, I consistently fail to exploit it); rather, because they are fascinating, successful people, as well as very good amateur Bridge players. I'm referring to London's Portland Club. I cannot be a member – no 'Pros' allowed, but am an occasional visitor, and regular participator in their away games.

One of my annual highlights is a week at Tessa and Stuart Wheeler's house in Tangier, where Rubber is played (almost) from dawn until (well after) dusk, only interrupted by the pouring of Pimms and the eating of delicious outdoor barbeques.

Although latterly I have introduced a few of the most useful conventions for such occasions (such as Transfers, Unassuming Cue Bids, Fourth Suit Forcing, Roman Key Card Blackwood, and Splinters), no conventions are allowed within the Club. Such an approach certainly hones your bidding judgement, as you have no tools to help.

This deal from the Portland sees me unable to ask for aces, instead guessing to pot slam. In the event, there were plenty of problems apart from aces. West led a heart, and East won the ace, then returned the seven of diamonds.

Reading West for the king of diamonds

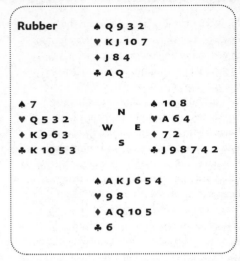

**Dealer: South   Vulnerability: North-South**

| | |
|---|---|
| **Rubber** | ♠ Q 9 3 2 |
| | ♥ K J 10 7 |
| | ♦ J 8 4 |
| | ♣ A Q |

West:
♠ 7
♥ Q 5 3 2
♦ K 9 6 3
♣ K 10 5 3

East:
♠ 10 8
♥ A 6 4
♦ 7 2
♣ J 9 8 7 4 2

South:
♠ A K J 6 5 4
♥ 9 8
♦ A Q 10 5
♣ 6

| S (ROBSON) | W | N | E |
|---|---|---|---|
| 1♠ | PASS | 4♠ (1) | PASS |
| 6♠ (2) | END | | |

(1) Not a shut out at Rubber.
(2) No Blackwood allowed.

**Contract: 6♠**          **Opening lead: ♥2**

(would East be crafty enough to switch away from his king?), I rose with the ace, drew trumps, finessed the queen of clubs, cashed the ace discarding a diamond, then ran all my trumps.

West was squeezed on the last trump, having to discard from ♥Q53 and ♦K. Away went a heart, but I could now lead my second heart to the ten, cash the king, felling West's queen, and follow with the promoted jack of hearts. Twelve tricks and slam made.

Note that the best return for East at Trick Two is a second heart. Now you have to play for a different squeeze-ending to win, delaying the club finesse until you have played all your trumps. I'm betting I'd have taken a simple diamond finesse and gone down.

# Crunch Time

Moroccan tummy had got me on the last night of a week chez Wheeler. I lay moaning in bed, reflecting on my task ahead. I needed to get back to London, then leave for Verona the very next day to play the World Individual.

This biennial event is one of my favourites, giving you the chance to play two boards with those you normally oppose. I have always done well, and enjoy playing a standard, simple system (French-style, using Five-card Majors and Strong Notrump). My best placing was third, in 1998, but it didn't look like I'd even make the 2004 event, though, let alone improve on third.

I'll cut short the unpleasantness of the travel, except to say that I did make it to Verona, and was able to nibble at white bread on my way to an opening 55% session (first of four). The next two sessions went like a dream: my partners were brilliant, and a 58% followed by a 64% session saw me well in the lead with a day to go.

I slept nervously and sporadically that night. Although my lead was big, breathing down my neck was the might of Italian many-time World Champion Norberto Bocchi, slightly taller than my six feet six inches.

I wanted a quiet start to the final session, but instead got this as the very first deal: West led the ace of clubs against my Six Spades, and switched to a diamond (best), to the queen and ace. I ruffed a heart, cashed the ace of trumps, crossed to the queen, ruffed a heart, ruffed a club, ruffed a third heart, ruffed a club, drew East's last trump, cashed the ace of hearts, then, at Trick Twelve led a diamond towards the king-ten.

Crunch time. West had cleverly kept hold of both his diamonds, but did he have the jack? I was tempted to go up with the king, because West might have been reluctant to switch to diamond away from the jack at Trick Two. But he had no other safe switch (a

**Dealer: South        Vulnerability: Neither**

| Pairs | ♠ A 9 8 7 4 |
| | ♥ – |
| | ♦ K 10 8 6 4 |
| | ♣ Q 6 4 |

| ♠ – | | ♠ J 10 3 |
| ♥ 9 6 5 4 | **N** | ♥ K 10 8 7 2 |
| ♦ 9 5 3 | **W      E** | ♦ Q J |
| ♣ A K J 9 7 2 | **S** | ♣ 10 8 3 |

| | ♠ K Q 6 5 2 |
| | ♥ A Q J 3 |
| | ♦ A 7 2 |
| | ♣ 5 |

| S (ROBSON) | W | N | E |
|---|---|---|---|
| 1 ♠ | 3 ♣ | 4 ♣ (1) | PASS |
| 4 ♥ (2) | PASS | 5 ♠ (3) | PASS |
| 6 ♠ | END | | |

(1) Good spade raise, unrelated to clubs (in the modern style).
(2) Natural slam try (again the modern way); perhaps hearts will make a better trump suit (4-4 as opposed to 5-4/5-3?).
(3) Slam try, asking for a club control.

**Contract: 6♠            Opening lead: ♣A**

heart would lead to a minor-suit squeeze on him – try it!), and after much pondering I inserted the ten.

Argh! East won the jack (I can still picture him doing it), and I was down two (he could cash a heart).

Three more bottoms came straight after, and, although I still held the lead, it was now a very slender one. I clung on until the very last deal, but Bocchi overtook me at the last gasp, and I had to settle for Silver.

# Ten Ways to Improve your Bridge

### (1) PLAY MORE

But not mindlessly. Focus and be self-critical; analyse your mistakes. Why did you go wrong? Was it faulty logic, a bad read of the opponents, or were you just unlucky? Would you make the same play if you met the situation again? You'll learn far more by such rigour.

### (2) DEVELOP A PARTNERSHIP

Learn together, through experimenting with new bidding ideas, training (you can practise partnership bidding on the excellent – and free – Bridge Base online (www.bridgebase.com), and carrying out post-mortems (constructively) after each session.

Find regular team-mates too. My team will go through every deal played, even the seemingly dull ones. It's surprising and illuminating just how much of interest can be gleaned. Your powers of analysis will sharpen hugely.

### (3) COUNT

The single most essential skill at Bridge is accurate and extensive counting. Most important are shapes: whether declaring or defending, count each suit, thinking in patterns, then build up a picture of the two missing hands.

Here would be an example of such mental reasoning: 'I know the spades are 5-3 with West holding five; diamonds are 4-2 with West holding two, and clubs are 3-3. Therefore hearts must also be 3-3.'

Also count high-card points: 'West has turned up with nine points, yet opened 1NT (12-14); he must have between three and five more points; that means he must have the ace of clubs. Aha, but if he has the ace of clubs, there is no room for him to have the queen of clubs.' Ideally you should end each deal by knowing exactly what cards each hidden hand contained, thinking in terms of their original thirteen cards.

## (4) TEACH THE GAME

There a few better ways to learn something than by teaching others. I can personally testify to this at Bridge, and have also been told so by many other teachers. A further advantage is that you might nurture a group of players who then spark off each other and all advance together, a most satisfying outcome.

## (5) READ

Rigorously. Test yourself – do not look at the answer to a problem without giving it proper thought.

Books for the less experienced:

*Collins need to know? Bridge* by Andrew Robson

*Times Bridge: Common Mistakes* by Andrew Robson (forgive the immodesty)

The *Really Easy* series by The English Bridge Union

*Begin Bridge with Reese* by Terence Reese

Books for the more advanced:

*Play these Hands with Me* by Terence Reese

*The Expert Game* by Terence Reese

*Why you Lose at Bridge* by Skid Simon

*How to Read your Opponents' Cards* by Mike Lawrence

I would like to mention four other writers, too: David Bird, Tony Forrester, Ron Klinger and Andrew Kambites. Buy anything written by them, and you won't be disappointed.

Subscribe to the specialist magazines: *Bridge Plus* (www.bridge-plus.co.uk), *Bridge Magazine* (www.bridgemagazine.co.uk), and the USA's *Bridge World* (www.bridgeworld.com), which is the best expert read.

## (6) USE COMPUTER SOFTWARE

There are CDs that enable you to play an endless supply of randomly generated deals. Amongst the best on the market, all of which can be programmed to play English Standard Acol, are: Blue Chip (the best British product), Q-Plus, Bridge Baron, GIB and Jack. And then there are CDs that do not have a playing engine, but feature structured learning based on set deals. My favourite of these are *Bridgemaster 2000 with Fred Gitelman*, and *Counting at Bridge with Mike Lawrence* (for declarer-play practice); and *Modern Bridge Defence with Eddie Kantar* (for defence).

## (7) PLAY ONLINE

Not quite the same as the real thing (but often more convenient), playing on the internet is nonetheless a very valuable way of gaining experience, plus developing flexibility (unpredictable partners) and concentration (many potential distractions). You will be hard pressed to better *Bridge Base*, although there is more British-style Acol on www.bridgeclublive.com.

## (8) BE PHYSICALLY AND MENTALLY PREPARED

If you have rushed to the game after a sleepless night partying late or looking after your children/grandchildren, you will not play well. Don't expect to. So, for an important game, you should make sure you are well rested with a good night's sleep behind you, and have eaten the right food beforehand (i.e. protein not carbohydrate). Then give it your all.

Also, understand your body. For example, if you need sustenance every two-and-a-half hours, carry a nutrient bar with you; a poor last half hour because the blood-sugar levels have dropped will sour the whole session for you.

## (9) LEARN FROM BETTER PLAYERS

The resident Club experts are always delighted to be asked their opinion – it's a great compliment. Further, some of these more experienced players will be only too pleased to play a session or two with you (it can't hurt to ask). Learn from their game – in particular follow their dummy play closely (not something you need to do when playing with a less experienced partner).

Try to play against better players too: don't sigh when your team draws to play Forrester's in the Gold Cup, be pleased at the opportunity to see some great card-play, and try to lift your game towards that level. At the very least try to watch ('kibitz') better players – this you can most easily do by logging on to Bridge Base and spectating at an expert game.

## (10) ENJOY THE CHALLENGE

Above all, enjoy the challenge of the greatest game mankind has invented. Play with a smile on your face, and you will be a popular partner and a great ambassador for the game.

Also by the same author:

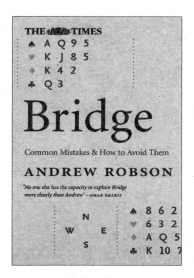

# Bridge
## Common Mistakes & How to Avoid Them
Andrew Robson

A compilation of Andrew Robson's acclaimed Bridge columns from
*The Times* to help the social or less experienced Bridge player to improve
their game and to stop repeating the same mistakes.

*Includes:*
A section outlining the key moves of the game
172 deals clearly explaining what happened
Tips to highlight the principal points to remember

Champion Bridge player, teacher and columnist, Andrew Robson, imparts
the essential know-how to play Bridge with confidence and to win the game.

ISBN-13  978-0-00-720410-6 • £9.99
ISBN-10  0-00-720410-8 • 208 pages